Don't Give Up on Me

Shedding Light on Addiction with Darryl Strawberry

D1417658

Don't Give Up on Me

Shedding Light on Addiction
with Darryl Strawberry

SHAWN POWELL

WITH

DAVID BLAIR MILLER, PSYD
RICH CAPIOLA, MD
JOHN PICCIANO, LCSW, MSW
RON DOCK, CAC

HENSCHELHAUS PUBLISHING, INC.
MILWAUKEE, WISCONSIN

Published by HenschelHAUS Publishing, Inc.
2625 S. Greeley St. Suite 201
Milwaukee, Wisconsin 53207
www.henschelHAUSbooks.com

HenschelHAUS books may be purchased for educational, business, promotional, or professional use or for special sales.
Quantity discounts are available through the publisher.

ISBN: 978159598-564-4
E-ISBN: 978159598-565-1
Audio ISBN: 978159598-569-9 (forthcoming)
LCCN: 2017953146

Publisher's Cataloging-In-Publication Data
(Prepared by The Donohue Group, Inc.)

Names: Powell, Shawn, 1964- | Capiola, Rich.
Title: Don't give up on me : shedding light on addiction with Darryl Strawberry / Shawn Powell, with Rich Capiola, MD [and 3 others].
Description: Milwaukee, Wisconsin : HenschelHAUS Publishing, Inc., [2017]
Identifiers: ISBN 978-1-59598-564-4 | ISBN 978-1-59598-565-1 (ebook) | ISBN 978-1-59598-569-9 (audiobook)
Subjects: LCSH: Substance abuse. | Addicts--Rehabilitation. | Strawberry, Darryl--Substance use. | Baseball players--Substance use. | Parenting--Psychological aspects.
Classification: LCC RC564 .P68 2017 (print) | LCC RC564 (ebook) | DDC 362.29--dc23

Project coordination: Lou Maggio
Editorial support: Kira Henschel
Cover photos: Jorge Alvarez (jorge@alvarezphoto.com)
Cover design: Whitney Smith

Printed in the United States of America.

*This book is dedicated to all those who never gave up on me
in hopes that this book will help others never to give up on
their loved ones who suffer from this terrible
Brain Disease of Addiction.*

—Darryl Strawberry

TABLE OF CONTENTS

FOREWORD

To hell and back! This is the story of Darryl Strawberry, an iconic professional baseball player who suffered the depths of abuse, addiction, recovery, and has now been clean for 12 years. *Don't Give Up On Me* illuminates the dynamics of addiction as seen through the eyes of a psychoanalyst, neuropsychiatrist, licensed clinical social worker, and an addiction specialist.

Dr. David Blair Miller, a board-certified psychologist and psychoanalyst, outlines the tragic beginnings of Darryl's life and the damage to his young psyche. Peer pressure, along with the "Monster" (Darryl's father) in his mind, controlled him.

Dr. Rich Capiola, a board-certified neuropsychiatrist, explains the circumstances leading to addiction and the brain damage that ensues. He also explains how addicts look to drugs and alcohol to release the adrenaline (dopamine) in their brains to function, and are constantly searching for the next high to feel better and reduce the pain.

Darryl needs to feel more than "being a nothing," as his abusive father, the "Monster" described him. Dr. Capiola also points out that addiction is a "brain disease," but can be treated if the addict is willing to face the hard work required.

In Darryl's case, it was the steadfast support of his mother, friends, and the Betty Ford Treatment Center, among other treatment facilities, that made it happen.

Dr. Miller asserts that addiction is an attempt to escape pain and conflicts at any costs. Destructive behavior (e.g., sex, gambling, robbery, etc.) is not uncommon. Addiction is a "runaway train" based on a lost sense of self, one's identity, and lack of empathy for others. Painful memories cause a fear of living and a search for peace through drugs and alcohol. Darryl's feelings of being an ugly, unloved person were based on the terrible physical and mental abuse he suffered as a child.

True hatred of self can result in becoming one's own worst enemy. Drugs and alcohol are a way to hide from the pain of life and the world. Darryl and his siblings grew up in the shadow of constant fear. The "Monster" tortured his family until the boys confronted him and forced him out of the family home. This background led to distrust and even paranoia in Darryl. While his mother later contributed to Darryl's recovery, her early distress from the abuse she witnessed within the home's walls disallowed the proper bonding and attunement.

John Picciano, CEO of Oglethorpe, Inc., and founder and sponsor of Darryl Strawberry Recovery Centers, described the "Monster" that continued to live in Darryl's mind as an entity that damaged his self-esteem and self-worth. His memories ultimately led to his need for alcohol and drugs to ease the pain of being "nothing." He was pursued by the brutal humiliation of the "Monster" that acted like a woodpecker in his head. He mistook the powers of addiction for "old friends." Though he tried, Darryl couldn't face his monster and go through recovery. In addition, he also suffered through bouts of cancer, but family and true friends never let him give up the fight.

Addicts begin their lives as innocent children. When they suffer the trauma of abuse and do not receive early treatment therapy, they may turn to drugs and/or alcohol as a means of escape. Picciano points out that over ten percent of our nation suffers from addictions, and that number continues to grow. Post-Traumatic Stress Syndrome (PTSD) from pathological child rearing, is as common in children as it is in veterans returning from war. Many times, PTSD can lead to a lifelong addiction! Darryl is a good example of such a pattern, but treatment is available, as long as there are those who "never give up on me."

Ron Dock, CAC, CIP, CRC, himself a recovering addict, was assigned to Darryl as a sponsor by the New York Yankees. Dock points out that addicts lie in the shadows of trauma and can never drop their guard regarding addictions. He reviews his own life as one who fought to survive and make happiness bigger than addiction. Ron became a sponsor of other addicts and has remained clean for many years. He is a devout follower of intervention and recognizes that sometimes addicts have to "crash" before they face the need for help.

Darryl Strawberry is now a spokesman for overcoming the "brain diseases" and together with John Picciano, has created the Darryl Strawberry Recovery Centers.

Dr. Miller, Dr. Capiola, John Picciano, and Ron Dock tell the story of Darryl Strawberry and his long journey to recovery (12 years clean). *Don't Give Up On Me: Shedding Light on Addiction* has to be the model for all addicts who have to face their diseases, accept intervention and therapy, and seek out recovery facilities like Darryl Strawberry Recovery Centers.

Arnold Pusar, PhD
Diplomate in Clinical Psychology
International Psychoanalyst

INTRODUCTION

I met Darryl Strawberry about five years ago. As a native New Yorker, I only knew what I had read about him. I knew he was a great baseball player, World Series hero and I knew he was a drug addict! Only later would I find out the extreme highs and devastating lows this man has lived through.

People stand in lines for the Major League All-Star Darryl Strawberry's autograph, but very few understand the torture that ruled his life, on and off the baseball field. I am one of the very few who know the reality of this man's lowest points and greatest triumphs.

When I met Darryl, he was neither an All-Star or a tormented soul. I met a man who had found peace. I met a man who possessed a crystal-clear perspective of himself. Darryl understood the horrors he had narrowly escaped and he was on a mission to help in the war against drug and alcohol addiction. He was eager to join forces with our company to fight for the millions of lives that have succumbed to the greatest enemy of our nation.

My name is John Picciano and for the past 40-years I have worked as an addiction specialist. I have watched as the substance abuse epidemic has spiraled out of control. I have watched people pleading for help and I have witnessed people ignoring the warning signs. But, the greatest pain has been the unnecessary deaths of so many.

When Darryl entered my life, I saw him as an ally in the fight. I saw a man who had been to Hell and back, but more importantly, I saw a man who could make a difference. I felt so moved by Darryl and his dedication to the mission that I invited him to join Oglethorpe, Inc. where he currently serves as a Director at two of our recovery centers in Florida.

Don't Give up on Me: Shedding Light on Addiction is the first step in Oglethorpe's "War on Drugs" initiative. We have recruited two of the finest psychiatric experts in the field of substance abuse as they shed light on the symptoms and treatment possibilities for those afflicted with addiction. Dr. David Miller and Dr. Richard Capiola understand this growing epidemic in our country. They share their expertise by breaking down the psychological components involved in those suffering from addiction.

Skillfully woven together by author Shawn Powell, Darryl's personal story of childhood trauma, drug abuse, and his battles against addiction is analyzed by Dr. Miller and Dr. Capiola, as well as Ron Dock, CAC, CIP, CRC, who became Darryl's sponsor and friend. The information gathered will help others learn the hard truths and hopeful messages for those suffering from this deadly dilemma.

Don't Give up on Me provides a simplistic look at the various issues involved with substance abuse. This book was written for addicts, caretakers, family members and friends of those suffering from substance abuse. It is a book of hope that will give you strength to battle onward.

John Picciano, LSW, MSW
CEO of Oglethorpe, Inc.

CHAPTER 1

WHAT IS ADDICTION?

Based on an interview with David Blair Miller, PsyD

Addiction is the compulsive use of a habit-forming substance that ultimately becomes an obsessed fixation in one's life. People with an addiction will exhibit great psychological dependency on a compulsive behavior or a harmful substance in order to escape underlying feelings of internal pain and conflict in their minds. Addiction will lead to defined physiological and psychological symptoms upon withdrawal of the substance.

According to Dr. David Miller, a board-certified psychologist and psychoanalyst, "Addiction is any thought, feeling or behavior that gives a person temporary relief or pleasure from a painful, internal emotional experience, despite the vast consequences involved." A person can be deemed an addict when he or she is unable to stop using a specific mechanism of addiction, even when the consequences result in serious illness, injury illness, or death.

Addiction is powerful. When a person is under the influence of an addiction or multiple addictions, the addictive substances have a vicious stronghold on the thought processes and decision making abilities of that person. People with addictions are attempting to cope with emotional pain that it so great, they are willing to harm themselves, just to find freedom from the afflicting pain. Addicts are in constant search for emotional relief. They live their lives in a continuous state of emotional deprivation and persistently search for various modes of escape.

The list of substances used by addicts is endless. Some addicts look to alcohol to numb their minds and escape the pressures of their internal world. Other addicts abuse illegal substances such as cocaine, crystal methane or heroin. Others rely on a supply of opiates to desensitize their pain. Some of the most popular opiates or pain killers being used today are OxyContin, Methadone, Percocet, and Vicodin.

Some addicts seek out psychological and behavioral distractions that can range from excessive sexual depravity to gambling binges. Other behavioral addictions include excess shopping, internet use, food, pornography, video games, tattoos, and plastic surgery. These addictions are common place in our society and if not kept in check, can destroy a family's financial well-being in a flash.

If addicts do not receive the proper intervention required to battle these addictions, they could ultimately lose everything in their lives. Addicts will lose their health, their youth, their beauty and their relationships with family, spouses and children. If an addict is unable to successfully redirect their actions, he or she could lose their wealth, and quite possibly their lives.

The reported deaths of those suffering from addictions resulted from HIV, various types of infections, liver diseases, Korsakoff Syndrome, Hepatitis C, strokes, and heart attacks. Korsakoff Syndrome is a persistent memory disorder most commonly found in those suffering from alcoholism. The worst-case casualty scenarios involve suicide and traffic deaths that commonly involve the deaths of other innocent motorists, passengers, or bystanders.

Addiction is reminiscent of a runaway train, and the addict, an emotionally handicapped engineer who is unable to bring the train to a complete stop. Often with addiction, the engineer has no idea the train is actually on the tracks, let alone speeding out of control.

Addiction is so powerful that people are willing to sell their own children for a hit of cocaine or an injection of heroin. Nothing matters to drug addicts; they have lost their sense of self and any empathy for those around them. An addict will go to the furthest extremes to find temporary numbness to the negative thoughts and feelings that relentlessly scramble their brains.

"Most people fear the idea of dying. An addict fears the idea of living because of the severe pain and personal duress they deal with on a daily basis," Dr. Miller states.

The most common questions asked of an addict are: *Why would anyone partake in an addiction that causes so many self-afflicting health problems? Why are addicts so afraid to live? Why are they so self-defeating?*

To properly understand addiction, we must ask this question: What is the etiology, or root cause, of a person's addiction? We must do our utmost to determine what an addict gains from drugs and alcohol. Yes, addicts gain temporary peace, serenity, and certain levels of mental relief from their chosen addictions. Why do you think 25 million United States citizens use illicit drugs on a daily basis? Addictions provide relief from painful memories, they quiet agonizing emotions, and provide a peaceful state of mind to those who are tormented.

Addicts suffer from chronic emotional torture that cannot be tamed by normal expression. With drug and alcohol use, addicts are able to avoid the overwhelming negativity that circulates within their minds. Addictions provide a temporary calm to an addict's damaged psyche. Addictions are an addict's security blanket. An addict finds solace inside its calming embrace.

Addiction is about escape. Addicts want to outrun their past lives and eliminate the mental anguish that constantly paws at them. They hold anger towards those who abused them or neglected them as children. It is extremely important to understand that addiction is not always the result of physical or sexual abuse, but from parental neglect as well. The people most vulnerable to addictions are those whose internal sense of self is fragmented. An addict holds a deep-rooted self-hatred in his or her mind and heart, and has no other choice but to follow these painful emotions.

One of the best analogies of a person suffering from neglect can be illustrated by the shattered mirror effect. When people stare into a shattered mirror, they do not truly see the person who stands before them. The person's reflection is distorted by the fractured glass that is incapable of presenting a complete and perfect image. A child who has been neglected often fails to be taught or fails to experience the act of self-soothing or internal emotional comfort. When neglected children stares into the shattered mirror, they cannot find their true identity—all they see is an ugly, unloved person before them.

Yes, the true hatred that addicts hold within is an undeniable hatred for themselves. Addicts suffer from self-esteem issues, self-loathing, and an overwhelming lack of self-worth. They are afraid to be alone, so they surround themselves with others who are suffering as well. Addicts are fearful of being alone with their thoughts and self-reflection, and in time, they become their own worst enemies.

Addictions serve the purpose of filling an internal void or emptiness that cannot be filled by the external world. Emptiness is often linked to either conscious or unconscious voids created in the childhoods of an addict. These children feel unloved, unwanted, and invisible. They feel as if they do not matter in this world to the people who matter most to them.

Why would children feel unloved? Why would children feel unwanted or invisible? What happened to these people? What occurred in their past lives to generate such self-hatred and self-defeated behaviors? What traumatic events caused these people to turn to drugs and alcohol to hide from the world?

DARRYL'S STORY

IN THE BEGINNING

If you have ever been to a Major League baseball game, then you are well aware of the distinct sound of a 95-mph fastball exploding off the barrel of a wooden bat. The sound is called "The Crack of the Bat," and it can bring thousands of fans to their feet with thunderous ovations and howling cheers!

Now, there are various types of sounds the ball and bat will make, depending on how hard the ball is hit. A line-drive to the outfield will make a much more distinct cracking sound compared to a pop-up in the infield, and a chopper in the infield is definitely not going to make the same sound made by a home run. In fact, a true baseball fan can be standing in line at the concession stand, hear the crack of the bat, and instantly know that a ball has been driven into the outfield stands of the stadium. The sound is that distinct.

When Darryl Strawberry entered the Major Leagues in 1983 with the New York Mets, his monstrous home runs instantly became those of legend. His long, fluid swing and incredible bat speed launched some of the longest home runs in baseball history. And the sound that erupted from the barrel of his bat was not only distinct, it was the sweetest sounding home run in the biz.

THWACK! THWACK!

Darryl Strawberry was an eight-time All-Star who hit 335 career home runs with the Mets, Los Angeles Dodgers, San Francisco Giants, and New York Yankees. His 17-year career produced numerous eye-popping moments that left his hometown fans hoarse from their screams of adulation. And if you think Strawberry's game time heroics were memorable, you would have been shocked with the long ball show he'd put on display, during batting practice.

His swing was so smooth, it looked as if he wasn't even trying when the bat whipped through the heart of his hitting zone. One ball after another would fly deep into the empty stands of the stadium. The baseballs ricocheted off empty seats and concrete walls, sending distinct echos throughout the confines of the playing field.

Yes, when Darryl Strawberry was hitting, people knew it. They didn't even have to be staring on to the field, to know that he was the one in the batter's box.

Baseball is a funny game. A Major League baseball player is considered an All-Star performer if he can maintain a .300 batting average over his career. To maintain an average of .300, a player must produce a hit, 3 out of 10 times at the plate. In fact, most Big League players usually manage to get 1.8 to 2.5 hits per 10 at bats. In most businesses, if an employee fails 7 out of 10 times, he is fired. In baseball he is a Hall of Famer.

Darryl Strawberry is no different. His lifetime batting average was .259, which means he failed to get a base hit 7.4 times out of 10 plate appearances. He failed in 75 percent of every Major League game he played in. Yet, he is considered one of the greatest home-run hitters and clutch performers in two decades of Big League baseball, in the 1980s and 1990s.

The reason for this analogy is simple. Darryl Strawberry created memorable moments. He is one of the few players in baseball history who could strike out nine times in a row and follow it up with a game winning dinger that would hit the roof of the stadium or completely clear the stadium.

Yes, Darryl Strawberry had a knack for creating the impossible. He had a knack for bringing fans to their feet with a single swing of the bat. He had a knack for giving New York baseball fans hope, even in the dire moments of a game. Fans understood that when Darryl Strawberry strode to the plate, with his stoic face and long body, their team still had a fighting chance. When Darryl took his stance against a pitcher, the bat became an extension of his slender self. It was if, bat and body were one in the same. He was a lethal hitting machine.

However, what most fans never realized about Darryl Strawberry during his All-Star slugger days, was that each of his plate appearances, were oddly reminiscent of his own personal battles and decisions off the field. Darryl was making bad choices for his life. He would then try to cover his mistakes with another mistake. He would try to hide his pain, but would only create further pain in the process. In life, Darryl Strawberry was failing 7.5 times out of 10. He had become his own worst enemy.

Darryl Strawberry had become a drug addict. He was an alcoholic, who was suffering from deep internal pains, that resulted in depression. He was in severe emotional pain, stemming from his agonizing feelings of self-doubt. His sense of self-hatred was instilled in him, many years prior to his days in a Big League uniform. The only refuge for his soul was swinging that wooden bat, and hearing that distinct cracking sound as the ball flew out of the stadium.

THWACK! THWACK!

As a young boy growing up in south-central Los Angeles, Darryl Strawberry faced issues much greater than those that surrounded his fleeting moments inside a batter's box lined with white chalk. The young Strawberry lived within a shadow of fear that haunted his every waking moment. As a child, he was afraid to close his eyes at night, for the fear that his mother would be beaten or killed. He was afraid to be heard sneaking down the hallway of his own home, for the fear of being noticed. Imagine a young child afraid to smile. Imagine a child afraid to breathe. This was a young Darryl's life in the Strawberry home.

For the sounds that echoed in his brain were not the sounds of his sweet swing connecting with a 95-mph fastball. No, the sounds that reverberated through his soul were the sounds of a belt or an extension cord being violently wielded across his bare back. The sounds were of his brother's screams, his mother's torture, and the pain that ripped his young mind apart.

THWACK! THWACK! THWACK! THWACK!

CHILDHOOD

Darryl Strawberry was born to Henry and Ruby Strawberry in 1961. Darryl was the youngest of three boys and the third of five children. His oldest brother was Mike, followed by Ronnie, then Darryl. His younger sisters were Regina and Michelle. The Strawberry children were very close in age and a very close knit group of siblings.

All five children were well behaved and they adored their mother, Ruby. The family was not poverty stricken, both parents held jobs and the children did not go without the essentials of life. Of course, with five children comes a multitude of bills: Groceries, Clothing, Utilities, and a Mortgage. But, the Strawberry family managed to meet all monetary expectations. Ruby made sure of that.

Ruby worked multiple jobs to help keep the family afloat. She worked and saved as much of her money as possible for the family. Henry made a good living working for the Postal Service, but his idea of saving money was usually replaced with placing bets on horses at the track or having drinks at the local dive bar.

Henry's wasteful spending left little for the Strawberry children. There were no brand new bikes or toys. But, the kids never complained. The boys would find junked bikes at the garbage dump and then restore them for their own personal use. The boys were resilient.

Ruby was the pillar of the household, but when it came to corralling her husband's spending or extracurricular activities, she was severely over-matched. Henry was a big, strong man who did whatever he pleased. At some point in their lengthy relationship, Henry and Ruby had obviously been in love, but as the years progressed and the children multiplied, Henry's love for Ruby and his children disappeared. Henry had emotionally checked out.

Henry did not want to be a father: he wanted to escape. He wanted to be free from all the monthly bills stacked on the kitchen counter of his home. Henry wanted to hide from the stresses of adulthood by taking an easier route. He wanted to take a selfish route that involved his caring for no one but himself. But, more than anything, Henry wanted freedom from the responsibilities of fatherhood. He was utterly lost when it came to being a father, and why wouldn't he be? Henry's male role model in life had been a violent alcoholic as well. In fact, Henry's father was the exact same person he had become.

Henry grew up in an abusive family environment. His father would beat his mother unmercifully; the young Henry could do nothing but cringe at the brutality. Henry was ill-equipped to save his mother. He was not strong enough to challenge his father, for Henry was just a young boy. He was an innocent child bearing witness to the unholy sounds of a tortured body and the wailing appeals of an obliterated spirit.

THWACK! THWACK!

Henry was well aware of the cracking sounds, too. But, it was the sounds of his mother's skull being cracked, not the sounds of a 95-mph baseball off the barrel of a wooden bat. The cracking sounds haunted his life, yet he could not rid them from his thoughts. He took the images, and the pain with him to the next chapter of his life.

But why? Why would someone who witnessed so many painful atrocities, repeat the same acts on the children he brought into this world? Why did Henry Strawberry feel obligated to repeat his own father's wrongdoings? Why did he become a monster? Did he have an undetected mental disorder? Were his alcoholism, gambling problems and violent traits passed down to him, genetically? Was he influenced by his environment, or pushed into his addiction through peer pressure? Or was it a theory of "We do what we see"?

Why did a young Henry Strawberry allow himself to fall prey to addiction in his adult life?

THE MONSTER

Childhood memories are supposed to be some of those most positive recollections of our lives. The memories do not have to consist of monumental happenings or outlandish gifts. Subtle flashbacks to your favorite ice cream concoction from Dairy Queen or learning to drive with your dad can be the moments that bring a smile to your face for years to come. In life, the little things create the grandest of memories. They are the reasons for our smiles.

But, what if the most rehashed memory of your childhood is pretending to be fast asleep in your bedroom when the Monster comes home? Or witnessing the rage of the drunken creature you refer to as "Dad" as he verbally lashes your mother with one fiendish threat after another? Or watching your mother be tossed, end over end, across the living room by the devilish ghoul who rules your home?

In the Strawberry home, not all children were treated with equality. The eldest son, Mike, and the two girls witnessed plenty of evil within the home. However, if Ruby wasn't the center of

Henry's physical and verbal abuse, Ronnie and Darryl were the alternate recipients of his violent outbursts. Mike and the young girls were never harmed by the violent hands of their father.

The physical abuse for Darryl began when he was nine years old. Ronnie was ten. Henry obviously felt discipline needed to be instilled into his two youngest sons. But, under the influence of liquor, Henry's idea of discipline would quickly turn into an all-out assault. Henry would wait for the young men to make a mistake, (as all children do), and then he would erupt into a whirlwind of expletives and physical violence. The words "I told you, I told you" would proceed a leather belt being ripped from his belt loops as if he were unsheathing a sword.

There was never rhyme or reason to the punishing strikes. Henry was a strong man, whose arms flailed wildly as the leather strap found its mark somewhere on the boys' bodies. The boys would attempt to block the belt or extension cord as it struck them, but it would only sting that much more when the strap wrapped around their arms before being wildly pulled away, as if Henry were starting a lawn mower.

Sometimes, it was not about the physical abuse, but the neglect of the young children. Ruby was once called by a neighbor while she was at work, because Ronnie and Darryl were wandering across Rosecrans Avenue in their diapers. The young boys were toddlers when they disappeared from their home, under the unwatchful eyes of their inebriated father, who was passed out cold in his bed.

As the boys got older, Darryl and Ronnie became private investigators. They would peer around buildings to see if their father's car was still parked in front of their house. If the car was there, the two boys would turn around and find a hiding place in their neighborhood until he had left. If the car was gone, they would sigh relief and race to their home. When Henry was at work, the kids could truly smile and laugh with one another.

Most children will have scars from their childhood upbringing. Kids get injured in their own backyards, on playgrounds, or during sporting events. But, the real scars of an abusive childhood run deep within a child's core. The welts Darryl and Ronnie received from their father's whippings and beatings were no comparison to the damaged mindsets of these young children. Darryl and Ronnie felt rejected by their father, as if they did not matter in this world. The feeling of rejection is a harsh, stabbing pain that is never easy to forgive or forget.

After a period of any type of constant abuse, an individual begins forming negative thoughts of self-worth and increased self-doubt. When one is constantly beaten down with hateful words or abusive fists, one ultimately starts believing he or she is indeed worthless in this world. If fear is added to the equation, then the negative feelings of self-worth and self-doubt are exacerbated. Darryl and Ronnie were both mired in this destructive thought process and fear ruled their young existences.

As time progressed in the Strawberry home, so did the beatings. But, Darryl and Ronnie were beginning to build a resistance to their father's brutal attacks. Although the boys were still of elementary school age, their tolerance towards their father's physical outbreaks was reaching a boiling point inside them both. The two boys were volcanic. Even at such a tender age, the boys knew they were nearing their breaking points as human beings.

Then it happened.

THE SKILLET, THE BUTCHER KNIFE, AND THE FRYING PAN

The sound was very familiar to Darryl. He and his brother Ronnie were jolted from their sleep. The sounds of a screaming maniac echoed throughout the young boys' home! Darryl and Ronnie sat up in their beds and listened as the sounds of shattering glass, accompanied the drunken rage of the Monster's dark voice.

The boys looked over to their 15-year-old brother Mike's bed, but it was empty. The boys crept into the kitchen, where they spotted Mike standing in the doorway of their parent's bedroom. Chaos filled the house! Their mother Ruby was screaming as a wide-eyed Mike backpedaled from the doorway.

Henry emerged from the bedroom toting a shotgun. Mike quickly turned and grabbed a skillet from the stove and turned to face the drunken menace. Darryl and Ronnie quickly joined their brother as they screamed at their father! Ronnie grabbed a butcher knife and Darryl grabbed a frying pan.

"GET OUT OF HERE AND LEAVE US ALONE," Mike bellowed.

Henry's bloodshot eyes spoke volumes as he charged the boys. The three boys scampered behind the dining room table, never relenting in their stand against the Monster.

"I'LL KILL YOU'ALL!" Henry screamed as he raised the shotgun.

The brothers did not back down. They stood their ground against the Monster. A skillet, a butcher knife, and a frying pan in the hands of three young, teenage boys. They made a stand against the horror that was their lives. The volcanoes had erupted.

Fear is the biggest enemy of our lives: The fear of change, the fear of loss, the fear of success. The young Strawberry men had feared for so long. They feared their father and his wrath. They feared for their mother's safety, and they feared for their own, simple lives. There comes a time in a person's life, however, when there are only two choices: Lie down and let the world trample over you or find your courage and chase fear out the door, even if it means grabbing a skillet, a butcher knife and a frying pan, to do it.

"JUST GET OUT OF HERE! AND NEVER COME BACK!" shouted Mike, holding onto the skillet as if it were a giant axe and Henry a tree.

The three boys stood united in their cause and found strength in their numbers. They were steadfast in their actions, showing a new-found power they had no idea existed. As the Monster stared at his sons, and then looked toward his wife and daughters, his fury was quietly snuffed. Henry calmly laid the shotgun on the dining room table and stared at his offspring one final time. He then turned and walked out of the house, never to return.

The family was instantly relieved, but now the young boys were the men of the house. They had never had a proper male role model in their lives and now they would be handling many aspects that would be completely foreign to their upbringing. How would they assist their mother from a financial standpoint? Who would hold them accountable for their teenage transgressions?

And more importantly, will the young Strawberry men follow in their father's footsteps and make the same horrible mistakes he had? Or, will they be able to find the strength to "Say No" and ultimately rise above the addictions that swallowed their father?

Darryl was glad his father was gone, and he knew in his heart would never be like the Monster!

Doctor's Notes and Comments to Chapter 1

with David Blair Miller, PsyD

When investigating the personal histories of drug addicts and alcoholics, a large percentage of those suffering from these and other addictions have been either physically abused, neglected, or encountered feelings of abandonment in their childhood years. Darryl Strawberry's life was no different as he and his brother Ronnie were physically and emotionally abused by their father throughout the early years of their lives.

In Darryl and Ronnie's cases, the fear of the unknown may have been a greater terror than the actual beatings they received. The two young boys snuck around their own home, trying to avoid the wrath of their father. They became private investigators to avoid any type of face time with their father.

Darryl and Ronnie were frightened of the one person who was supposed to be their protector. The young boys did not receive any type of love from their father. There would be no hugs or kisses for the little boys, nor were there any signs of unconditional love shown to them by their father. Love was a four-letter word to Henry Strawberry.

Addicts like Darryl and Ronnie have experienced persistent ruptures in the emotional attunement that is meant to be shared between parent and child. Emotional attunement is not only a necessary requirement between parent and child, it is a vital cog in the mental and emotional development of the child. Emotional attunement is the act of understanding the needs of a child, then putting yourself (the adult) into a position to fill the void of the child in a positive manner, while maintaining parental control. When people experience emotional attunement from others, they feel understood and soothed. This type of mental affirmation has a positive effect on our brains.

When we are born, our central nervous system and brains are extremely primitive. Have you ever noticed that mountain goat kids can actually walk and keep up with their nannies hours after they are born? Can you imagine a doctor delivering a newborn baby, then immediately placing the infant on the floor, so it can stand up and wobble to its mother? Babies need to be fed, changed, and cleaned. Humans are helpless at birth, and totally dependent on others for everything in their lives to survive.

At birth, a baby's mind is a clean slate. The baby shrieks, cries, and whimpers to communicate its needs. When parents hear their baby's cries, their minds immediately shift into high gear as they attempt to recognize the specific need or needs of the infant. Parents go through an entire mental checklist of possible solutions to their baby's cries. Do you need changed, my love? Are you hungry, baby girl? Does someone need a nap? Babies rely on their parents or other adults for everything!

As the baby grows, parents are responsible for protecting, soothing, and teaching their child. But, more importantly, parents are relied upon for the extremely important task of understanding the child. During the emotional and mental development of a child, parents must be able to convey information in a loving, caring, and consistent manner. Children need to feel they are loved, and when they realize they are sincerely loved, their minds are freer to expand, create, and grow.

When a baby cries, a parent responds with a soothing voice, changed facial expressions, and a more comforting body language. A parent soothes the baby with a loving touch or by picking up the baby and holding the child. "Oh, baby, are you okay?" These actions are examples of emotional attunement, which is the most important emotional and psychological experience the infant child can have at such a young age.

If parents have sleep deprivation or fails to take care of themselves, or are lacking much-needed sleep, this can negatively affect the emotional attunement between a parent and child. Caregivers must take proper care of themselves if they are ever going to be able to properly care for their children. As the grouchy parent picks up the baby and holds it to his or her chest, the unnatural rhythm of the parent's heart can actually signal anxiety to the baby. The baby can pick up on the stress, and in turn, feels an overwhelming level of stress as well. In other words, the parent's heart rate actually has an integral effect on the baby's developing nervous system.

When a parent is emotionally or chronically stressed, this can result in an anxiety and sadness within the baby. When a baby does not receive the proper amounts of love, patience, compassion, or nurturance, it will not develop a true or healthy sense of itself. It will not receive a true emotional attunement from its mother or father.

If parents drink, do drugs, or are involved with any other type of addiction that selfishly takes them away from their child, then the baby's ability to properly bond with the parent is severely diminished. The baby needs to be able to connect with the caregiver to bond. If the parent and child do bond, this creates a sense of mutuality. Experiences of mutuality affect the baby's capacity to attach to others. This form of relating will carry through the entire life of the child.

If a parent is stingily involved with his own life, the baby will not receive a much-needed dose of emotional nurturance. If a parent neglects the needs of a baby, the infant will be void of any source of emotional nurturance. In basic terms- a baby is a living organism. A tree is also a living organism. If a tree does not receive proper attention (sunlight and water) the tree will eventually die—this is exemplified within many forms of addiction.

The human brain operates in a similar fashion. If the brain is not fed with security, nurturance, and emotional attunement, then the psychological development of the child will become stagnant and be unable to grow and thrive properly. Young children rely on secure attachment with the parent; attachment is an important milestone in the development of a child's emotional sense of self. Children need to be emotionally fed and watered. They require emotional nurturance. They require a parent's warmth and light.

Children with secure attachment know they can rely and depend on their parents. This can be witnessed when dropping a young child off at daycare. The baby will cry for its parent as they leave, but in time, the tears will stop because of the secure attachment the child has with that particular parent. The baby trusts that its caregiver(s) will return and they will be reunited once again. Young children have the experiences or understanding that their mother or father will not let them down.

When a baby receives proper maternal and paternal attunement, it can maintain a feeling of secure attachment throughout his or her adult life. Securely attached adults have an easier time relating to others, feeling comfortable with others, and trusting in others. A securely attached adult creates harmonious relationships that involve happiness, friendship, loyalty, and trust. People who are securely attached have fewer fears of being abandoned, and are more likely to become close to others without insecurity or fear. These people also have healthier self-esteem, which helps them properly navigate the adversities of their future lives.

Babies with insecure attachment may show intense emotions when the parent drops them off at daycare. Insecure, ambivalent attachment refers to parents who are inconsistent in their child- rearing behaviors. Such caregivers will respond *quickly to a baby's needs one day and ignore its needs the next day. This type of attachment causes the baby to become emotionally confused and anxious during emotional development, and quite possibly throughout their entire lifespan. These types of attachments are damaging and closely associated with neglect, which can be just as devastating to a child's emotional state as physical abuse.*

In the case of Darryl and Ronnie, their upbringing was damaged early on due to the lack of emotional attunement between the two boys and their father. The neglect and physical abuse was unwarranted and highly destructive! Henry's lack of emotional nurturance and unconditional love destroyed the young boys' self-esteem. In the minds of these children, they were nothing more than unworthy, unloved burdens.

The acts of physical, emotional, verbal, and sexual abuse destroy the necessary emotional bonding required between parent and child. Proper emotional attunement between parent and child is imperative throughout the growth of a child. Parental attunement helps a child establish trust, recognize needs, and form a stronger sense of empathy for others. Proper attunement also provides a child with a stronger sense of emotional attachment, which is needed in establishing and maintaining relationships, as well as succeeding in life without resorting to alcohol or drugs.

When a child is neglected or abused, the child is unable to connect to caregivers with emotional attachment. Worse yet, the child is robbed of individual authenticity. When children are unable to connect with their individual authenticity, they have difficulty becoming honest with themselves. If children cannot be true and honest with themselves, then their ability to truly connect with their self-identity is seriously stunted, resulting in various character disorders.

Adults who were abused or neglected as young children can suffer from either "avoidant attachment" or "anxious ambivalent attachment." A person who experiences avoidant attachment will tend to have anxieties about emotional intimacy and closeness. These people have difficulties with the concept of trust, and have a difficult time depending on friends and loved ones for help.

An anxious ambivalent person's life is usually filled with emotional extremes and an obsessive preoccupation toward friends or a love interest. Due to their anxious emotional state, they tend to jump into relationships with little thought or consideration to circumstances or needs. These people live with constant paranoia and fear that their relationships will be ended by their friends or significant others.

Anxious ambivalent people have a tendency to suffocate others with their overbearing needs for love and acceptance. As stated earlier, people with addictions often withstand certain arrests in their emotional development as children. Such developmental arrests were most likely caused by abuse, trauma, or neglect. These same people will tend to have *avoidant and anxious ambivalent attachment styles that will create havoc in future relationships and friendships.*

Darryl and Ronnie were emotionally damaged by the physical abuse and neglect they received from their father. They were robbed of the emotional attachment required from a loving father figure to its child. Darryl and Ronnie's abilities to connect on an emotional level was markedly impaired, but most of all, these young boys were being unknowingly led into a self-identity crisis that would become excruciatingly difficult to overcome.

It is important to realize that a vast majority of parents are loving people with good intentions. They long to see their children happy and healthy. Other parents come from homes that were riddled with drug and alcohol abuse by their caregivers. These people were raised with a forced sense of acceptance to addiction, and ultimately parent their own children the way they themselves were parented.

Parents who were raised in such unhealthy environments must not perceive themselves as bad parents and condemn themselves because their child is addicted to drugs or alcohol. They must identify the situation before them, assess the severity of the problem, and provide educated assistance to those affected by substance abuse.

The healthy development of self-esteem and self-care is a complex process that can take many years. Unhealthy self-esteem does not develop simply from parental neglect or abuse. In fact, sometimes unhealthy self-esteem develops from a parent's excessive praise or perpetual idealizations. Parents who praise their children with excessive compliments that are inconsistent with the child's own self-perception can actually damage that child's self-esteem.

How can this happen? When children receive conflicting messages from parents and other important people in their lives, they will actually be forced to negotiate between each message. For example, if parents tell their child that he or she is the most talented baseball player on the team, when the child actually is a bench warmer, the child could develop a false sense of reality.

A false sense of reality, or "False Sense of Self" leaves a child quite confused and vulnerable to later substance abuse and addiction. A person's self-perception becomes that person's reality, regardless of another person's intentions. Self-esteem is highly correlated with the quality, empathy, and consistency of emotional attunement from caregivers.

Self-esteem is interchangeable with Ego and is developed through emotional attunement and nurturance provided by loving parents. When love and trust are established between a child and his mother and/or father, the child has a greater chance of rising above adversities and troubling times in future years. This is because children learn to trust in the notion that their parents will always be available to them during times of woe.

Here is an example of how it works: The mother loves, protects, acknowledges, teaches, and guides her son during the child-rearing years. She completes these tasks with compassion and respect, which ultimately provide her son with a healthy sense of self-esteem. The mother's positive nurturance weighs heavy in the child's life and helps guide the child to a better understanding of his own emotional needs.

When a child is properly prepared to understand his own emotional needs, he has a better chance of making wiser decisions during future trials and tribulations. When children have received emotional attunement, they learn to prioritize their personal needs and desires. These children become better students. They study for tests and complete their homework. They listen to their bodies when they do not feel well and make adjustments in their sleeping and eating patterns. They avoid things that are not good for them, including unhealthy relationships with friends and their significant others.

Darryl had a strong relationship with his mother. In fact, his relationship with his mother ultimately paved the way for his recovery against the many addictions that imprisoned him.

Darryl's father was an opposing influence in his life. Henry's actions were detrimental to Darryl's self-esteem, which undermined his mother's valiant efforts to raise a confident son, free of inner turmoil. Henry created fertile ground for Darryl's mistrust, anger, and resentment. But worst of all, Henry's actions provided the seedlings that would create the future self-destructive behaviors and substance abuses Darryl would come to know.

CHAPTER 2
NATURE OR NURTURE?

Based on an interview with David Blair Miller, PsyD

D arryl grew up in an environment that made him believe he was worthless. He grew up in an environment that made him feel unworthy of love. And, unbeknownst to this young child and his abusive father, was an innocent life that would one day be consumed with addictions. The adverse actions of a parent and/or the unfavorable environment of a young child can spearhead the negative thoughts, feelings, and behaviors of a future addict.

When a father or mother abuses a child, the messages sent to that child are, "You are a bad person!", "You are no good!" and "I don't love you!" Through these vicious words and brutal physical attacks, the child is relegated to the lowest levels of inadequacy. The child feels devalued, deflated, and unloved. When Henry Strawberry beat his young boys, his message was not only cruel and sadistic, it was devoid of any possible depiction of love.

Parents who punish their children with a physical act (spanking) often confuse discipline for physical abuse. Common sense should tell you that beating your child with a closed fist or an object (belt/switch) that leaves welts or raised marks upon a child's body is the act of a loveless victimizer. If you injure a child or you constantly resort to violence as a form of intervention, then you are without question guilty of physical abuse. In fact, the acts of beating your child are not only a criminal act, it unfortunately sends a message to the child that he is worthless, unwanted, and unloved!

Children long to feel validation from their parents. They want to be liked by their parents, they want to feel important and valued, but more than anything they want to feel loved. People want to be appreciated in their lives. People of all ages are constantly searching for approval. Why do you think the Facebook/Selfie is so popular amongst our society? People actually get upset when their friends fail to "like" their social media posts. This happens because people want reassurance and approval.

A child's brain develops with the collaboration of genetics and its environment. A parent can significantly help influence a child into the type of character or person he or she will one day become. A parent's actions can help influence a child's ability to appropriately treat others. A parent can also guide children when they are choosing friends and in the way children are perceived by others. But the child's brain does not simply develop based on its gene pool or the advisements of its parents. Nor is a child's brain development the result of some sort of 50/50 split between nature and nurture.

If we use computer terms as an analogy, the hardware of the child is the genetics and the software of the child is the environment. The computer will not properly function without the proper binding of both entities. The combination of the hardware and software will co-create the desired choices and actions of the individual. However, the combination of both entities could also provide the means to a person's character and future addiction(s).

As human beings, we all have the same neurochemicals in our brains. We have dopamine, endorphins, oxytocin, and serotonin, which are associated as the "Hormones of Happiness." These neurochemicals are correlated with a person's motivation, desire, and overall well-being. When people reach goals or accomplishes feats, they receive a boost of reinforced pleasure from the "Hormones of Happiness."

The "Hormones of Happiness" are highlighted by dopamine, better known as the reward molecule of the brain. Dopamine is responsible for the reward-seeking or pleasure-driven behaviors of our psyches. All reward-seeking behaviors increase dopamine transmission in the brain. Dopamine flows when we are excited, motivated and curious. Dopamine is mostly transmitted when we are seeking the pleasures of food or sex.

Without dopamine, people lack motivation and face underlying feelings of nothingness. When addicts use cocaine, nicotine, or crystal methane, they are receiving a tremendous release of dopamine, which defends against their overwhelming feelings of emptiness. But, contrary to belief, drugs alone are not addictive. Many people can take a hit of cocaine or crystal methane and not become addicted to drugs whatsoever. So how do people become addicts? And why are addicts more vulnerable and susceptible to drugs and alcohol?

When a child has been traumatized at a young age, the child seeks various outlets that will hopefully lead to an increased release of dopamine. The reason for this search is to find pleasure, but more importantly, to hide or mask the internal pain he or she is constantly battling. With every dopamine hit, the reward system becomes more activated. When a person uses drugs like cocaine or crack, the limbic system of the brain is flooded with excessive dopamine levels that are five to ten times greater than its normal homeostatic state.

The artificially-enhanced elevations in dopamine levels (due to the drug intake) become so high that the only way a person can continue reaching these heightened levels is by increasing the frequency or quantity of the drugs being used. Drugs create a need that only drugs can meet. In time, the neurons of the brain are so desensitized to the drugs being used, they have no choice but to increase the drug use. The drug-induced desensitization eventually leads to a failure in the brain's neurotransmission, which results in people taking more and more drugs to reach the rewards they are desperately seeking. When this happens, the drug *user* becomes a drug *addict.*

Endorphins are known as the pain-killing molecules of the brain. Endorphins are endogenous, morphine-like neuropeptides that our pituitary glands produce as natural pain killers and stress releasers. Endorphins resemble opiates in the chemical structure and are produced during strenuous exercise, physical exertion, the act of sex and most notably, sexual climax.

A perfect example of how endorphins work can actually be found in action movies. Have you ever watched as the action hero of a movie runs for his life while being chased by a band of gruesome zombies? You watch the man running and running and running, and you think to yourself- "There's no way this guy can run this long without falling over in pain or exhaustion!"

Well, during the heightened stress of the chase, the endorphins are released in the man's brain, allowing him to run through the pain! The fact that the man is able to continue running until he finally escapes the clutches of the walking dead, tells us that the neurochemicals of his brain have successfully completed their mission as well. It also tells us that a sequel is most likely in the works.

Endorphins can also be released by eating and gossiping. Endorphins are also a major contributor to our experiences of love and attachment. Young children rely on endorphins to secure bonds with their parents and siblings.

Drugs like heroin and morphine play a significant role in the endorphin system by aiding in the soothing effect of a person's agitated state. But why do people gravitate to the soothing effects of drugs like heroin, when their bodies are already producing natural pain-killers? When a person possesses a history of being abused or neglected, his or her ability to self-soothe during times of distress is seriously impacted and adversely affected. This is because that the abused individual's brain circuitry has been prevented from fully developing due to the emotional or physical trauma endured by that particular individual. When a child's brain circuits are not properly developed, the child will have significant trouble connecting with love and affection. Therefore, the ability to develop and sustain meaningful relationships will be negatively affected.

Abusive conditions result in developmental arrests in the brain, causing a decreased release of endorphins from the pituitary gland. When a child lacks the natural endorphin release, he or she is ultimately more susceptible to the effects of drugs like heroin and morphine. In fact, many addicts describe an overwhelming feeling of love when they are under the influence of drugs. These drug-induced feelings of love are the same emotions a non-drugging person experiences when he or she is raised in a healthy, loving environment.

Oxytocin is another bonding hormone used as a neurotransmitter in the brain. Oxytocin is biologically linked to a person's trust levels and loyalty. Once trust is established, the release of oxytocin allows a person to be comfortable with the idea of being romantically held, cuddled, or touched. Romantic contact further increases the production of oxytocin in the brain. This is the reason oxytocin is referred to as the "Bliss Hormone." When parents touch or caress their child, oxytocin is released, helping the development of the child's parasympathetic nervous system.

A child who has been the victim of physical or sexual abuse, traumatic stresses, or severe illnesses will be less likely to feel the effects of an oxytocin release in later years. Although hormones are being released in a normal pattern, the oxytocin itself becomes less potent and less receptive to external cues. The body relies on a fully developed oxytocin system to promote trust, which in turn leads to a meaningful and loving relationships. When the oxytocin system is not fully developed, adults may rely on drugs and alcohol to find the bliss they are seeking.

Serotonin is commonly known as the true "Happiness" molecule. The release of serotonin ensures a more positive outlook on life. Normal serotonin levels allow people to become more sociable and less challenging in school, business, and relationships. People with low levels of serotonin often suffer from feelings of emptiness and loneliness, resulting in depression.

There are several medications used to increase the reuptake levels of serotonin in the brain. Examples of these medications include Prozac, Zoloft, and Lexapro.

Oftentimes, teenagers will join gangs to feel better about themselves. These young people often suffer from inadequate levels of serotonin, which triggers the need to be surrounded by other people. The teenagers feel empty and alone, so they seek out comfort in a group setting even if the group is involved in illegal activities.

Gamma-Amino Butyric Acid (GABA) is an inhibitory neurochemical that creates the opposite effect in people. GABA slows down the excitability in the central nervous system and helps to relax or soothe us. Another neurochemical is adrenaline, the hormone that kick-starts the body's energy and excitability! Adrenaline is a highly potent neurochemical that can activate a reaction or decision within seconds. Adrenaline may also serve to defend against underlying feelings of sadness, emptiness, or inadequacy.

GABA is known as the brain's inhibitory hormone. This molecule slows the neurotransmission in the central nervous system, creating a calming effect in the body. It is known as the body's natural tranquilizer. Benzodiazepines such as Valium and Xanax work in conjunction with the GABA system.

Adrenaline is the final hormone or neurotransmitter in the brain. It is known as the energy or stress molecule, otherwise known as "Fight or Flight." The "Fight or Flight Response" is usually engaged when a person is under harmful attack, or when he or she is faced with a survival situation. Heart rate and blood pressure will soar as people attempt to fight their way through the imposing attack or flee the situation altogether.

Darryl, Ronnie, and Mike Strawberry were faced with a "Fight or Flight Response" with Henry. When they grabbed the skillet, the butcher knife, and the frying pan, they were standing up to the threat. They were ready to put their young lives on the line and fight for their lives, and the lives of the females of the house.

Even though all humans possess the same neurochemical systems, a negatively influenced emotional environment can prevent a child's brain from properly developing a strong, positive sense of self. When abused as a child, the negative messages received by that child- "I'm stupid!" "I'm a burden!" or "I'm worthless" will ring loudly in that child's mind. This relentless persecution will contaminate the child's perception of himself.

Darryl and Ronnie were bombarded with this negativity by their father. The years of abuse ultimately affected the neuro-chemical releases in the young boys' brains. When children do not grow up in an emotional safe haven, their neurochemicals may not function properly, when compared to children with a more stable, emotional upbringing. When children have been emotionally damaged by abuse or neglect, they are more susceptible to addiction in later years.

The emotional development of Darryl and Ronnie would be tested in years to come, due to the lack of emotional attune-ment received from their father. The hardware and software of Darryl's life were impaired greatly by both nature and the lack of nurture by their father.

DARRYL'S STORY

TEENAGE YEARS

Darryl and his family were free. They were free from having to tip-toe through the house to avoid being verbally or physically abused by their father. They were free of the nagging fear that filled their minds on a nightly basis before finally falling asleep. The boys did not have to pretend they were private investigators any more. The act of searching for their father's car in front of the house was not a part of their lives, at last.

But was this freedom, a good thing? Would the absence of an adult male in the house affect the children? Yes, there was freedom to breathe and to laugh and smile, but would there be too much freedom? Would the young teenagers become less disciplined in their personal choices?

Ruby had always been the mainstay of their young lives. She provided stability and balance to a group of kids who knew nothing but horror from the other side of the parenting equation.

With the financial burden of the family falling square on Ruby's shoulders, her time at home with the children would be considerably less. The kids would be on their own more often, and the daily chores of the household would fall into the hands of all five Strawberry siblings. The children loved their mother and made a vow among themselves to never let her down.

A vow is a promise. A promise is a declaration that an act or task will be done or not done, based on the word of one to another. Vows mean nothing in our society today, especially when they are made by children. Ruby would realize this truth very soon.

THE DOWNFALL

The oldest Strawberry child, Mike, was twelve years old when he took on the role of "Man of the House" and he proved to be a strong, positive force for the family. Mike always had a great head on his shoulders, and he was bound and determined to make a positive, meaningful life for himself. Mike was a great athlete, but was more intrigued by law enforcement after listening to a policeman speak in his high school classroom, Mike knew what he wanted to do with his life. He wanted to become a police officer.

Mike was very conscientious about his decisions. He worked hard and kept his nose clean throughout his high school years in Los Angeles. Mike worked diligently at being a solid role model for his younger siblings, but had a difficult challenge ahead of him. For Mike had not lived through the same horrors that befell his younger brothers. His mind was not cluttered with the same levels of pain that had been inflicted upon Ronnie and Darryl. As "Man of the House," the young Mike had a difficult task ahead of him, indeed.

As much as Mike wanted to create a positive environment in the Strawberry home, Ronnie was on the other side of the equation. After the departure of his father, Ronnie's actions quickly became destructive. His defiant personality brimmed with wrath, and every moralistic value he may once have possessed was now spiraling out of control.

Ronnie was backsliding. When he did attend school, he was disruptive and was often expelled for his disruptive behaviors. In fact, Ronnie's multiple expulsions did not faze him in the least. He was beginning to embrace the "thug life" persona, and all the dastardly attention that surrounded it. He was not having a difficult time staying in the right lane, he had already crossed into the other lane and was driving into oncoming traffic.

Ronnie was being arrested and charged for numerous misdemeanors. If he wasn't smoking or selling dope, he was stealing, fighting, or damaging other people's property. In Ronnie's mind, he was already damaged goods, and had no desire to change that moniker. His father didn't care about him— why should he care about himself?

Ruby had lost control of her middle son. She tried to discipline him, but he would just scoff at her. If she grounded him to his room, he would just laugh and climb out of his bedroom window and escape into the neighborhood. The more she demanded, the more defiant he became.

Ronnie was living for the nights. He had stopped attending school altogether and was now spending his time with his gang compadres, under the light of the moon. Drugs had become a big part of his young life. He was smoking marijuana and drinking alcohol at an alarming rate. He and his gang were all about getting high and causing mischief throughout the 'hood.

They would light up their PCP-laced "Sherm sticks," which are joints that have been dipped in phencyclidine, also known as "angel dust." When smoked, Sherm sticks produce a hallucinogenic high that causes users to lose control of themselves. Soon, the young thugs would be in all-out brawls with rival gangs or people within their own group. The night had captured Ronnie and locked him away, just as it had done with so many others.

Darryl studied his brothers' two opposite personalities and was terribly conflicted in his heart. Darryl admired his older brother, Mike. He knew that Mike was living his life on the right side of the tracks. Mike possessed two outstanding traits: self-assurance and fortitude. When Darryl looked at Mike, he saw the person he wished he could be.

On the other hand, Darryl and Ronnie had a bond. They had been pitted against the Monster their entire lives and bravely battled through it together. When Darryl envisioned welts caused by a severe beating, his first thoughts were of his brother Ronnie.

Darryl witnessed the cause of Ronnie's welts, and he knew of his pain all too well. The bloody stripes on Ronnie's back and legs were mirror images of his own wounds.

Ronnie and Darryl's scars were buried deep in their fibers. They were both emotionally maimed and both began taking their resentment and pent-up frustrations out of their home and into their schools and neighborhood. As, Ronnie wreaked havoc in the neighborhood, Darryl started his negative outbursts at his new junior high school in San Fernando Valley.

As a new 7th-grade student at Sutter Junior High, Darryl was a lot bigger than the other students. The combination of his large physical stature and the fact that he was a black student bused in from the inner city made Darryl an instantaneous power force in the school's hallways. Within days, Darryl began strong-arming students for their lunch money. He even started threatening kids for their watches and anything else he desired.

Darryl's intimidation tactics did not last long at Sutter Junior High, as he was expelled from the school within weeks. Darryl then attended Audubon Junior High, but that did not last long either, when he was expelled for skipping school.

His mother was heartbroken when she found out about his multiple truancy infractions. Ruby had no idea Darryl was cutting classes to smoke weed, drink beer, and hang out with some of the riff-raff of the neighborhood.

There are four main reasons teenagers begin to take drugs:

1. To feel good: for pleasure, to become fearless
2. To feel better: to escape life and chase away stress
3. To do better: improved focus/improved strength
4. Curiosity: peer pressure/boredom/vulnerability

Did Darryl use drugs out of boredom? He couldn't have been curious about drugs, since he was well aware of how drugs were negatively affecting his brother Ronnie. Would he allow himself to become a drug addict like many others in the neighborhood or was it more about the old mantra: "Why do you climb a mountain? Because it's there."

Was this casual drug use a warning of things to come? Was he using drugs to escape his own life? Was he using drugs to fit in with the people he had surrounded himself with? Or was he sincerely using illegal substances to power through his blasé existence? Only time would tell if his early drug usage would become detrimental to his life in later years.

Darryl's junior high struggles continued at his next school, Horace Mann Junior High School. At Horace Mann, Darryl was constantly in the principal's office for fighting, truancy, and insubordinate behavior. He was nearly expelled again when he was nabbed for setting fire to the bathroom outside his classroom.

Darryl did not want to attend his first-period class, so he took insulation from the bathroom's ceiling and lit it on fire, inside the bathroom's garbage can. Within minutes, the school was evacuated and Darryl got his wish—missing his first-period class. Darryl was in big trouble with the school for his defiant behavior, but was miraculously allowed to finish the school year.

Both Ronnie and Darryl were venturing down darker paths with every step. Ronnie was involved in several criminal incidents—theft, assault, drugs—you name it. If Ronnie wasn't beating someone up in the neighborhood, he was being sufficiently whipped by someone else. He was once hospitalized after being pummeled by a group of gang members wearing brass knuckles. His face was badly disfigured and he could not see out of his swollen eyes for weeks.

Darryl was a complete mix of his two brothers. He was not walking the straight and narrow like Mike, but he wasn't getting arrested like Ronnie either. He cared about his mother's feelings, which kept him from totally crossing over to the dark side with Ronnie. But, he did like the feeling of being a tough guy—it felt much better than being afraid.

At the age of 14, Darryl began shooting craps in shady parts of the neighborhood. He would win some and lose some. When he did walk away with a wad full of winnings, his gang of on-lookers became instantaneous winners as well. Darryl would use his victory stash to buy marijuana and beer for the entire group. He was a hero in their eyes!

The impact of a home environment carries great weight towards the emotional and mental development of a child. The abusive actions of a parent can certainly increase a child's risk of addiction. A problematic home environment can also stem from the negative influences of an older sibling in the family. This fact is especially true when the older sibling is fondly looked upon by a younger sibling.

Darryl had two choices in his young life. He could follow the lead of his oldest brother Mike or go down the dark path set by Ronnie. Darryl was choosing the dark path. And although Darryl was not overly keen to undertake most of Ronnie's dangerous activities, he was connecting with Ronnie's method of pain concealment. Darryl was also finding acceptance with his bad choices. He felt a sense of invincibility amongst his peers.

Every time Darryl won a craps game, he also quenched his thirst for self-worth. Every time Darryl bullied another student man for his lunch money, he was building a wall around his true feelings of self-doubt. Darryl's self-worth had been destroyed by his father, and he constantly swam in a pool of self-doubt. Darryl's lack of self-worth and abundant feelings of self-doubt, was the biggest battle of his young life.

Ronnie was hiding from his pain, and in the process, was leading his little brother down the rabbit hole. Ronnie was endangering his younger brother. Mike knew it and so did Ruby.

The only thought that raced through each of their minds was: What was next for these two young teenagers? They both needed to find something to take them out of the environment they were being sucked into before it was too late.

THE REFUGE

Darryl was in dire need of finding a refuge from his current life choices and actions. He needed to find an activity that would be fun and challenging, but it had to be something that could also satisfy his strong desire for self-acceptance. He needed a venture that would highlight his physical attributes. He needed a pastime that could generate self-assurance and a hopeful future. But, more than anything- Darryl needed something that could provide him with an elevated sense of self-worth.

Darryl Strawberry found that refuge and his refuge was sports!

For months, Darryl had secretly longed for an escape hatch that would allow him to step off the dark path he was traveling. When he discovered the games of football and basketball, he was instantly transported to a different mindset. He was now spending time on the other side of the tracks—a greener side, with trees and grass and games.

Darryl's father had been a strong, hulking man, but he had never taught his sons any type of sports skill. The young men had to learn how to play sports on their own. Darryl enjoyed the competition on the football fields and the basketball courts. As the gangly southpaw continued growing taller and taller, he was also continuing to elevate his athletic abilities.

Darryl was throwing four to five touchdowns every pick-up game he played in. On the basketball courts, Darryl was shakin' and bakin'! He was breakin' ankles and skyin' to the rim for finger rolls and leaners in the lane. But it was not until Darryl began playing baseball at Rancho Park that he found the sport he fell in love with and in which he ultimately flourished.

Darryl could do it all. He was an outstanding pitcher, with a lively, hard-throwing arm. He could run and steal bases. He could track down fly balls, then turn around and nail a runner trying to advance to the next base. Darryl could hit the ball like no other kid in the area, and the power he possessed in his long, skinny body was becoming legendary in the California Little League ranks.

As Darryl's baseball prowess continued developing, his need for alcohol and drugs simultaneously diminished. His mind was clear when he was competing. He was able to block out the negative images of his life and momentarily forget the anger that still clung to his brittle soul. Sports was truly a refuge in his life.

LEARNING DISCIPLINE

Although sports had now become an influential part of Darryl's life, he was still dealing with issues regarding discipline. He was growing up in a single-parent household with a loving mother, who was unfortunately absent for gaping moments of he and his siblings' lives. Ruby's life was devoted to her children, and she was a determined woman who would not allow her children to go without food, clothing, or a roof over their heads.

Darryl respected his mother and Mike, but he was still dealing with the destructive obstacle course being run by Ronnie. Darryl's high school years were upon him, and he was in need of more positive role models for his life. He needed a father figure in the worst way and out of the blue, he found people to fill that role.

When playing on a sports team, boys and girls receive life-changing lessons on a daily basis. They learn the importance of teamwork and camaraderie. They learn of sacrifice and selfless-ness. They also learn of discipline and courage. Darryl was no different.

When John Mosely and Brooks Hurst entered the young outfielder's life, Darryl's outlook on discipline and self-restraint were positively altered. Darryl's views on true courage and humility were also changed for the better because of these two men. Darryl needed a gut check. He needed to have his heart confronted and his mind stripped of the selfish habits that were sewn deep within his current state of thinking.

Coach Mosely was his Junior League coach. Mosely made sure that Darryl respected his God-given gifts. He taught Darryl that by becoming a better person first, a better player would surely follow. He inspired Darryl, and refused to let him fall into the teenage traps of laziness and listlessness. He demanded timeliness from Darryl and provided motivation to the young sports phenomenon. Above all else, he gave Darryl hope.

Coach Hurst was his baseball coach at Los Angeles Crenshaw High School. Hurst demanded tenacity, work ethic, and hustle at all times during a game and practice. Darryl's baseball abilities were becoming legendary at this point, but Coach Hurst would not allow him to feel as if he were some sort of untouchable prodigy. He would not allow Darryl to be free from discipline and instruction.

In the middle innings of one game during his sophomore season, Darryl was pulled to the side by Coach Hurst and asked about his lack of hustle when coming off the field. Coach Hurst was in Darryl's face as he barked at his star player. Coach Hurst not only wanted to relay his disappointment, he wanted Darryl to know that his rules on hustle were non-negotiable. He wanted Darryl to know there are always consequences for one's actions.

After the on-field confrontation, Darryl took the ball cap off his head and handed it to his coach. He then promptly removed his baseball jersey and handed it to Coach Hurst as well.

"FORGET THIS! I QUIT! I'm done. I'm not playing for you!" screamed Darryl.

Darryl stared at his coach, but Hurst never blinked a single eyelash. A disgruntled Darryl turned and stormed off the field, never to return that season. Mike also quit the team out of respect for his brother. However, both Darryl and Mike missed the games, their teammates, and even Coach Hurst. Darryl felt bad about leaving and even worse that Mike quit the team in his final senior season because of him.

The following year, Darryl met with Coach Hurst and apologized for his actions, then asked if he could come back to the team. Coach Hurst calmly explained the reasons for his tone on the field, and he made sure that Darryl understood that he would do it again if rules are broken. He told Darryl that he was one of the most talented high school players to ever come out of Southern California, but Darryl needed to become more disciplined.

Coach Hurst stressed the importance of a good work ethic and the significance of playing with energy, on and off the field. He wanted the best for Darryl and was willing to push the young man to the limits. He wanted to see Darryl's talents blossom to their fullest. Coach Hurst saw great things in Darryl Strawberry, but Darryl Strawberry was his own worst critic.

Darryl knew he had talent. At 16 years of age, he could already wallop a ball farther than most people in professional baseball. That said, it was difficult for him to buy into the crazy hype that surrounded him. Ruby also had trouble buying into the extravagant baseball tales of her youngest son. She found her son's incredible sports feats difficult to believe.

Because Ruby kept Darryl grounded, her youngest son kept looking into the mirror and seeing a worthless person. He was buried to his neck in self-doubt. Even when the crowd screamed and cheered his name, a little voice in Darryl's head kept reminding him that he was a NOTHING and would never be anything but, NOTHING. Darryl's self-esteem was at an all-time low.

Maybe his self-esteem was low because he had never accomplished anything like this in his young life. Maybe it was because his mother kept him grounded. Or maybe it was because he was well aware of his father's presence at his ball games, yet was never spoken to by the elder Strawberry. The pain he endured as a youngster still haunted his thoughts, but knowing he had a father who had nothing to do with him as a young man, was heartbreaking.

THE PROSPECT

As Darryl's senior year progressed, so did the hype surrounding his game. He was being featured in newspaper articles and magazines. *Sports Illustrated* claimed that Darryl was "the Black Ted Williams" because of his slender build and his long, sweet swing.

At the completion of Darryl's senior baseball season, the big talk in Los Angeles was the Major League baseball draft. According to multiple sources, Darryl had a tremendous chance of being taken in the first round of the draft. Of course, Darryl and his mother could not and would not buy into the build-up created by the media in Southern California.

Then it happened! Darryl was called to Coach Hurst's office during the middle of the school day. An excited Coach Hurst delivered the fantastic news that Darryl had been selected by the New York Mets with the very first pick of the Major League Baseball draft!

Coach Hurst was bubbling over with pride for his young outfielder and Darryl couldn't help but smile. It was quite possibly the most exuberant smile of his 18 years of life. Within minutes, Darryl was whooshed into a classroom for a press conference. He was handed a New York Mets jersey as dozens of camera strobes flashed in his eyes.

Darryl was a New York Metropolitan and his family was ecstatic for him. His mother and sisters blushed with pride for their professional baseball man. A delighted Mike was filled with joy for his little brother. Ronnie may have been the happiest of them all. He embraced Darryl with honor, respect, and a brother's love. His kid brother had made it, and he was incredibly ecstatic for Darryl's success.

Darryl had achieved one of the highest forms of sports accomplishments by being selected as the #1 amateur player in the world. He had achieved it through hard work and dedication to his craft. He accomplished it because he had been pushed every day by his coaches, his mother, and his brothers. And, he accomplished it without the aid of drugs.

For the first time in his life, Darryl could look into the mirror and see the shadows of his former self lifting from the reflection. He could see a smile. And although the smile was but a faint whisper in the reflecting glass before him, it was a smile nonetheless. Moreover, it was a new beginning for a kid brother who was now a man.

The looming question for the young teenage superstar would be, "How will Darryl handle the new pressures of a world outside of the neighborhood in which he grew up?" Will the exposure of drugs and alcohol at such a young age have any further impact on Darryl, now that he is out on his own? Drug and alcohol addictions can happen to anyone at any age, but addiction is more likely to happen to those who were introduced to such vices as adolescents.

Was Darryl Strawberry ready for this meteoric jump to professional baseball? The world would soon find out.

Doctor's Notes and Comments to Chapter 2

with David Blair Miller, PsyD

When Henry Strawberry left his family, his young teenage boys were left to run the household with their mother and sisters. Darryl and Ronnie felt freedom for the first time in their lives. But living without the guidance of a father figure is a difficult arrangement for any young teenager, especially when the maternal parent is working extra jobs to provide food, shelter, and clothing for her children.

Setting boundaries for adolescent children is a complete necessity for parenting. A line in the sand must be drawn if a child is to comply with the regulations, rules, and moral obligations deemed appropriate by the caregivers of the family. If a child has a healthy mind, he or she will be better able to stay within the confines of a parent's wishes.

But what if the child's mind has been negatively affected by abuse? As stated earlier, children who have been abused or have been raised in a home of chaos, may not be able to properly release the neurochemicals needed to provide internal happiness or bliss. Therefore, in lieu of this inability to find joy, the young Strawberry teens were free to roam the schools and streets in search of their own happiness.

Adolescents need consistency, love, and boundaries! They need sleep to learn, and they need to learn in order to excel.

They need nutritional guidance to maintain strength, so they can excel in extracurricular activities. Boundaries create a healthy sense of self, even when the child has experienced physical and mental atrocities.

When Darryl and Ronnie gained freedom from their abusive father, they each began acting out in different ways. Ronnie was out of the house and gone! He did not feel comfortable in the home anymore because of his painful recollections. The memories of his torture were fresh in his mind, and he could not separate himself from the brutal reality that had rocked his younger existence. So, he ran away!

Darryl handled his freedom in a much different fashion. He became a bully in his middle school, stealing money and jewelry from his fellow pupils. He did attend classes, he was starting fires in school, and basically living life on his own terms. Darryl was disruptive, and his behavior was bad. However, bad behavior is not a true indication of a bad character or person.

A good person can make a mistake by doing something bad. Good people do bad things out of desperation, environmental pressures, sadness, anger, and irrational emotions. Young people do bad things for attention, or because they simply do not know any better. These types of young men and women are generally lacking parental guidance and discipline.

Darryl and Ronnie felt shame in their lives. They felt this way because they were told they were bad and no good! When one is told over and over- "You're no good!" and "You're worthless!" in time, one will tend to buy into those beliefs. Darryl was acting out as a bully, because he felt small inside. By acting out as a bully, he felt powerful and in control of his life, or was Darryl unconsciously emulating his father? Was he identifying with his father? We all need to identify and connect with others even if it results in poor consequences.

Truth be told, Darryl and Ronnie both lacked guidance and discipline in their lives. Now that their domineering father was out of their daily life, the young men were provided uncontested leeway to roam and explore. It was during these moments of unrestraint that the two teenagers began experimenting with drugs, alcohol, and gambling. The two were experiencing new, exciting feelings. They had discovered a way to tap into the "Hormones of Happiness."

During their teenage years, Ronnie's drug use was much more accelerated than Darryl's. Ronnie's hardcore use of illicit drugs was generating an emotional release that surpassed any joy he had ever known. To use a quote from an anonymous drug user, "Getting high was like waking up on Christmas morning and finding out that all the presents under the tree were addressed to me."

Could Ronnie's drug abuse have been avoided had his abusive father remained in his life? No one will ever be able to truthfully answer that question. But for all intents and purposes, it would have been difficult for anyone to overcome such emotional and physical damage without the assistance of intense psychological therapy. Therefore, when people do not *have the proper resources to assist them, they turn to other sources of relief. This act is commonplace. It is human nature.*

Both Darryl and Ronnie lived through their childhood completely devoid of a father's love and nurturance. Both their hardware and software systems were severely damaged and without proper psychological attention, the boys were wildly grasping at straws in a wind tunnel. Nature or Nurture? All the Strawberry young men wanted to do was survive. All they needed was a father's guidance, love, and discipline.

The concept of discipline is often misinterpreted. Discipline means behaving within the guidelines of rules and regulations. A disciplinarian is the person who teaches self-control and leads by example. Henry Strawberry was not a disciplinarian to Darryl and Ronnie—he was an alcoholic who used rage and physical abuse to mind-trap his children. The violent beatings did not represent discipline; they exuded hatred.

When Darryl acted out as a bully, he was kicked out of school. Why? Because, Darryl lacked discipline and self-respect. Darryl began smoking, drinking, and gambling at twelve years of age. Why? Because, Darryl lacked discipline and self-respect. On the other hand, Ronnie was defiant. He not only lacked discipline, he laughed in the face of rules and regulations. In Ronnie's mind, he was untouchable. He felt omnipotent.

During these critical teenage years, their mother Ruby became the family's disciplinarian. Ruby wore many hats—she was the breadwinner, the cook, the maid, the provider, the protector, and now the disciplinarian. Ruby was a single mother, overwhelmed by the many roles she was fulfilling in the home.

Ruby's main priority to her children was providing them with food, shelter, and clothing. Ruby's priorities were sound. She did the best she could. But, to be a true disciplinarian for teenage children, there must be ground rules, structure, and a consistent approach regarding reward and punishment.

Teenagers constantly test their freedoms and the authority over them. In the case of most single-parent providers, teenagers tend to push the envelope more frequently than those who have two parents standing guard. Parents must be able to set the rules of the house and expect their children to comply. If the children do not comply then a suitable punishment for their disobedience must be administered, but not by withdrawing love. It is important that parents explain their points of view; otherwise their discipline can come across as cruel and sadistic.

Single parents have difficulties with structure and punishment, because oftentimes, they are working two or more jobs to make ends meet. Therefore, children takes advantage of the parents' absence and either serve a portion of the punishment, or ignore the punishment altogether. Such inconsistency causes the framework of discipline to crumble.

Darryl and Ronnie both lacked discipline through the early parts of their teenage years. The two young men also lacked *attention and positive regard. Let's examine some of the reasons for this inadequacy. Henry was physically abusive to Darryl and Ronnie, but he was not abusive to his other three children. This is a major inconsistency issue for a disciplinarian. Why would a father physically abuse two of his children, but show love and nurturance to his other three offspring?*

Perhaps in the mind of Henry Strawberry, Darryl and Ronnie were born during a terrible time in his life. Was Henry associating Darryl and Ronnie's births to a painful time in his own life? Were there unconscious, negative connections between Henry and his children? Any way you slice it, Henry's ability to show consistency through discipline while providing love and nurturance was extremely limited and flawed.

Darryl would not encounter the true meaning of discipline until he started playing sports. On the other hand, Ronnie never experienced true discipline at all. Is there a correlation?

When Darryl began looking to sports as a refuge, he became more in-tune with the structure and consistency of discipline. He understood the expectations of his coaches, and he had no other choice but to comply. Coach Mosley and Coach Hurst both provided tough love to Darryl. The coaches set rules and regulations that had to be adhered to by all players. If the players did not obey the rules, then the consequences to their particular infractions were fully enforced.

Darryl understood the rules. He knew he had to be on time, listen, and hustle on and off the field. Coach Hurst's rules were non-negotiable. When Darryl quit the high school baseball team because of his disagreement with Coach Hurst, he took two steps backwards from the disciplined person he was becoming. As much as Coach Hurst wanted his star outfielder back in the lineup, he would not and could not back down from the rules he had established for the entire team. Coach Hurst was consistent in his discipline. Coach Hurst was teaching Darryl important life lessons, but sometimes there are underlying circumstances that led to the teenager's negative response to authority.

When Darryl was a young child, he was violently reprimanded for his mistakes. He was chastised by a loud, enraged voice. When Darryl made mistakes, his mind would be tortured by the mental images of being whipped by his father's belt! This was a terrifying image for Darryl, as it would be for any human being.

Verbally drilled by Coach Hurst for his lack of hustle, Darryl responded by removing himself from the situation. It was his way of escaping his coach's stern confrontation. Darryl missed the remainder of his sophomore season because he was unable to properly rationalize the message that was animatedly delivered by his coach.

Coach Hurst was attempting to instill the importance of a disciplined approach. The coach knew that if he could convince Darryl to improve his work ethic, the sky was the limit for the young man. On the other hand, Darryl shied away from the confrontation because he correlated making mistakes to physical and verbal abuse.

Darryl was reinstated to his high school team the following year and dominated in every capacity. Darryl had taken time to reflect on his own actions, as well as the reaction of his coach, and realized that he needed proper discipline and structure as much as Coach Hurst needed his superstar's bat in the lineup. Player and coach gained mutual respect for one another and never had another confrontation.

Children of all ages need structure. They all need rules and regulations, but more than anything else, children need consistency in the administration of discipline. Ronnie never understood discipline because all he ever wanted to do was escape. True, loving discipline is the life-line between a parent and a child. Respect and honor are born from this connection. That said, this process begins with the parent!

When a child is consistently exposed to an unsafe emotional environment, the neurochemical and psychological development of the brain may be notably altered. Therefore, the emotional development of the child is not likely to occur normally and this is a crucial factor leading to a child's future concepts of trust, love, and happiness. The software downloaded into the computer is responsible for the viruses, not the hardware. The environments of abusive homes are altering the life courses of our children.

The emotional attunement between a parent and child is vital to the prevention of addiction. Nurture trumps nature when it is related to addiction. When the abused child is unable to properly release dopamine and endorphins, he or she will undoubtedly search the corners of the world for happiness. We need to ask ourselves this question- "What software am I downloading into my child's computer?"

No one in this world has ever awakened from a long night's sleep and thought to themselves, "I think I want to be a crack addict." Addictions are a release from pain. Ronnie and Darryl never set out to be troublemakers or drug abusers. They never asked to have an addiction. All they ever wanted was to be understood. They want to be heard and loved, and most importantly, they wanted to be valued.

CHAPTER 3

COPING MECHANISMS

Based on an interview with David Blair Miller, PsyD

C oping mechanisms are methods used to avoid anxieties and stressful emotions or painful memories. Most young people listen to music, read books, or play sports to elude the anxieties that chase them. When it comes to those who have been abused or neglected, however, listening to music and reading books is just not enough. Many abused children will eventually resort to using drugs or alcohol to tame the stresses of their lives.

Darryl and Ronnie coped with their painful emotions in two different ways. Darryl was well-guarded against the abuse he had endured. He purposely blocked out (through the process of disassociation) the ugliness of his younger years by the following two approaches:

1. He developed his own "Character Armor," which is a habitual pattern of organized defense mechanisms used to protect against fears or anxiety while maintaining the individual's self-concept, and;

2. He relied upon several defensive mechanisms, which will be discussed further.

Ronnie coped with his painful emotions by falling deeper into the world of hardcore drugs and alcohol. He was attempting to disconnect from his pain, but the memories continued to claw at his brain. His mental battles were loud and vibrant. He could not block out the screams that violently ruled his mind.

As a teenager, Darryl would build up walls against possible emotional threats in his young life. He learned to shield himself from the negative images of his past by plugging into his own specific, character armor. Creating character armor is like building a giant fort. The fort is strong and tall and capable of defending against King Kong or rival armed forces eager to attack. Character armor is best described as a defense used to disguise a person's underlying weaknesses from himself and others.

Inside this imaginary fort, the individual is protected against ill-will or painful abuse. The fort seals the person inside a private vault of protection. No one is allowed inside the vault without his or her permission. A child feels protected and secure within the walls he or she has constructed. In the movie *The Sixth Sense,* the little boy Cole (played by Haley Joel Osment) made a fort in his bedroom to protect himself from the ghosts that constantly haunted him. He felt safe inside his fort, even though it was made from flimsy sheets held together by clothes pins.

Character armor can also be detected in bullies. Whenever you see a kid or an adult talking about how he is going to beat someone up or bragging on the number of guys he has beaten up in the past, you are actually witnessing a person who is fully dressed in character armor. Character armor is a false representation of oneself. It is an attempt to hide one's vulnerabilities and perceived shortcomings by creating a false façade of strength and domination.

The people who talk the most are usually the ones who cannot stand behind their words. These are the bullies of our society. Bullies are afraid of their own shadows and talk a huge game to hide their insecurities and weaknesses. In the animal kingdom, cats are known for arching their backs when they feel threatened. By arching their backs, the cat appears larger and thus less vulnerable for an attack.

Darryl was arching his back in the junior high hallways. He felt bold and powerful when he was taking his schoolmates' money or other valuables. Not one single classmate or peer had a clue that Darryl was riddled with self-doubt and extensive insecurities. In fact, Darryl worked hard to ignore his ingenuous front as he was fully protected in his own character armor.

All defense mechanisms have a fundamental purpose in the self-preservation of an individual's mind. Each defensive mechanism guards an individual from the overpowering anxieties, stresses, and fears that can attack them. Examples of defense mechanism include:

1. PROJECTION occurs when individuals are unable to acknowledge their own personal difficulties and project

their problems, struggles, or substance abuse onto another person.

EXAMPLE- An alcoholic goes to a billiards hall with several friends, who are also suffering from substance abuse. As the night progresses, his buddies get into a brawl with other bar patrons over a pool table infraction.

When the alcoholic is questioned about the altercation, he talks freely about his friends' alcoholism, and how their actions were responsible for the fracas. By deflecting the situation towards his friends, the alcoholic is denying his own alcoholism and dismissing the fight as someone else's problem.

Projection is the act of attributing one's disavowed troubles or issues on to another person.

2. **PROJECTIVE IDENTIFICATION** occurs when a person projects his own issues or problems into another person's mindset.

   EXAMPLE: A food addict who is suffering from body weight issues will run into an old friend, and say "Hey Buddy, you've put on a few pounds, huh?" The food addict is projecting his own poor body image onto a person who may or may not have a weight problem. By making this offensive statement, the food addict has denied his own problems by projecting them onto another person.

   Projective Identification is an unconscious process of a negative self-image being forced upon another person.

An addict using Projective Identification causes another person to internalize the same feelings of rage or unhappiness the addict is feeling.

3. DISASSOCIATION involves a detachment from reality as a means of coping with emotional pain or trauma.

4. REPRESSION involves blocking out or pushing unpleasant feelings or experiences away to avoid feelings of fear or anxiety.

5. IMPLICIT MEMORY is a type of long term memory that is in direct contrast to explicit memory. Implicit memory does not require conscious thought. Implicit memory affects a person's thoughts, feelings, and behaviors.

   Explicit memory is a conscious, intentional recollection of factual information based on previous experiences and concepts.

   Implicit memory is the unconscious, defensive process used by Darryl as a teenager. Implicit memory is an unconscious process used in the recollection of events that are the result of an automated response. Perhaps you have heard the old phrase, "It's just like riding a bike." The ability to jump on a bike and start riding it like you did as a child is an example of implicit memory. Another example of implicit memory is the ability to recall lyrics to a song after hearing the first note.

Implicit memory also involves disassociation, which allows a person to function in life without being constantly reminded of the traumatic situations that may have taken place in the past. Implicit memory uses past experiences to remember things without thinking about them. The performance of implicit memory is enabled by previous experiences, no matter when they occurred. Implicit memory is primal.

Here is an illustration. There was a news report about two Englishmen who bought and raised a lion cub. The men loved the baby lion. They played with the lion cub and wrestled with it. The men fed the lion cub and nurtured the young lion through his first full year of life. The men loved the lion cub and the lion cub loved them back.

One day, the men decided to free the young lion and reintroduce him to his real home in the African Bush. Three years later, the men went to the Serengeti to visit their young lion, who had become an adult lion. The adult lion immediately recognized the two men and raced to them! The men played with the lion and wrestled with him. The men loved the lion and the lion loved them back.

Watching a video of this report was a truly touching experience. However, the implicit memory that was triggered was not of the lion reconnecting with the men. No, the significance of the memory was felt by a select few (people) who actually watched the video. These specific individuals were emotionally affected by the video because they had never experienced such unconditional love in their own lives. The memory of being unloved was hidden away by the individuals' implicit memory.

Implicit memory is raw and intense. Therefore, a defensive mindset is established through disassociation to block out the traumatic events of one's past. This action allows a person to concentrate on his present life, while avoiding the negative memories of the past. Implicit memory allows people to properly function in adulthood.

Disassociation is the act of disconnecting from painful memories of the past. This action protects individuals from painful images and sadness related to the anxieties of their early childhood. Disassociation allows them to separate emotional experiences from their physical presence.

Darryl was aware of his painful past, but instead of confronting the pain with intense psychotherapy, he unconsciously disassociated himself from the memories on his own. Darryl had a job to do, and he could not be bothered with emotional experiences that constantly highlighted his negative self-images and internal shame. Darryl chose to split off from his past memories to survive as an adult.

The act of disassociation is commonly used by those who have been physically or sexually abused. It also takes place in the minds of those who are neglected or abandoned. Social distress or trauma can also trigger disassociation. This is because our brains cannot differentiate between physical pain and emotional pain. In our brains, pain is pain.

If you witness a horrific car wreck, and are asked to make a statement regarding the horrifying sights of the crash, your brain can process your painful recollection in the exact, same way as if you were the one injured in the crash. Neuroimaging technology has demonstrated that physical pain, emotional or social distress, and recollections of neglect and abandonment, can all be detected by similar brain reactions.

When we are physically injured, we are treated with opiates or opioids. These pain-killing narcotics are used to comfort the person who has been injured. The opioids, which are commonly known as Oxycodone, Hydrocodone, and OxyContin, attack the limbic system of the brain, creating feelings of pleasure and relaxing contentment.

When people are emotionally injured, they treat themselves with drugs, alcohol, and opiates to find the same neurochemical release. An increased dopamine release will provide a serious escape from a person's pain and inner-anguish. In time, the brain requires increased dopamine release. People crave the feelings associated with the release. It is only a matter of time before the addiction is in full force.

* * * * *

DARRYL'S STORY

DECISION TIME

One of the best ways of preventing drug abuse is by not trying drugs and alcohol in the first place. This is an "easier said than done" proposition for some teenagers in our society. It is simple math—"Drug use leads to drug abuse." As stated earlier, the environments of one's home, school, and neighborhood can be strong contributors to drug use for teenagers.

For adults, the risk of drug and alcohol addiction can be accelerated during divorce, the death of a loved one, the loss of employment, or the overbearing stresses of one's daily life. One of the leading reasons for accelerated drug use among teenagers can be attributed to life-altering changes. Overwhelming adolescent stresses include the death of a parent and/or loved one, the social stresses associated with changing schools, or dealing with stressful, life-altering decisions.

For Darryl, being drafted as the #1 player in the Major League baseball draft, carried burdens that 99.99 percentage of all teenagers would never realize or comprehend. It is one thing for individuals to be the center of attention in their family, or their school or neighborhood. It is a whole different scenario to be the center of attention within the New York media. And 18-year-old Darryl Strawberry was smack dab in the middle of a media firestorm.

Darryl was offered $200,000 to sign with the Mets. With that amount of money, he could instantly help his mother with all monetary burdens. The freedom from financial burden is a sure-fire way of releasing stress loads in a family. The money was important to Darryl, but he had many other factors to consider before signing upon the dotted line of his baseball deal.

Darryl already held a scholarship offer from Oklahoma State and the thought of playing in the obscurity of Stillwater, Oklahoma actually sounded heavenly to him at times. Stillwater was a simple place with a simple plan. The Big Apple's media madness was much like a twisting, spinning vortex twirling him about like a mailbox in a tornado.

There is an abundant amount of pressure on adolescents who are expected to make adult decisions. Life-changing decisions are overwhelming for a person of any age, let alone for a person just out of P.E. class. Why do you think so many childhood entertainers struggle and fail in their attempts to continue acting careers as adults?

Darryl worried about leaving his mother and siblings. He worried about being on his own. He was worried about where he would be playing in his first season. The unknown can be frightening for anyone, let alone for a baby bird being pushed out of the nest. Moving away from Los Angeles was a life-altering change. With every step toward this tough decision, Darryl seized up with the painful premise of leaving his brother, Ronnie.

Would Ronnie be okay? He wondered if he would receive a call about his brother being incarcerated or worse. He felt as if he was leaving his family unprotected. It took all three Strawberry brothers to chase the Monster away. Mike would be all alone in the next fight.

Ruby encouraged him to let go of his fears. She gave him the motivation he needed to pursue the chance of a lifetime. She pushed her son to reach for the stars and never give up hope. She wanted the best for her Darryl, and she made it clear that she would always be but a phone call away.

After much thought, Darryl took the pen from the Mets General Manager, Frank Cashen, and signed his named on the dotted line of the contract. Darryl Strawberry was officially a New York Mets baseball player.

Within days, Darryl was handed an airline ticket to Kingsport, Tennessee, where he would begin his minor league career. Ruby's youngest son was on his way!

MINOR LEAGUES IN THE SOUTH

To say that the town of Kingsport was somewhat of a culture shock to Darryl Strawberry—well, that would be an understatement. Kingsport was a town nestled in the mountainous region of Eastern Tennessee. The population of Kingsport was 42,000 and 95 percent of those people were white. Three percent of the Kingsport population was African-American and less than one percent was Hispanic.

Growing up in south-central Los Angeles, Darryl was accustomed to a more diverse population. Black, White, Hispanic, and Asian people from all corners of the world, were a part of the Southern California population. It took a while for the south-central teenager to feel comfortable in a town so different from the area in which he had been raised.

Kingsport was a sleepy town, with beautiful scenic views, but little entertainment value. If one enjoys car races and putt-putt golf, then the bedroom community of Kingsport is a wonderful place to explore. Los Angeles was always hopping with action. It was loud and boisterous, and there was always something to do, at all times of the day or night.

Sometimes, ordering lunch from a fast-food restaurant in Kingsport was difficult for Darryl. The slow, mumbled drawl of the Eastern Tennessee region sounded weirdly slurred to his ears. He would often ask people to repeat themselves so he could better understand them. The thought of ordering food through a restaurant's drive-thru window made Darryl cringe. He would have a better chance ordering a meal in Shanghai, China.

When Darryl reported to Kingsport, he thought the New York media frenzy would finally come to an abrupt end. Darryl was wrong. Every night in Kingsport, the New York media was there in full force! And the chaos did not stop with the reporters and camera lights. Darryl was inundated with autograph seekers who packed the Kingsport Mets stadium.

Darryl was totally happy to sign autographs for the fans, but the plethora of questions that accompanied the autographs was always the tough part of the assignment.

"How do you like Kingsport?"

"How long 'til you hit your first home run?"

"Are you as good as they say?"

"How tall are you?"

Answering the same questions over and over, each and every night, can become challenging at times for celebrities. In time, celebrities become less human with their answers. They become robotic, and are often considered rude for their short answers.

"It's fine."

"I don't know?"

"I hope."

"Tall."

Some fans feel that celebrities are unfriendly when they give such curt answers. But the fans fail to understand that these "celebrities" are in fact, real people, just like them, and when someone has to answer the same questions over and over, it becomes a tad bit tedious.

Let's put this in perspective. When any person hears the same questions over and over, the answers will naturally become as humdrum as the duplicated questions being asked. For example, take parents who are asked the same question over and over by their 3-year old child.

"Mommy, what is that?"

"Nothing"

"Daddy, are we there yet?"

"No."

"Mommy? Mommy? Mommy?

"WHAT?!! WHAT!!? WHAT!!?"

"Daddy, how tall are you?"

"Tall."

The point of this illustration is that public figures and celebrities get a bad rap sometimes, because they come across as disinterested to their fans. It is also extremely difficult for baseball players to be overly thoughtful to fans, when they know they will most likely be heckled by them and their cohorts later in the evening.

Darryl started receiving heckles early on for the Kingsport Mets. When he struggled at the plate or made an error in the field, the stands would erupt with echoing jabs like, "YOU SUCK!" or "OVERRATED!" or "WHAT WERE THE METS THINKING?" Such taunts were rough on an 18-year-old's psyche, especially for someone who is already suffering from negative self-esteem issues.

The racial slurs yelled from the stands then became the proverbial icing on the cake for Darryl. He had heard racial slurs throughout his life, but the distasteful smears he received in the Appalachian League cut like a jagged Rambo knife. The words that echoed through the park were filled with an ugly hatred.

Darryl wanted out of Kingsport!

At the conclusion of each of his games, he would lock himself inside his apartment bedroom and not come out until it was time to report to the field the following day. He called his mother every night when he returned to this room. He was lonely and homesick, and never ventured far from his apartment bedroom. He was a shut-in and just wanted to get back to Los Angeles and his familiar surroundings.

The following year, Darryl played for the Lynchburg Hillcats in Virginia. The Hillcats were a Single-A affiliate of the Mets farm system. The town of Lynchburg was very similar to Kingsport. It was a predominately white township with the same impatient, raucous fan base. It was another year of autographs, jeers, and cruel racial taunts, but it was In Lynchburg that the onslaught of racial slurs against African-American ballplayers was beyond hateful. The Bible Belt was speckled with viciously spiteful hate-mongers.

Darryl labored mightily in Lynchburg. He struggled at the plate, which in turn led to his difficulties in the outfield. If he wasn't striking out with the bases jammed, he was overthrowing second base, allowing one run after another. He questioned his abilities from the time he opened his eyes in the morning, until the time he shut them for the night. Darryl had entered a new, all-time emotional low. In his mind, he was failing.

Darryl's lowest moment as a Mets farmhand came on a day he decided not to play in the game. He also decided not to go to his workouts or batting practice or anything else associated with the Lynchburg Hillcats. He completely shut himself off from the world and had no intentions of being part of the team on this particular summer day. Darryl was a no-show.

Instead of showing up for work at the park, Darryl decided to get drunk and smoke some weed. He was not a heavy drinker or smoker in the minor leagues, but his underlying stresses were pushing him toward both methods of escape. His overwhelming feeling of rejection was taking charge of his life once again.

Was Darryl falling into the same bad habits that nearly destroyed his junior high education? Would his decision to skip practice and a game lead him into a pattern of skipping more games? Was Darryl backsliding? Or were the racial taunts of his hometown crowd weighing heavier on his mind than he wanted to admit?

The next morning, Darryl was met with the headlines of the local Lynchburg newspaper- "Mets #1 pick goes AWOL!" The article slammed him for skipping both his workouts and the game. At least the newspaper was blind to the fact that Darryl spent his entire day off smoking weed in his bedroom. Had they gathered that kind of scoop, Darryl would really have had some explaining to do.

Darryl knew he was going to be in serious trouble with the Mets organization for his actions, but he was fed up with the vile mouths of the Lynchburg fan base. Fortunately, Manager Gene

Dusan was extremely understanding of Darryl's situation. He could see the pressure under which Darryl was playing, and he wanted to help the young star rise above his challenges. The speech he delivered to Darryl was compassionate, understanding, and remarkably positive.

Gene wanted Darryl to know he had the tools to make it big in the game of baseball. He told Darryl he was putting too much pressure on himself, and that he needed to have more fun with the game. Gene told Darryl to ignore the racist idiots in the stands and play the game for himself and no one else. Darryl needed to let go and play the game in the exact way he had for Coach Hurst at Crenshaw High School.

Darryl took the words to heart. He was one of the first arrivals to the park from that day forward. He never skipped out on a game or practice again. The positive speech delivered by Gene Dusan was one of the most important player/coach meetings Darryl would ever have in his career. Gene was truly like the captain of a ship, steering his young vessel through rough waters.

Darryl also received major assistance from Lloyd Mc Clendon, who was sent to Lynchburg for a rehabilitation assignment. Lloyd's presence in Lynchburg was an important move made by the Mets organization. His company was the best medicine for Darryl's strife, and it couldn't have happened at a better moment.

When Lloyd arrived in Lynchburg, he saw Darryl's sunken eyes. He could tell Darryl was smoking weed because of the hazy look in his eyes.

"Man, what are you doing to yourself?" asked Lloyd.

"Man, this place sucks! Nothin' but hate in those stands," answered Darryl.

"Well, that shit's gonna stop. Lloyd McClendon's here now!" Lloyd's declaration was followed with a smile.

Darryl grinned from ear to ear. Lloyd's words rang true in his heart and it was the first time Darryl had been able to breathe in what seemed like forever. In fact, Lloyd McClendon was the first person to keep Darryl Strawberry from running away from the game of baseball. Darryl needed Lloyd's strength and confidence, and it was well received.

Darryl finished the season strong in Virginia. As the season continued, Darryl refused to let the negative hatred spewed by Lynchburg's "Hateful-Few" affect him anymore. He owed Lloyd much gratitude for becoming a protector in his life.

The following year, Darryl played AA ball in Jackson, Mississippi, and was named MVP of the Southern League when he hit 34 homers and drove in 97 runs. He also stole 45 bases—not bad, when you consider they play 22 fewer games in the Minor League circuit.

Darryl's next Minor League assignment was in Tidewater, Virginia, which was the AAA affiliate of the Mets. It wasn't long before New York fans were asking- "Where is Darryl Strawberry?" and "When is he coming to New York?" After playing in 16 AAA games, Darryl was given the news that he was being called up to the Big Leagues!

At 21 years of age, Darryl Strawberry had made his way from an apartment in Watts to the rural communities of Kingsport and Lynchburg. He braved the humidity of Jackson and journeyed to the Atlantic coast, before finally being called up to "The Show"! Not bad, for a kid who was one wrong turn away from spending his life on a dark street in the 'hood.

Not bad for a kid who had nearly been kicked out of Horace Mann Junior High for starting a fire in the boys' bathroom. Not bad for a kid who was persecuted for the color of his skin. Not bad for a kid who went to bed each night with tears in his eyes and fear in his heart. Not bad for a kid who wore the raised welts of a belt strap on his back. Not bad for a kid who felt he was a NOTHING!

In the blink of an eye, Darryl was on a plane headed for New York City. In his brief time in the minor leagues, Darryl truly found himself. As a player, Darryl learned the game of baseball. He worked on his trade with thousands of swings in batting practice sessions and during his cage work. He learned the art of fielding through thousands of pop flies and grounders hit to him by multiple coaches and their trusty fungos.

A high school baseball player has a 0.5 percent chance of being drafted by a Major League team. Once drafted, a baseball player has a 9.3-percent chance of making it to the Big Leagues. Darryl Strawberry was not only the #1 pick in the 1980 draft, he made it to his Big League affiliate within three years of signing his contract.

Darryl Strawberry accomplished this grand feat without any type of illegal substance. He did not rely on weed or beer to make it to the top. He did not use any type of "bully" mentality to push his way to the summit. He did not have to roll the dice or set anything on fire to escape reality. Darryl completed his tasks with hard work, self-sacrifice, and patience.

When Darryl arrived at Shea Stadium, he was placed in a familiar scenario. He was once again the center of attention: Lights, cameras, action! But, this time he was ready for all the hard-hitting investigative reporting of the New York press!

"How do you like New York?"

"How long 'til you hit your first home run?"

"Are you as good as they say?"

"How tall are you?"

Welcome to the Show, Darryl Strawberry.

* * * * *

DOCTOR'S NOTES AND COMMENTS TO CHAPTER 3

with David Blair Miller, PsyD

Darryl battled through a few tough years as a minor league baseball player. Minor League baseball is a mental challenge for any young man, especially one who has lived through an abusive upbringing. Fans of the game see the glamour in the sport. Those who have worked in professional baseball as a player, coach, or trainer refer to their profession as "The Grind."

In professional baseball, there is no such thing as a day off, or a vacation day, or a holiday weekend. Professionals in baseball work ten to twelve hours a day, and when they're not working, they are either sleeping or traveling to their next series destination. Professional ball players are expected to perform at their highest levels every single time they take the field. They battle through various aches and pains throughout a season. The players will also contend with sleep deprivation and unfavorable nutrition sources, but onward they grind.

Darryl was a teenager when he entered the minor league baseball circuit out of high school. He was not prepared for the strenuous schedules and itineraries of a professional ball player. Professional baseball was his first and only job and he had no idea there was so much practice time involved with each game day experience. His stress levels were becoming more intense with every game he played.

If you do the math, Darryl was carrying the emotional baggage from his past, he was battling the intense workload and stresses of a difficult game in an unfamiliar environment, and to top it all off, he was now dealing with the emotional strains of racism and hate-mongering. That is a heavy load for anyone, let alone a teenager.

Darryl was equipped with his character armor. While his subconscious mind was attempting to stave off the demons that pursued him, how does a young man stay focused on his task at hand, with so many emotional land mines littered on the path before him? He first started his defensive stance by building a fort.

His fort was his bedroom at the apartment. When he closed his bedroom door, he was locked away and protected. No one could negatively affect him or hurt him when he was sealed off from the rest of the world. His second line of defense was to block out the hurtful words and actions of the racist fans. There is always one bad apple in every bushel.

Darryl was his own worst enemy. He lacked self-confidence and his self-esteem was already severely damaged, so the revolting words from the stands merely exacerbated his negative self-image. He did not feel accepted or loved by his own father, so the deplorable jeers of the unruly fans were a constant intrusion on his implicit memory.

A person in this situation has two choices:

1. *He can stand his ground and fight or*

2. *He can fly away, run away, or hide. This type of action was referred to earlier as the "fight or flight" response. When a person is faced with a "fight or flight" scenario, the sympathetic nervous system is immediately activated, triggering a physiological response within the adrenal medulla of the brain.*

Once the adrenal medulla is charged, a hormonal rush occurs in the body. Adrenaline or epinephrine, along with several neurotransmitters (serotonin and dopamine) and hormones (cortisol, testosterone and estrogen), are released into the body like a swarm of bees. The release of adrenaline and cortisol causes increased blood pressure and elevated blood sugar levels, while suppressing the immune system. This hormone bump results in an explosion of energy and increased muscle tension to either fight or run.

The sympathetic nervous system regulates the emotional response to a threatening situation or stress. Darryl's mind was being emotionally attacked and he had the choice to rise up and defeat it, or hide away and let the problems eat him alive. Darryl chose to hide away in his fort and smoke marijuana. He allowed the overwhelming anxieties of his life to dictate his misguided actions.

Darryl faced an abnormal amount of stresses as a teenager. In fact, he faced more emotional dilemmas than most people his age. Darryl was seriously thinking about giving up and letting go of his baseball dreams. Thank goodness, Lloyd McClendon showed up in Lynchburg when he did. His presence helped calm Darryl, while also giving him encouragement. The stress was momentarily relieved, but for how long?

Stress has serious effects on a person's immune system. We all have natural killer cells we use to fight off toxins, viruses, and infections. When we are stressed out, our natural killer cells are unable to properly fight off the toxins, viruses, and infections introduced into our bodies. The reason this happens is because our natural killer cells are compromised by our own levels of excessive stress.

During high levels of anxiety and stress, our natural killer cells are pulled away from their function of fighting off disease and infections so they can assist in the restoration of a person's heart rate and blood pressure. In other words, our anxieties and stresses prohibit our natural killer cells to accomplish their duties. When this happens, we become sick, infected, or worse. The connection of mind and body is phenomenal. Taking care of one's mind is just as important as taking care of one's body.

When young parents are chronically stressed, their young infant children can actual feed off their stresses and become stressed themselves. When a mother is stressed, her heart will race and her blood pressure may soar. Here is an example of how stress can be shared between a mother and her infant child: A stressed mother hears her infant child crying. The mother picks up the baby and holds it to her chest to quell her infant's tears. However, when the baby feels the unrhythmic pounding of its mother's heart, the baby does not feel comfort at all.

The erratic heartbeat of the mother is not soothing to the child, so the child experiences the same stress the mother is undergoing. The mother is unable to properly comfort her baby's cries, because the baby is now equally stressed.

This experience has a direct effect on the baby's nervous system and developing brain. The overwhelming stress felt by the baby impacts a very important aspect of the infant's brain, which is known as the parasympathetic nervous system. The parasympathetic nervous system is responsible for self-soothing and is a total necessity for a person's ability to cope with anxiety while restoring calm. Most addicts have a difficult time restoring calm and inner peace, which is why relaxation techniques, deep breathing, and yoga are useful exercises for those suffering from addiction.

Stress is a silent killer. It is one of the many reasons drugs and alcohol are used in our society. And how do we battle stress? Many people choose to run. They choose to hide away inside their character armor or behind the imaginary walls of their fort. Some people ignore the stressful moments of their past through memory disassociation. These people are choosing flight instead of fight.

In addition, there are four additional defensive mechanisms teenagers use to block out stress, sadness, and painful memories of the past. These defense mechanisms include:

1. *Denial,*

2. *Minimization,*

3. *Intellectualization and*

4. *Rationalization.*

DENIAL is a defense mechanism that regulates the intensity of a person's actualities. Drug abusers and alcoholics are notorious for denying their actual levels of consumption. Denial is a huge part of addiction. That said, the act of denial is not limited to addictions of drugs and alcohol. The most common form of denial happens among people who are obese.

Obese people do not see themselves the way others view them. They live in a state of denial for various reasons:

1. *Food is the main source of their "Hormones of Happiness" release.*

2. *Willpower is a very difficult state of mind to achieve and/or*

3. *Laziness. People use hundreds of excuses to avoid losing body fat. They live in a world of denial, so they never have to face the reality of their existence. Food addicts make excuses to avoid the work needed to positively alter and improve their health and lifestyle. Many people rely on denial because they are often unable to cope with real-life situations due to their extremely low self-esteem.*

MINIMIZATION is a defense mechanism used to minimize the intensity of a situation in life. People will use minimization to justify an action that is completely harmful and unsafe. An example of minimization can be found in an abusive marriage. A woman can be punched and thrown down a flight of stairs by her terrorizing husband, but she will minimize the altercation by calling it a spat or quarrel.

People who use minimization as a defense mechanism will often downplay a situation or make light of its intensity. People who suffer from depression will minimize praise. Darryl suffered from self-esteem issues, and would frequently minimize his accomplishments. He never truly believed in the overwhelming hype and enthusiastic praise he received for his baseball talents.

INTELLECTUALIZATION is a defense mechanism that involves a person using reasoning and/or logic to block the emotional stresses and painful memories of his past and present life. An example of intellectualization can be found during a divorce. A woman divorces a man. The man is devastated by the loss of his wife, but instead of focusing on the painful visions of his broken home, he sits down and recalculates his financial budget. He completes this task in an attempt to find something positive or logical to his loss. By checking his financial ledger, he finds that he is now saving $820 a month. This is an intellectual, logical mode of escape. It is the man's defense mechanism against a powerfully sad moment.

RATIONALIZATION is the most common defense mechanism used by teenagers. When individuals rationalize their choices, they are merely making excuses for their actions. There was on old adage "Preacher's kids are always the wildest!" This saying applied to those teenagers who partied during their high school years, then blamed their uptight, religious upbringing for their rebellious acts.

Rationalization can be a dangerous defense mechanism, because it allows teenagers to commit unacceptable acts, only to justify that action later with an excuse or reason for their action. The following is a dramatized illustration, but it will prove the theory of rationalization.

A teenage girl is driving her terminally ill, elderly grandmother to the hospital. As the girl motors down the highway, she accidentally runs a red light, nearly crashing into a garbage truck. The car spins out of control before coming to an abrupt stop. When she looks at her grandma, the girl realizes the old woman has just died from a heart attack.

When asked about the incident later, the girl responds, "I don't know what the big deal is. She was going to die anyway." The teenage girl comes across as a cold individual with her remarks, but she is rationalizing her feelings to defend her sadness of the situation. This is rationalization.

* * * * *

No one is immune from psychological disruptions, stressful incidents, or painful recollections. Darryl had lived through some extremely tough moments during his young life. Had Darryl been given the opportunity to receive intense psychological treatment, he might have been able to cope with his stresses in a much safer and complete fashion.

Darryl was a teenager when he was pushed out of the nest and into the world. He had to learn quickly if he was going to survive. He used several coping mechanisms to block his painful recollections. The important message for parents is to be alert and cognizant of their children's signals. Parents need to see the signs, read between the lines, and be wary of the behaviors of their children.

The teenage girl who ran the red light was in great pain. She never wanted her grandmother to die. She made a mistake and compounded that error with her uncaring remarks.

Parents and caregivers, look deep inside your children's hearts, ask questions, and be open-minded to their struggles. Our children require a parent's light.

CHAPTER 4

UNDERSTANDING THE MIND

Based on an interview with David Blair Miller, PsyD

D arryl progressed through his minor league years much more quickly than most athletes in his profession. He faced many challenges and numerous stressful situations in his three minor league seasons, but managed to overcome all the challenges and obstacles in his path. By the time Darryl finished his minor league career, he had mastered the ability to defend himself against loneliness, racism, and the day-to-day pressures of a professional baseball player.

Many people believe the greatest milestone for a baseball player is to make it to the Big Leagues! "If you make it to the Bigs, then you have truly made it! You have conquered the world!" Truth be told, making it to the Major Leagues is only the first step of the journey.

To illustrate this point, imagine you are playing a video game like *The Legend of Zelda* or *Super Mario Brothers.* Conquering each minor league level is reminiscent of an animated superhero defeating a barrel-throwing gorilla or a fire-breathing dragon to advance to the next level. As the character battles his way through each heart-stopping sequence, he eventually arrives at the final level of the game. He has made it to the top! He has conquered the world! Right? Not necessarily. The superhero still has to defeat the final gruesome creature who is guarding the princess! The key to saving the princess has one critical component: "Stay alive in the process!"

The goal of the superhero is not just making it to the final level, it is about conquering the final level and saving the princess. What good is making it to the final level if you keep getting burned alive by the fire-breathing dragon in the process?

Baseball players who arrive at the Big-League level want to excel and survive. They need to avoid the dragon's fire, stay alive, and contribute as long as they can because the pay-off at the end of the final level is the true reason they began the journey in the first place.

This mindset creates all types of increased mental stresses for a major league baseball player: the constant worry of contributing on a daily basis, the perpetual threat of injury, and the consistent pressures of the front office and fans. Players have been known to play with broken bones to retain their spot on the major league roster. These players understand that if they pull themselves out of the line-up, there is a chance a younger player in the organization could take their place at any given moment.

Darryl makes his grand entrance into the Majors on a team that is in last place. He is surrounded by older players who are holding onto their decaying careers by their fingertips. Many of these players are going through severe anxieties, and are compensating for their stresses by engaging in senseless sexual encounters, illicit drugs, drunkenness, and frivolous spending. Such behaviors are the first indications of a damaged emotional structure.

Darryl enters an unhealthy environment and must be alert to the dangers that will prey upon his own vulnerabilities. Darryl will encounter men who are combatting the same insecurities Darryl has felt throughout his career and his early life. He will also be introduced to men who have the same addictions his father possessed. As stated earlier, addicts are often those who are emotionally empty and searching for an escape from the constant pain they are enduring.

Addictions are not limited to drugs and alcohol. People have behavioral addictions with food, pornography, Internet use, video games, and gambling. But how can gambling and video games cause addiction if they are unable to stimulate a dopamine release? The answer to this question is remarkably important. Gambling and video games can absolutely trigger dopamine and adrenaline releases in the brain. Addictions to pornography, tattoos, or surfing the Web can also trigger a dopamine release.

If you blindfold a gambling addict and walk him into a casino, his brain is immediately stimulated! The bells, whistles, and clanking sounds of the slot machines will cause an automatic neurochemical stimulation in a gambling addict's brain. The oxygen pumped into the casino can also trigger a dopamine response.

Believe it or not, people can actually get addicted to television shows. Let's use the game show *Wheel of Fortune* as an example. A person who is addicted to this show can be busy painting in the back room of the house, hear the *WHEEL! OF! FORTUNE!* Chant, and be in the living room before Vanna White flips her first letter. The whirring, cracking sounds of the spinning wheel and the audience's *WHEEL! OF! FORTUNE!* chant can absolutely transmit a dopamine release in a person who is addicted to this particular show.

The gambling addict will bet his entire life savings on a single wager. Such addicts have been deprived of a sense of self-confidence as a child. People who lack self-esteem as children will be unable to self-regulate, self-soothe, and self-gratify as adults. They are in constant search of the "Hormones of Happiness" release, and once they have identified a particular drug or activity capable of creating such desired neurochemical responses, they have a very good chance of becoming addicted to that mode of release.

It is important to note that abuse does not necessarily cause addiction, but people who have been exposed to childhood pain and trauma are more vulnerable to manufactured dopamine releases, which in turn, could lead to an addiction.

Darryl is vulnerable to drugs and alcohol. He is vulnerable to the pressure of fitting in, and going along with the actions of his peers. He is a young rookie who wants to fit in with his older teammates. Would he be strong enough to combat the temptations that would ultimately confront him?

Darryl has relied on defense mechanisms to fend off the pains that have flooded his soul. Will the future actions of his teammates trigger the explicit memories currently hidden in his mind? Will he rationalize his decisions to use drugs and alcohol? Will he fall prey to the newest temptations of his life—beautiful women with underhanded agendas?

Darryl has a strong need for connection. Will this need become the downfall of his young life?

* * * * *

DARRYL'S STORY

HAVE FUN

"Have fun, kid!" Those were three dangerous words of advice for a 21-year-old athlete entering into his first games as a Major League professional ball player. The pressures of performing in the Minor Leagues were stressful enough, but now Darryl was entering a new realm of work-related tension. If he thought the heckling of a random few in the southern cities of Kingsport and Lynchburg were tough, how would he handle the relentless, booming jeers of the 40,000 fans packed into the Big League stadiums across the National League territory?

When faced with the pressures of his adolescent years, Darryl did not exactly handle those stresses in the best ways possible. He turned to alcohol and marijuana at a very young age, because he thought it was the best way to deal with the pain and self-doubt he wrestled with on a daily basis. He relied on illegal substances to numb his heart and mind.

Luckily for Darryl, he did not totally rely on the same escape route during his Minor League days. He was more of an introvert throughout his three years in the minors, and although he did drink and smoke marijuana, he refused to fall prey to the distractions of hard drugs and desirable women.

He kept his nose somewhat clean, and walked as straight and narrow as possible, just like his brother Mike would have hoped for him. He learned to release his frustrations by calling his mother and siblings back in Los Angeles.

Now that he was in the Big Leagues, though, what would he use as an outlet for stress? He was now living in the city that never sleeps. He had more money than he could have ever imagined. He was staying in five-star hotels in major cities around the United States, and was surrounded by temptations he never knew existed.

But Darryl's greatest feeling was now developing. Darryl was being viewed as the predestined, slugging savior of New York City's sports scene. These words lay heavy upon the shoulders of the 21-year-old outfielder from Los Angeles. How would he respond? How could anyone live up to such predetermined standards?

"Enjoy yourself out there today!" Those were five dangerous words of advice for a 21-year-old who suffered from self-esteem issues. To enjoy oneself is to be free of internal negativity, external stress, and self-afflicted pressures. Darryl was completely swallowed up by all three of these entities.

How do you enjoy yourself when you are expected to hit a home run with every swing of the bat? How do you enjoy yourself when you have fans screaming and cursing your name, because you struck out four times in one game? How do you enjoy yourself when you have started your rookie campaign with zero hits in 11 at-bats? Which is exactly what Darryl did in his first 11 plate appearances.

Players have to develop a thick skin to endure the abusive outbursts from ruthless fans. Believe it or not, playing professional sports is a person's occupation. Can you imagine if a baseball player leaned over an office cubicle and berated an account-ant for typing a wrong number into his general ledger account? Or if an NFL football player screamed at a waitress for fumbling her tray in the restaurant?

If the accountant and waitress received this type of idiotic scrutiny, they would both struggle to perform their jobs. In fact, the stresses of being heckled throughout their workdays would cause both people to search for a job as a toll booth operator in the isolated wilderness of the Upper Yukon—far, far away from people!

Darryl started his Big League career by going 0 for 11 with seven strikeouts. Thankfully, hitting coach Jim Frey was there for Darryl in his rookie campaign. Frey took Darryl under his wing and explained the importance of finding a hitting plan that worked for him, practicing hard to perfect his swing, and focusing on the goals he was ultimately striving toward. Frey told Darryl that the biggest deterrent to a player's success is losing focus, because outside distractions can ruin a player's career more quickly than anything else.

"Stay focused!" These two words needed to be the center-piece of Darryl's aphorism. These two words were an observation of truth and a mantra for success for the young rookie. He needed to stay focused! He needed to stay alert! He needed to avoid external distractions! He needed to apply these two words to his personal life, let alone his occupation.

He needed more people like Jim Frey in his life.

FIRST TASTE

Darryl started his Major League career with the cellar dwellers of the National League. The last-place Mets had been struggling for years, and Darryl was looked upon as the key liberator of the organization. Front-office personnel and fans looked to him and another rookie sensation as the two men who would one day lead their beloved Mets to the Promised Land. The other rookie was 19-year-old Dwight "Doc" Gooden, a right-handed flame-thrower from Tampa, Florida. Gooden would join Darryl within a year.

In 1984, Darryl was officially introduced to the nightlife of the Big Leagues. It all started slowly for Darryl with innocent card games, cigars, and beer. As the last-place Mets started racking up wins, though, the post-game celebrations started becoming more frequent and more rowdy. Card games and beer were now being replaced by gorgeous women and hard liquor.

Darryl and his teammates were now spending their nights in bars and nightclubs. Women threw themselves at the players. Picking up a girl in a bar or nightclub was like shooting fish in a barrel for Darryl. He and his teammates could take a girl back to their hotel room on a nightly basis if they wanted to—and on most nights, they did just that.

Darryl's nightly jaunts through the nightclubs of National League cities had become a nightly occurrence. He was living the dream! Or was he? Unbeknownst to Darryl, these moments would give him his first taste of alcoholism and drug addiction.

Was Darryl using alcohol and women as his stress outlet? Was he using alcohol to reduce the anxiety that was swimming through his mind? Was he sleeping with random women to satisfy his lack of self-confidence? Or was he using both alcohol and women out of boredom? When he was younger, his uses were attributed to boredom. Why was he using them now?

Maybe the pressures of being the Savior of New York's sports scene was becoming too much for the young rookie. Darryl was being overrun with requests for his time and person. If he wasn't being followed by the high-powered lights of news reporters, he was being hounded for autographs and photographs by sports fans everywhere he went.

Darryl did not enjoy being the focal point of a news story. He suffered with the new pressures that surrounded him. He once walked the streets of New York City with his mother, and pointed to a homeless man. Darryl said he envied the man's existence because nobody paid attention to him.

Darryl was handling his anxiety in the same way he had as a teenager. He was trying to escape the pain, instead of dealing with the issues head on. He needed to apply the work habits and discipline he had learned to his life habits. He needed to apply the words of Jim Frey to his daily grind: "Stay focused." In Darryl's mind, though, he was handling his life the way he felt it needed to be handled.

As his first major-league season came to an end, Darryl proved that he was destined for great things. That said, Darryl had far more important concerns after being informed of some disturbing news by his family.

Ronnie was in serious trouble back in Los Angeles.

THE CRACK HOUSE

When Darryl arrived in Los Angeles, he was met with the news that Ronnie was living in a neighborhood crack house and was in drastic need of assistance. The crack house was deplorable. The smell that escaped the dwelling was reminiscent of rotting flesh. If the Grim Reaper owned a home, this would be it.

Mike was now a Los Angeles police officer. He and Darryl headed to the rat-infested house in Mike's patrol car. Once the two men arrived at the house, Mike ordered another man to bring Ronnie outside. Several minutes passed and then Ronnie stumbled from the decrepit abode.

Darryl and Mike were in shock as they laid eyes on their middle brother. Ronnie's eyes bulged from his gaunt face. He was strung out on drugs, his body was thin and frail. He looked as if his skin was pulled tight across his skeletal frame. He was walking death.

Darryl and Mike burst into tears at the sight of their brother. Ronnie would have nothing to do with them. His voice was hostile as he told them to leave.

"Y'all ain't me! Look at you, a big-time ball player. Look at you, a cop! Who am I? I'm NOTHING! I'M NOBODY! This is who I am. Y'all don't know me! Go away and leave me alone!"

Ronnie's words scorched his brothers' hearts.

"I'm NOTHING!"

Those were the same painful sentiments that had polluted Darryl's mind when he was growing up. He knew Ronnie's pain all too well, for his brain had tricked him into thinking the exact same thing about himself for years. The Monster had done a great job of destroying these two young men's self-images.

Mike and Darryl finally convinced Ronnie to leave the house and come home with them. They feared that as long as Ronnie was in that crack house, the Monster would be right there with him. Ronnie felt trapped in the bright rays of the sun, yet felt curiously safe inside the darkness of the house.

Ronnie longed to escape the sounds of the vicious attacks howling in his brain. However, he felt exposed to the outside world because of the nasty scars sprawled across his back, still visible in the light of day. The crack house was dark and dreary, just like Ronnie's self-respect. The dark house was a place where he could conceal the raised marks upon his skin. The drugs were a mask that he wore so no one could see the pain that lived within his tears.

Despite his brothers' best efforts, in time, Ronnie would relapse and return to the dark world. He was too damaged. The Monster remained victorious in Ronnie's life, and the Strawberry family had no choice but to let him find his own way. Letting Ronnie go was a very hard decision for them all.

It was up to Darryl to keep fighting for his own life. He had to battle hard to keep the Monster out of his brain. He knew that he had to control his drinking and his extracurricular activities with the women. He had to make sure he owned his life once again, and did not allow it to fall in the hands of the Monster as Ronnie had done.

The genetic patterns of drug use within families is difficult to comprehend. How did the three Strawberry men evolve into such different people, with such different habits? Mike had no involvement with drugs or alcohol, even though he saw the effects of its abuse every day in his home. Ronnie fell hard, and was held captive for most of his teenage and adult life by the brutal grip of drugs and alcohol. Darryl had difficulties with addictions since he was a teenager, but would never fall into the deep troubles that Ronnie faced in his life.

Darryl had to stay strong! He had no other choice.

NEW RELATIONSHIPS

In February of 1984, Darryl would finally be introduced to baseball's next ace hurler, Dwight "Doc" Gooden. The two became best pals instantly. Dwight was a shy teenager with a tremendous sense of humor. Dwight had an infectious laugh that would jumpstart the entire clubhouse once he started to giggle.

Darryl and Dwight were the up-and-coming superstars of the Mets. Just as Darryl had been looked upon as the Mets' "Hitting Savior," Dwight was deemed the Mets' "Pitching Savior." Two young kids were ballyhooed by the New York media as the sparkling sensations of the Big Apple.

Many of the older players started resenting Darryl and Dwight. However, veteran players Keith Hernandez and Gary Carter helped quell most of the internal jealousies within the Mets clubhouse. Hernandez was a strong figure in Darryl's life because of the mutual respect the players had for one another.

Darryl added another new friend to his life, Lisa Andrews. Darryl met Lisa in Los Angeles during the 1983 off-season and they immediately hit it off. The two became an official couple by the first of the year. It didn't take long for Lisa to move in with Darryl, in Long Island later that spring.

Playing baseball is a very stressful activity. As stated before, the levels of failure in professional baseball outweigh the successes by a long shot. Couple that anxiety with the constant scrutiny involved in a celebrity's life, and then further compound that stress by adding a live-in relationship—well, you are certainly asking for some enormous hurdles to overcome.

As the 1984 season began, Darryl's swing was mired in a deep slump. Everything Darryl tried, backfired. He was being booed by Mets fans at home and heckled by National League fans on the road. He could not escape the ridicule and it was wearing on his mind. The negative chants of "Dar-ryl, Dar-ryl" and "Strawberry, You Suck!" were deeply etched into his brain.

His struggles at the plate then translated into struggles at home with Lisa. The two were constantly fighting. Lisa was a live wire, and when she fought, she was relentless. Darryl did not have the energy to fight all the wars being waged upon him. He was having trouble clearing the hurdles of his life.

With every spat, Lisa became less tolerant of Darryl's struggles at the ball field. She added fuel to a fire that had been burning out of control since Darryl was a young child. When the two fought, it was not a friendly disagreement—it was an all-out verbal onslaught.

Darryl loved Lisa, but he was not ready for this type of fiery relationship in his life. He already had too much on his plate, and one too many dark travelers hiding inside his mind. The Monster was still there traipsing through his thoughts, and reminding him that he was a NOTHING.

Darryl found himself trapped. He had two choices: 1) He could dig in and fight with all his might. He could make the necessary changes to turn his season around and finish on a high note. He could fight to save his relationship, and find a peaceful middle ground between the two of them. 2) Or he could drop his head and run!

Darryl chose #2 and sought escape. He started drinking again, and as the games progressed, so did Darryl's drinking. He started going out after every game and partied until the wee hours of the morning. Often, Darryl would never make it back to his Long Island home. These actions did not bode well for the relationship. The more Darryl partied, the fiercer the fights with Lisa became.

Darryl partied in his hometown and on the road. That is where he was introduced to the newest friend in his life—"Greenies." Amphetamines or "Greenies" would become Darryl's first major addiction. Amphetamines are a dominant central nervous system stimulant used for people suffering from Attention Deficit Hyper-activity Disorder (ADHD), narcolepsy, and obesity. They are drugs that can enhance performance and cognitive thinking.

After a long night on the town, a hungover Darryl would stumble into the clubhouse. He would retrieve his jar of Greenies, and pop a "friend" or two—and miraculously, he was good to go. The drug provided him with pure focus! Focus? Where had he heard that word used before?

After popping a Greenie, the baseball looked more like a white beach ball as it sailed through the strike zone. Darryl found his focus, but it was not the same type of focus Jim Frey preached about in Darryl's rookie season.

Instead of decreasing his party mentality, Darryl was strictly relying on the effects of the amphetamines to get him through each day. He was grabbing Greenies out of the glass jar and crushing them like they were M&Ms.

Darryl relied heavily on his amphetamine fix. If he didn't have access to the Greenies, he would be a mental bust for the game. When the Greenies began losing their potency, Darryl just started downing more of them. This was truly the onset of Darryl's future drug problems. He had allowed himself to be sucked into a precarious situation. He was in the danger zone and refused to admit he had a problem.

"Have fun, kid!"

"Enjoy yourself out there!"

Is this what they meant by having fun? Is this fun? Are you enjoying yourself, Darryl?

Darryl was burning the candle at both ends, and his game was suffering because of it. The Mets were playing well, but Darryl was not. He was the integral cog in the team's wheel; if the Mets were ever going to push for a World Series title one day, Darryl would have to be at the top of his game.

He was spiraling out of control, but just before he was about to crash and burn, his veteran teammate, Keith Hernandez, stepped in. Keith told Darryl to knock it off! He told him he was too talented to let alcohol and drugs consume him! He cared for Darryl and his words were aimed to protect Darryl, not hurt him.

The words hit Darryl hard. He understood that Keith truly cared for him, and that meant the world to him. Darryl started the arduous task of turning his life around. He began working toward his goals, but more importantly he was working toward the team's goals. Darryl was bound and determined to follow Keith's lead and make a positive impact on the team once again. He had made a new life choice, and decided to fight for his life, and not run away from it.

Once again, Darryl was in a fight against the Monster. He reminded himself of Ronnie and the crack house that held his brother captive. His soul ached with visions of Ronnie and Darryl sharing a room inside a crack house redolent of the stench of rotting corpses. Darryl knew he could not let that happen. What would his mother think of him if he did? He could never let her down.

He knew that he and Lisa had most likely jumped into a live-in situation prematurely, but he was determined to improve that relationship as well. He understood the importance of having Dwight's back, and working together with him, for the purpose of leading their Mets to the "Promised Land."

When people first start using drugs and alcohol, they believe they can control their use. It is definitely safe to say, "Drugs are not your friends." Every time Darryl gobbled up a handful of Greenies, the Greenies were in turn gobbling the life from him.

Darryl did not feel normal when he was without his Greenies, which is why he increased the quantity taken. Even in the earliest stages of drug abuse, people have the need for higher and more frequent doses.

Darryl had one important job in front of him.

"Stay focused!"

Doctor's Notes and Comments to Chapter 4

Understanding the Mind—The Id, the Ego,
and the Superego with David Blair Miller, PsyD

Darryl was introduced to many new faces, new surroundings, and most importantly, a new source of defense against the painful memories of his past life. His bold, new life was filled with money, fame, and every vice known to mankind. But, more than anything else, Darryl just wanted to fit in and feel valued. He wanted to be liked by his teammates, loved by his new girlfriend, and adored by his fans, especially the female ones.

Darryl was on a slippery slope. His emotional or psychic structure had never fully developed due to the emotional strains of his childhood. Darryl had done an admirable job in the minor leagues of completing his work, taking care of his mind, paying bills, and fulfilling regular duties, but now that he has been introduced to harder drugs, he was inching closer and closer to addiction.

Before addiction becomes a factor in a person's life, it is important to first understand how we believe the mind develops, forms, and functions. The word "mind" here is used interchangeably with "character." A person's character is formed by a combination of genetics and the numerous exchanges and experiences created within that person's environment and personal history.

The expression of genetics is a co-constructed relational matrix with human experiences as it comes into contact with an individual's nature. Each experience is superimposed upon previous experiences, creating layers and layers of our past experiences. These experiences do not suppress genetics, but rather combine with genetics to form individual thoughts, theories, and feelings about life. The combination of genetics and experiences form the character of an individual.

The core essence of one's self is termed the Ego. The Ego will properly develop with positive emotional attunement between parent and child. Unfortunately, people suffering from addictions will normally have tremendous deprivations in emotional attunement. A child who does not receive satisfactory emotional attunement will suffer greatly, and the development of that child's Ego will be profoundly affected.

A well-developed Ego provides individuals with a defined sense of who they are and what they stand for as a person. People who possess a healthy Ego are more capable of caring for themselves, protecting themselves and, most importantly, loving themselves. People who do not have an intact Ego are less capable of self-soothing and often lack self-respect and the ability to love or be loved.

"Reality Testing" is an important emotional developmental achievement that occurs as a result of adequate nurturing from the mother, father, or caregiver. Reality Testing is a person's ability to differentiate between fantasy and reality. Reality Testing is an important function found in a healthy Ego

system. People with fragile Egos will have trouble differentiating between fantasy and reality. Addicts are extremely vulnerable to poor Reality Testing because their Egos are underdeveloped.

A person's most primal needs are to survive, eat, drink, reproduce, fight, play, and enjoy life. These particular actions can provide immediate gratification for human beings. By realizing gratification through such actions, mental functioning, which is referred to as the "Id," is promoted. The Id is the only personality component that is instilled within a human being at birth. The Id is driven toward satisfying human needs, wants, desires, impulses, and urges towards pleasure.

Because addicts often have devastating personal histories of abuse, neglect, rejection, and abandonment, they are much more vulnerable to burying themselves into the pleasure-seeking world of the Id. This is where the powerful dopamine surges come into play. Addicts consume themselves with pleasure releases to ward off the haunting memories of pain, loneliness, and emotional frustration. Addicts are typically attracted to hedonistic activities and experiences that result in immediate relief from their internal suffering.

Our minds develop a system whose main responsibility is the management and removal of painful memories, constant anxieties, and recurring frustrations. This system is referred to as a person's "Unconscious." Without our Unconscious, we would be unable to live our lives in peace or harmony. The Unconscious minimizes frustrations and painful memories, which allows us to function in all facets of daily life. Without our Unconscious, we would not be able to escape the painful happenings of our past lives or the ongoing taxing pressures of our current lives.

As our minds become more psychologically sophisticated, we develop an ability to differentiate between right and wrong, or good and bad. This aspect of the psyche is referred to as the "Superego." Although the Superego is only partially conscious, it represents the internalization of parental regulations, as well as the rules of our society. The Superego supervises, judges, and supports the Ego.

The Superego is the moral consciousness that dwells within our being. When we receive an overwhelming sense of guilt for something we have done or are planning to do, we are receiving signals from our Superego. When we feel a twinge in the pit of our stomach as we attempt to make a decision, we are experiencing a "Gut Feeling" or a Superego moment.

Addicts tend to be more impacted by emotional attacks (real or imagined) due to their lack of self-esteem and self-worth than non-addicts. Therefore, an addict's Superego becomes more critical in its response or self-judgment of one's self. The Superego causes increased self-doubt in addicts based on the history of emotional abuse or physical trauma endured by the individual.

When a person (especially an addict) suffers from low self-esteem, the Superego can allow a person to fall into a maso-chistic state. Masochism can be best described as an inward anger that leads a person to self-destructive behaviors associated with substance abuse. When an addict reaches a state of emotional inadequacy, the results can range from substance abuse to behavioral self-destruction.

These acts of bad behaviors can be unconscious or conscious acts and are directly linked to an unhealthy Ego and a harsh-attacking Superego. Many addicts suffer from a harsh-attacking Superego. When addicts suffer from overwhelming thoughts of unworthiness, ugliness, or self-hate, they will rely on their addictive substances or behaviors to chase the harsh-attacking Superego away.

When individuals feel loved, supported, and validated, they will develop a strong Ego. However, when they feel unloved and are filled with self-doubt, they are suffering from a poorly developed Ego and Superego, and the Id may ultimately lead them to substance abuse and an addictive lifestyle.

Our minds are constantly being twisted and pushed and pulled by the complex interactions of our experiences and our individual genetic makeup. We all have wishes, fears, and frustrations. We all have the capacity for loving and hating. We judge and we are judged. We are accepted and we are admonished. When our life's interactions are positive, we live in relative peace. If our experiences are difficult, our emotional state is alerted and we live with constant anxiety, pain, and fear.

If we are unable to properly manage the difficult thoughts and moments of our lives, we will be unable to change our *course of response and will ultimately experience symptoms such as sadness, irritability, agitation, helplessness, and hopelessness. People who are unable to change their negative mindset will become obsessive, angry, isolated, and emotionally void and empty, which often results in mood disorders such as depression.*

When a person becomes distraught, the Ego diligently utilizes any and all defensive maneuvers in an effort to find relief or feel better. Individuals will attempt to self-soothe by attacking the perceived culprits of their particular anxiety or pain. Example of such actions include crying, isolation, ignored feelings, denial, excessive work, intense exercise, eating disorders, avoiding love and affection, and more. If individuals do not learn to regulate their feelings, they will suffer from a misaligned idea of happiness and wholeness.

Darryl's drug use was a runaway train, and he was the emotionally handicapped engineer who was unable to bring the train to a complete stop. Darryl desperately needed intervention at this point in time. He needed someone to take control of the train and pull it back upon the track. Up ahead, a dark tunnel awaited him.

CHAPTER 5

THE ONSET OF ADDICTION

Based on an interview with Rich Capiola, MD

D arryl Strawberry was introduced to alcohol and marijuana at an early age. Darryl looked at drugs and alcohol as something to do out of boredom. Sometimes he used drugs because of peer pressure and sometimes he used them to escape the memories of his past. But Darryl's casual experimentations with drugs and alcohol were unknowingly priming his brain for future drug abuse and addictions.

Most people believe that drug and alcohol addictions arise in adults due to the various stress loads and demands associated with an adult's daily grind. Stresses such as divorce, death, or job loss are often blamed for a person's increased use of drugs and alcohol. Excuses are constantly made to justify an adult's negative actions, outlandish behaviors, and serious substance abuse issues.

In truth, an individual's addictive processes actually begin much earlier in a person's life. The acts of drinking and drugging first begin with curiosity. A teenage boy may notice that his father has a liquor cabinet that is mysteriously locked.

The teenage boy wonders to himself- "What's in the cabinet? Why does he lock it? Why can't I have some too?" The locked cabinet tells the teenage boy that the bottles inside the cabinet are taboo or forbidden, which instills a deeper curiosity in the teenager.

The teenage boy understands the limitations and abides by the rules set by his father. He understands that the liquor cabinet is to remain locked at all times or there will be severe consequences. As the teenage boy becomes older, he begins hanging out with friends from the neighborhood or from his school. The group of teenagers congregates in its own private space, far from their parents' watchful eyes. This lack of parental control allows a teenage boy to explore, experiment, and fulfill curiosities.

The social connectivity within the group allows the teenage boy to become more comfortable with the idea of taking a sip of beer or a hit off of a joint or cigarette. The boy's environment can become a viable instigator to the onset of drug and alcohol use. On the flip side, these same environments can also be the driving factors that keep young men and women from abusing drugs and alcohol.

If the teenager has a great experience with a certain drug, drink, or behavior, that person will become more likely to repeat this action in the future. If a person receives a pleasurable reward reaction from a particular drug, the person will store this positive feeling in his or her brain as a positive recollection or "ghost memory." On the other hand, if young individuals have a negative reaction to a certain drug or drink, their brains will remind them of their horrible experience.

Here are a couple examples of this principle: If a teenage boy tries Tequila for the first time in his life, then spends the rest of the night violently vomiting as he hugs the rim of the toilet bowl like it's his soulmate, that negative memory sequence is stored away inside the boy's brain. Therefore, the teenager will be less likely to use Tequila as his "go-to" drink from that day forward. An ugly response to Tequila or any other substance will most likely prevent a person from using that type of alcohol again.

On the other side, if a teenage girl breaks her arm and is prescribed OxyContin to diminish the pain, she could receive a mellow high that not only lessens the pain, but gives her an overwhelming sense of relaxation and peace. This pleasant response rewards the brain circuits of the girl, and stores a positive memory. This action begins the initial process of cementing an addiction inside the girl's brain.

"This OxyContin is great! I feel so good!" The ghost memory of this particular opiate is automatically stored away in the brain, and if the drug were to be offered to her again (perhaps outside the boundaries of healthcare), an overwhelming feeling of bliss will immediately flood her mind. The ghost memory of the positive experience will also tie in specific details associated with the recollection. She will remember her drug dealer and the people who shared the experience.

The majority of substance abuse cases have a strong connection to social gatherings. The old adage, "the more, the merrier" truly applies to this theory. When a young person is a part of a group setting, that person has a better chance of utilizing different types of drugs or alcohol. In fact, a person who becomes addicted to a drug will actually receive a dopamine release at the very sight of his drug dealer or drug-using companions.

Although Darryl began his alcohol and drug use during his teenage years, he did not become a true addict until he made it to the Major Leagues in New York. Darryl began partying with his Mets teammates early in his big-league career. He and his teammates were constantly drinking, smoking marijuana, snorting cocaine, and womanizing.

Darryl was experimenting with all types of psycho-active drugs, but his first real addiction was with potent stimulants called amphetamines. These drugs were referred to by various names like "Bennies," "Uppers," and "Speed." One of the most potent stimulants used by the team was a Mexican diet pill called Asenlix. This drug was better known by its street name, the "Greenie."

Darryl was drinking and drugging in the wee hours of the night, and was relying on amphetamines and Greenies to maintain productivity on the field. The fact that he needed Greenies to focus and deliver was a sure sign of his addiction. If Darryl was unable to use one of these stimulants prior to a game, he was left with a feeling of sluggishness. His mental state was unfocused and foggy.

The New York Mets' clubhouse was a bad environment for the 21-year-old Darryl Strawberry. Inside the clubhouse, Darryl was provided with stimulants on a daily basis and was encouraged to use them by his older teammates. Darryl relied heavily upon the amphetamines and Asenlix to perform. When one is in an environment where drugs are made available and encouraged as part of the team's daily routine, this environment will further aid in the cementing process of one's addiction.

Darryl was relying on his stimulants for concentration and focus, and he was savoring the energizing qualities of his post-game social interactions. He was attending dinners, parties, and private penthouse soirees in the city. He was combining the social energies of his entourage with his intense neuro-chemical releases provided by the drugs and booze. This was a lethal combination for a 21-year-old man with pockets full of money.

Some of you may be wondering how social interaction can be a factor in addiction. Let's explore this notion a little deeper. Why do we like to go to dinner with friends or hang out at a sports bar with our buddies on the night of the big game? We receive energy from social gatherings! Social connectivity energizes our spirit. We feel alive. The dopamine surge has been triggered.

It was no different for Darryl's brother Ronnie when he was locked away in a crack house filled with junkies. The group setting provided him with energy. He felt welcomed, desired, and in an odd way, loved by those who shared in his debauchery. When Ronnie shared a spoon with another crack addict, he was connecting his chemically-enhanced pleasures with those sharing his moment. His fellow addicts were a great part of his momentary bliss.

As Darryl continued his nighttime social romps, he was inadvertently priming his brain with insatiable pleasures. Inside chic New York City penthouses, hardcore drugs were being presented like beautifully plated meals at a 5-star Madison Avenue restaurant. High above the city streets was a smorgasbord of drugs, drinks, and women. Darryl had no idea he was cementing the pathways of his future addictions. He was blind to the power of the temptations.

"Priming" is the act of setting up the brain so the neuro-chemical processes associated with addiction are ready to kick into action. For example, let's say you are being set up on a blind date. Your body is already signaling a dopamine re-sponse as you prepare for the date. The idea and thought of connecting with someone generates energy, nervousness, and happiness. You are priming your brain with the thoughts about the planning and the expectations of the upcoming rendez-vous. You are priming your brain for a pleasurable encounter.

"When you attach the idea, 'I did a substance and it affected the biochemistry of my brain, and I received a positive feeling from it, and I am having these feelings with a group of people or friends,' then you are promoting the act of cementing an addiction," states Dr. Capiola, a board-certified psychiatrist.

It is important to note that once a person's brain has been primed, and the pathways and connections have been established inside the brain, the ability to stop drug and alcohol use becomes extremely difficult. The people, places, and things are the entities that support the bold culture of addiction. These three entities will always be the strongest factors in our journey. An individual must learn to properly manage his or her actions to preserve positive recollections in our brain.

Ghost memory is a strong force in the human mind and it plays a major role in Darryl's future.

* * * * *

DARRYL'S STORY

1986
THE VIKING WARRIORS

It was the final home game of the 1985 season and the standing ovations from Shea Stadium could be heard echoing throughout the neighborhoods of Flushing, New York. The Mets had finished in 2nd place in the National League East behind the St. Louis Cardinals, but the Mets' fan-following had a sixth sense about next year's season. The Mets legion of fans could feel that a World Series championship was within reach.

The Mets players were also aware of the grand possibilities that awaited them in the upcoming baseball season. Darryl was playing great ball. Dwight was unhittable. But, most importantly, the team was gelling as a family on and off the field.

Team chemistry is the key to any championship run. Whether it is in high school, college, or professional athletics, team unity must be established to win titles. The Mets were the epitome of team chemistry. When the St. Louis Cardinals fans created T-Shirts that read, "The Mets are Pond Scum," the Mets players embraced the message! They ate it up! Those shirts were like wood for the furnace.

Each player had his teammates' backs. If someone made an error, there were ten guys at the steps of the dugout, providing encouragement. If someone hit a home run, the entire bench would greet the player as he crossed home plate. If someone was involved in an on-field scuffle, the entire team was ready to fight like a pack of pit bulls.

The Mets were a cocky bunch of guys who played the game with chips on their shoulders. They ran the bases with undeniable aggression. They were not afraid to disrupt a double play, even if it meant driving the shortstop into shallow left field. They dove, crashed, and flew for balls with abandon. They were one tough band of hombres.

Mets Manager Davey Johnson told the 1986 Mets that he did not just want to win every ball game, he wanted to dominate every ball game. And dominate they would. Had Major League Baseball approved the use of war paint, the Mets would have worn it. They were on a mission to win it all, no matter what the cost.

The personalities of the 1986 Mets squad can be best described as "hard core." They played the game like a crew of Viking warriors. They also partied like a crew of Vikings—minus the boiled goat meat. They were drinking, drugging, gambling, and fornicating like they were a Hall of Fame rock band. The Mets were the talk of the country and they loved the attention.

The question looming over this band of hombres was: Could they maintain the frantic pace in which they were operating?"

THE HOMEFRONT

In 1985, Darryl married Lisa, who was pregnant with their first child. Although Darryl's family had doubts about his marital union with Lisa, he was not about to let his newborn son be raised without him. Darryl understood the importance of a positive father figure in a child's life, and only wished he could have had the same in his younger life.

During the 1985 season, Darryl was a doting father and husband. He was still popping Greenies and drinking from time to time, but was definitely more attentive to family needs. He made sure he was with his family on the nights after home games and pushed his partying to the side to be the best family man possible. However, the drugs and alcohol were never far from his thoughts. His "old friends" were hiding in the darkness, right beside the Monster.

During the 1986 season, the family game plan was put on the backburner for the season. As the team began to pound the opposition into the ground on a nightly basis, a feeling of invincibility swept over the team. Darryl felt the excitement and it was electric. He had never felt such love and camaraderie in his life.

Crazed Mets fans chanted his name as if he were a god. The fans hung on every pitch thrown to their cleanup hitter, hoping he would hammer a ball deep into the outfield seats. Admirers came to the Mets' batting practice session, just to observe Darryl clouting one magnificent long ball after another.

With every deliberately slow home-run trot, Darry Strawberry became more powerful. Sexy groupies braved the wrath of the Shea Stadium security guards, just to deliver their phone numbers to #18. He was unknowingly reverting to his junior high bully days, but now he was taking a "meal per diem" from every player in the National League.

When the team won a game, they partied until the early light of morning. When the team lost a game, they partied until the early light of morning. They partied in New York and in every other National League city. They drank any liquor or beer that was offered to them. They smoked anything they could get their hands on and they slept with any woman who grabbed their shirt sleeve.

The wives and girlfriends of the players just turned a blind eye to the situation. They buried their heads in the sand and pretended that it was not happening. Why? Because, they were living a plush lifestyle, so why on earth would they want to upset the apple cart over a few drunken affairs? Money truly is the root of all evil.

The Mets players were treated like royalty. They were invited to million-dollar high-rise apartments where they were provided women, cocaine, and $50,000 bottles of Macallen scotch. The team was definitely a modern-day crew of Viking warriors. They even had a chant they yelled when their plane landed on the tarmac of an opposing team's airport.

"WHAT ARE WE GOING TO DO?"
"WE'RE GONNA DRINK ALL THEIR ALCOHOL,
SCREW ALL THEIR WOMEN AND
KICK THEIR ASSES ON THE FIELD!"

Darryl and his teammates had graduated from amphetamines to cocaine. Cocaine is a stimulant. When taken, the high from cocaine is immediately followed by feelings of power, self-confidence, increased energy, and invincibility. These side-effects felt wonderful to Darryl. And although he was still using speed, it was cocaine that truly fed him.

Cocaine was a dangerous drug for Darryl, because it not only gave him an instant source of self-esteem, it provided him with Superman powers. When he was flying on cocaine, he was the speeding bullet. On cocaine, Darryl was incapable of being hurt or abused—the ammo rounds bounced off his chest. On cocaine, he was strong and virile, God's gift to women. On cocaine, Darryl was not only a Viking warrior, he was the Mighty Thor, with his powerful thunder stick!

During the different stages of Darryl's life, his reasons for drug use had run the gamut. As a young teenager, Darryl needed the high to lessen his feelings of distress. He suffered from depression and social anxieties and he was stressed out from his awful upbringing with the Monster. Boredom also was a major factor for his drug and alcohol use.

As a young rookie in the Big Leagues, Darryl turned to drugs to escape stresses, but he also took drugs to help increase production. He chose amphetamines to have better focus while hitting the ball. As an All-Star performer, Darryl switched gears and started using cocaine and other harder drugs because they made him feel good. The drugs made him feel invincible and powerful.

There is one common thread through all the different reasons for using drugs and alcohol. In all cases, Darryl started using drugs based on vulnerability and the influence of others. Peer pressure is not just an adolescent issue. Adults are notorious for leading others down a dark path. The adult pushers want to see others fall to the depths in which they already find themselves.

Darryl was sucked into the social influences of drugs and alcohol nearly every time he began using them. Was this the same thing that happened to Ronnie? Was peer pressure the reason for his demise? Or did he just use drugs to sleep through the pain that consumed his soul?

ADDICTED

It was in 1986 when Darryl officially became a hardcore drug addict, a sex addict, and an alcoholic. Darryl knew he had a serious problem, but he had no intentions of changing his lifestyle. He had the world by the tail, and anything or anyone he desired was at his disposal. He was living the life of a king!

Much later in Darryl's life, he realized that with every decision he made, there was always a consequence. Most bad decisions have negative consequences, and nearly all decisions made under the influence of drugs and alcohol result in the ugliest of outcomes.

Darryl and Lisa's marriage was stomping on thin ice. If Lisa wasn't screaming and yelling at Darryl for his drunken, sexual exploits, they were arguing about their money woes. Darryl hated to argue and fight; it brought back bad memories from his childhood. He would argue, then shut her out. It was the only way he could deal with her hysterical rants.

He knew he was guilty of everything she was claiming. That said, he would not give in to her furious interrogations. He knew he was not an ideal husband and was failing miserably as a father to his son, but he would not admit guilt to her allegations. He was not ready to confess his transgressions.

Darryl also knew they had financial issues. He was living high on the hog, and so was Lisa. If they wanted a new car, they bought a new car. They never checked a price tag; they just bought it. If Lisa wanted 60 pairs of shoes, she purchased 60 pairs of shoes. Darryl did not have an accountant; he just knew he was making insane amounts of money, and he wasn't afraid to spend it.

Darryl was well aware that his life decisions had to change, but all personal transformations would have to be put on hold until the season was complete. Darryl was locked into his team's successful run and he was determined to direct his energies towards the team's unified mission. He wanted a World Series title. He owed it to his fans. He wanted it for his team. He needed it for himself.

A BAD DECISION

The Mets finished their regular season with a record-setting 108 victories. The team was primed and ready for their first-round playoff matchup with the Houston Astros. The Mets players made a decision to invite their wives and girlfriends to Houston for the first round of the playoffs. This turned out to be a bad decision!

After winning Game 2, the players were in mid-season form. They resumed their hardcore party activities, leaving their wives and girlfriends to fend for themselves back at the team's hotel. When Darryl arrived at his room in the middle of the night, he discovered he had been locked out. The chain on the door was firmly secured, and Lisa was not about to open the door for her inebriated husband.

The two bickered through the door, their words gnashing at one another. Darryl ordered Lisa to open the door, but she would not. The shouting match was waking up the entire floor of the hotel as Darryl's deep, angry voice echoed through the hallway.

Darryl rammed his way through the door, and immediately confronted his wife with fire in his eyes. They screamed and shouted at one another, their quarrel the most intense yet. The couple stood eye to eye, as built-up anger and frustrations exploded from both. Lisa was seeing red, and Darryl saw the Monster.

In a split second, Darryl made a horrible mistake. With an open hand, he smacked his wife across the face, breaking her nose. Silence filled the room. Time stood still. The piercing, bloodshot eyes of his father flashed into his brain. This was a bad decision!

As blood poured down Lisa's face, Darryl stood silent. He had crossed the line, and he knew it. He had slipped into a shadowy realm he swore he would never enter. As he stared at his sobbing, bloodied wife, a feeling of remorse rushed through his veins. How had this happened? How had he sunk this low? Was the Monster alive in him?

The next few days were empty and hushed between the two. As the hours passed, sorrow filled Darryl's heart. He was fraught with emotions and deeply disturbed by his actions. The blood, the screaming, the hostile exchanges—all weighed heavily on Darryl's mind. Yet, he knew he had been captured by a greater force. He was snared by addiction, controlled by the demons that had claimed his father's soul so many years ago. Darryl had never been so lost in his life.

The Mets defeated the Astros in six games. All Darryl could think about, though, was how he had let down his family. The Mets captured the World Series title by defeating the Boston Red Sox, but Darryl was caught up with the possibility of losing his wife and son. He felt doom inside his heart, and a dull, pounding ache inside his brain. Or maybe he was just drunk again.

A ticker tape parade was held in the Mets' honor. As the team made its way through the streets of New York City, there were very few sober champions. Most of the players had not even slept the night before, and those who had found a moment to doze off, woke up just prior to the starting time of the parade. They were unshaven, grungy, and hungover.

Once again, Darryl popped Greenies to get through the moment. His palms were sweaty and his head banged as he squinted through his sunglasses. As the motorcade made its way down Broadway, the fans chanted for their favorite son.

"DAR-RYL! DAR-RYL! DAR-RYL!"

Darryl Strawberry was a world champion. He and his Viking warrior teammates had overcome astounding circumstances to stand tall amongst the buildings of the City. The Mighty Thor and his powerful thunder stick would forever live in New York sports infamy. The Viking warriors had divided and conquered! Would the casualties of their wars far outweigh the spoils of their victories in days to come?

"DAR-RYL! DAR-RYL! DAR-RYL!"

Darryl squinted upwards toward the thousands of exuberant fans waving their arms and cheering his name. He listened as the screaming voices faded, before oddly disappearing into a muted whisper. He could still see their faces and their swinging arms, but all he could hear was the growling voice of the Monster, deep within his being.

"YOU WILL NEVER AMOUNT TO ANYTHING! YOU ARE A NOTHING! AND YOU WILL ALWAYS BE NOTHING!"

Darryl's head was pounding from the hangover. Or maybe it was a sense of his own impending doom.

* * * * *

DOCTOR'S NOTES AND COMMENTS TO CHAPTER 5

with Rich Capiola, MD

Darryl's initial addiction was with amphetamines, but as the 1986 season progressed, so did his desires for cocaine, alcohol, and sex. Darryl was quickly forming addictions for numerous substances and activities. However, unlike most addicts, Darryl had money to burn and paying for his numerous addictions was not an issue for him.

Many people wonder how celebrities, sports figures, and the wealthy people of our society always seem to suffer the most with addictions. The rise and fall of celebrities are a huge part of news reports, talk shows, and gossip programs like TMZ. They have everything they could ever want or imagine, so why are they ruining their lives with drugs?" and "They have all the money in the world. Why can't they just stop!" are constant quotes delivered by the show hosts and echoed by those viewing the program at home.

Well, first of all, celebrities and sports figures are exposed to the media much more than someone in the general population. However, the main difference between celebrities and average citizens is the fact that celebrities have more money, more resources, and more people trying to take advantage of them.

If the average addict had a vault full of money, he or she would be in the same exact predicament as someone who is wealthy or famous. If an addict has millions of dollars in his bank account, he will continue to spend that money until he gets psychiatric help or goes broke. All addicts (rich or poor) share a common denominator. They have lost their abilities to control impulses. Once a person loses impulse control, his logical thinking process also becomes severely impaired.

Addicts who are wealthy have no conscience when it comes to spending money on their addictions. Wealthy individuals can afford to get high every single day, which is a primary reason for their monumental falls. Addicts who are poor will spend their entire paycheck on a drug binge. An impoverished individual will go broke and turn to crime and prostitution to fuel a drug addiction. This is due to a person's absence of impulse control and irrational logic. Rich, poor, or somewhere in between, an addict is an addict.

When a person takes his first hit of marijuana or snorts his first line of cocaine, the initial high received by these drugs is extremely intense. The brain remembers this intense high and stores the memory in the frontal lobe of the person's brain. Each and every addict will search the world, high and low, for an equal or greater high. The initial high is the carrot that keeps drug addicts coming back for more, even when the pleasure granted by that initial high is unattainable.

Drug users or addicts will always seek to replicate their initial high. That said, this constant search of a more powerful experience is not limited to drugs. The same search also applies to behavioral addictions such as sex, food, and gambling.

Although Darryl was in a relationship, he was constantly searching for a greater experience in his sexual life. The novelty of each sexual experience was a driving force in his next sexual hook-up. The thought of becoming intimate with different women causes a major dopamine surge in a sex addict's brain reward system.

The addict does not think logically. "I know I should go home to my girlfriend right now, but the girl I'm with right now is drop-dead gorgeous!" A sex addict's mindset is strictly primed on the idea of becoming sexual with the woman in the short skirt, across the room. This single moment is all about the sexual conquest and fantasies running wildly in the sex addict's mind.

The dopamine surge is initially ignited by the man's attraction to the woman. The brain pathways are intensified by the chase while the drugs are busy, eliminating all inhibitions. The dopamine surges provide the sexual urges.

Humans are always looking for the more powerful response. If the sex addict was to avoid the girl at the party and go back home to his girlfriend, he would not receive the same, intense dopamine burst. The novelty of a different woman appeals to a sex addict because he is seeking the overwhelming feelings that accompany the initial sexual high! When individuals begin seeking out different sexual partners, they are cementing their addictions within that particular behavior.

Sex addictions are often triggered by pre-existing addictions. If an addict has a desire to be sexually active with another person, he may also need his alcohol fix to complete the sexual conquest process. The alcohol addiction helps fuel the sexual cravings by numbing the logical thought process and releasing the addict's impulse control.

Darryl was sexually driven by the women, the chase, and the idea of having a novel sexual experience. His sexual desires were fueled by the dopamine release. Yet he needed the drugs and alcohol to push him toward his ultimate desires. The dopamine responses for both sex and alcohol resulted in one giant package deal for the addict. Cocaine was definitely a libido-enhancing factor for Darryl.

Ruby Strawberry said it best, "Actions dictate actions. If you would stop chasing women, you would stop drinking."

Let's say Darryl had taken his mother's advice and stayed home with his girlfriend instead of going to all the drug and sex parties. This idea sounds logical. But an addict does not think logically. He would most likely have found another avenue to satisfy his desires and needs. For instance, if a person has an on-line pornography addiction, should you take away his computer? If he truly has an addiction, he will find another computer.

Food, sex, drugs, and alcohol are all connected to positive outcomes in an addict's mind. Each type of addiction uses the same brain pathway reward system. These addictions are all powered by a unique dopamine surge within the individual addict. So, if a person is already tied into an addiction, and his addiction is taken away, he or she will eventually seek out other ways to produce a dopamine charge.

It is difficult for addicts to generate a feeling of happiness through life experiences, so they rely on biochemical releases to realize elation or joy. What if a sex addict was told to stop fooling around with women? "Son! Stop doing this!" the mother scolds. But the son does not want to stop. He feels fear and anxiety when he stops chasing women. In his mind, he cannot stop! The novelty of the women is too powerful!

This is the moment that a sex addict's defense mechanisms begin to kick in. Defense mechanisms like rationalization and denial begin their job of protecting the addict's illogical thought processes. These rationalizations are unconscious thoughts that successfully bend the limits of logic and make sense of the addict's irrational decisions. These defensive mechanisms are so powerful that an addict has no idea he is actually applying these perceptions to his current situation. Sometimes, the only way to convince an addict that he is making major mistakes in his life is through a horrible accident, injury, or near-death experience.

"How do you combat the illogical mindset of an addict?"

The first step in the process is finding the addict a proper intervention program or drug recovery facility. Each individual possesses his own personal framework of addiction. This framework of addiction reveals an individual's priming mechanisms and dopamine trigger mechanisms. The addict must place his life under a physician's microscope for the purpose of uncovering the person's underlying history.

It is extremely difficult for an addict to reveal the origins of his pain and the reasons for his personal torture. Reality is a difficult cross to bear. It is so much easier for an addict to just have sex with women or shoot up or drink, rather than facing the "monsters" who roam within their minds.

This process of self-reflection takes work! An addict will never be able to say "No" to drugs, until he can he say "Yes" to living.

CHAPTER 6
STRESS AND ANXIETY

Based on an interview with Rich Capiola, MD

When a person is saddled with addiction, there are several types of incidents and actions that can generate a biochemical release in that person's brain. We have discussed several of these dopamine-charged scenarios, from the bells and clanking sounds of the casino, to the anticipatory responses of a possible love connection.

The addict's brain is constantly searching and priming itself for a possible dopamine release. Anxious situations can also prime an addict's brain pathways. In fact, couples who possess a powerful sexual relationship will often have aggressive and chaotic personal relationships as well. This is due to the high-powered energy that can be shared in both sexual aggression and contentious confrontations.

Fighting, quarreling, and arguing release dopamine. This surge of adrenaline will be kick-started by a nose-to-nose argument and finish with a phenomenal bout of make-up sex! If this pattern repeats itself, the act of fighting is actually priming the brain for something wonderful once the dust has cleared. Make-up sex is one of the most intense reward systems provided in human beings. Now you know why fighting couples stay together!

Couples will unconsciously pick fights with their spouses or significant others just for the chance of getting their hands on that bucket of gold at the end of the rainbow. In time, this action/reaction sequence becomes ingrained in their relationship. If love is eventually lost between the two, then fighting and arguing become their only mode of expression to one another.

When we pick a partner, we always set out to find the things we like about that person. Is she smart? Is she pretty? Is she funny? Will she get my jokes? What we should be asking is: "What does she see in me?" Often, a person will unconsciously choose a partner who is a reflection of that person's own self. The couple shares similarities in their personalities, which causes them to constantly pick at each other's common deficiencies.

To illustrate this point, why does a father yell at his son for the same things he did as a child? The father sees his own fallible actions in his son. A father doesn't want his son to make the same mistakes he did, so he chastises the youngster. Could this be a possible reason for Henry Strawberry's actions toward his two youngest boys? Did Henry see himself in his two boys? Did he physically abuse the two boys because that is what his father did to him?

Frequently, a father who was physically abused as a child will punish his children in the same aggressive manner. Henry felt unloved as a child, and quite possibly saw a reflection of himself in his two boys. Henry's angry reactions toward his boys may have been due to a deep-rooted hatred for himself and the overwhelming stresses attacking his own life. Henry Strawberry's anxieties were poorly managed. He was combining his personal distress with alcoholism, resulting in the destruction of a family and two young boys' self-worth.

Men and women exhibit anxiety in various ways. Sometimes, a parent will respond to anxiety with anger. An example of this behavior can be illustrated in the following manner: A family spends a day at the State Fair. Thousands of people are milling about the fairgrounds, eating gigantic turkey legs, and pointing at enormous livestock bursting from their pens.

While Dad is being wooed by a carnival worker to test his strength with a sledge hammer and a ringing bell, Mom discovers that her 8-year-old son is missing. She is frantic! She shouts his name as she races from one game booth to the other. When she turns the corner, she finds her son clanking rings off of soda bottles.

The hysterical mother races to her son, grabs his shoulders, and screams at him! "Don't you ever walk away from me again! DO YOU HEAR ME?" Was the mother angry with her son? No, she was not mad at him—she was upset, fearful, and worried. In this case, her anxieties emerged as anger.

When spouses argue or fight, the man becomes angry because he feels that his spouse does not understand his feelings. A woman becomes hysterically upset because her spouse is not connecting with her emotional needs. Emotions run high in any spousal altercation, but if alcoholism or drug abuse are involved, the interactions have a greater chance of becoming volatile or violent. The intense altercations are the results of an addict having poor impulse control and/or impaired logical thought process.

When Darryl was locked out of his hotel room by his wife, the anxieties of being shut out quickly turned to anger. When he broke into the room and found his wife talking on the phone, he flew off the handle because in his substance-altered mind, she was cheating on him. Why did he think this? Because, a guilty person will automatically assume she is cheating on him, especially since he had been doing the same to her. Guilt, jealousy, and paranoia are the most commonly used tools found in an addict's tool box.

The assumption that his wife was cheating on him hurt his feelings, causing him to react with anger. As stated before, when an addict gets angry, he is already void of any type of impulse control. If he is high or drunk, his illogical emotions will override any semblance of rational thinking and verbal or physical violence may ensue.

Darryl was fighting off demons from all corners of his mind. He had graduated from addiction to a polysubstance dependence. His need for psychological or psychiatric assistance was paramount at this point for his marriage and his life. If he failed to pursue help, the marriage was destined to come to an abrupt and violent end.

* * * * *

DARRYL'S STORY

THE RECKONING

When Darryl Strawberry first started taking drugs as a teenager, his decision to do so was strictly voluntary. When he decided to start partying with his Mets teammates at the onset of his Major League career, his decisions to do so were strictly voluntary. In 1986, Darryl's decision to use drugs and alcohol was no longer a voluntary choice. Darryl was suffering from full-blown addictions to drugs, alcohol, and sex.

The drugs and alcohol had taken a hold on his life, and his ability to exhibit self-control was diminished greatly because of it. Darryl's decisions and behaviors were turning increasingly destructive. His highs were extremely high and his lows were at the bottom of a black abyss. When addiction strikes individuals, their judgment, decision-making, and behavior control are greatly impaired. This state of mind ultimately leads to other addictive activities, such as gambling and seeking sexual pleasures.

Darryl and Lisa managed to hold their marriage together for a few months following the 1986 season, but Darryl could not resist the temptations of drinking and drugging. He would get high and they would argue and fight. He would get drunk and they would fight and argue. It was a never-ending battle between the two.

Lisa ultimately filed for separation from Darryl and moved back to California with their son. Darryl was alone in New York City. This was a perfect situation for Darryl, right? He could party without having to report home to the wife and family! He would have freedom to hook up with chicks on a nightly basis! He could really live like a king now!

In actuality, Darryl crashed. By that time, the drugs and drinks were scrambling his brain. He went into a deep depression, and was lonely and ashamed. He still partied, but it was for much different reasons. In his earlier days, he partied to push down the horrible memories of his past. Now he was partying to hide from the pain he had caused his own family and himself.

Feeding his addictions was an around-the-clock pity party and Darryl Strawberry was its honored guest. Sports had always been Darryl's refuge from the stresses of life. Now he was finding less joy in the game that had once saved him. The team was undergoing major scrutiny after winning it all the year before. He and his teammates were expected to rise up as the conquering heroes with every plate appearance and every pitching performance. If they failed, they were met with the unyielding "Boo-Birds of Shea."

Darryl was under the most scrutiny. He felt pressures from the media, the Mets organization, as well as his teammates. Combine those stresses with the strains of his personal life and you had yourself a ticking time bomb of emotions. Darryl loved the New York fans, so he was capable of shutting out the ugly few who tried to get under his skin. He always wanted to be the best he could be, but his self-loathing continued to be his biggest opponent.

One particular evening, Darryl unknowingly partied through the night and into the following morning. When he finally emerged from the bar, he was met with the blinding light of the morning sun. He blocked the bright, yellow rays from his face as if he were a vampire. When he looked at his watch, he realized it was 8 a.m. He didn't even sleep, but drove straight to the stadium for the game's noon-time start.

He played the day game with a belly full of amphetamines and Tylenol, but was in such pain, the hair on his head hurt. As each excruciating inning limped along, all Darryl could think about was curling up in the corner of the clubhouse and falling asleep for a month.

His good friend Dwight was also plunging into the drug scene. He was performing well, but when Dwight wasn't pitching, he was either drunk or stoned out of his mind. Dwight had been arrested for an airport gun charge and failed a mandatory drug test before the 1987 season. He would ultimately be checked into a drug rehabilitation and detox center in New York before rejoining the club later that spring.

Why didn't Darryl do the same? Why didn't Darryl check himself into Smithers? What held him back?

The Mets 1986 clubhouse had great team chemistry. There was an unnatural harmony among the players regarding their nocturnal identities and uncivilized nighttime behaviors. The 1987 clubhouse was different than the year before. Many of the players from the championship season were no longer in the organization and many of the remaining players were trying to clean up their unconscionable acts from the previous year.

The Championship Mets were amazing! The team was arrogant, and they knew they were going to win the moment their cleats met the playing field. However, the team's off-the-field antics damn near put them in their coffins.

As the 1987 season proceeded, so did the internal issues between the present team's player personnel. The fights that ensued between teammates that year were unfathomable. It was a team of drug addicts and alcoholics. It was like a group of clean-cut sailors living with a band of blood-thirsty pirates. A drug-induced paranoia ran rampant inside the clubhouse, while jealous rivalries began unfolding on the field.

Darryl had his fair share of run-ins on the team, and so did Dwight. But, they were still the super stars of the squad, and as long as Darryl was cranking out home runs and Dwight was setting strike-out records, most players had to swallow their animosities and suspicions, no matter how true they may have been.

The '87 Mets failed to make it to the playoffs. They were defeated by the St. Louis Cardinals. Maybe their arrogance caught up to them. Maybe there was too much paranoia and jealousy within the make-up of the team. Or maybe it was the end of the party-hearty Mets and their band of blood-thirsty pirates.

RECONCILIATION?

When Darryl played well, the Mets played well. He was always the focal point of the team's offensive scheme. It was 1988 and a brand-new season for the Mets. Darryl Strawberry was starting the season on fire! He had managed to survive the previous season's drama, and was now leading his team with some impressive displays of power. He was driving in runs, stealing bases, and hitting some majestic long balls. Darryl was carrying his team on his back, just like he had done so many times before.

When Darryl was playing well, happiness was easier to find. The Mets were on top of the Eastern Division once again, and the only other thing on his mind was getting his family back. Darryl and Lisa had reconciled in the off-season of 1987, but Lisa did not join her husband until the spring. She was pregnant with their second child.

Later in the season, Lisa gave birth to their daughter. Darryl felt blessed to have been given a second chance with Lisa and his children. He was ecstatic about the birth of his daughter, and his family was becoming a first priority in his life. He understood the importance of family, and he wanted to be the best father possible.

The last thing Darryl wanted was to be labeled as a bad father. He wanted his mother to be proud of his actions. He wanted his siblings to smile, knowing their Darryl was the head of a loving home. Darryl had learned so many important lessons during the childhood chaos that nearly destroyed him as a person. He could not let himself make the same mistakes.

Darryl wanted his two children to know that they were special gifts from God. He wanted them to know they would NEVER be a NOTHING in his eyes. He needed them to know how much he loved them.

He had to STAY FOCUSED. He had to FIGHT OFF THE MONSTER LURKING IN THE DARK SHADOWS OF HIS MIND. Was this possible? Or were his addictions buried too deeply in his being?

A BOMB IS DROPPED

In April of 1989, Darryl Strawberry had a bomb dropped on him. A woman was suing Darryl for child support for a child they created during a one-night stand in St. Louis the year before. Darryl agreed to a paternity blood test, and was more than willing to cooperate with the woman's attorneys.

When the paternity results were announced, it was determined that Darryl Strawberry was indeed the father of the child. Darryl was stunned. A million thoughts buzzed through his brain, and none of them was pleasant. He knew his marriage was already on shaky ground, and dropping a bomb like this would surely send his wife over the top. He knew the dreadful fate that lay before him. He knew.

Without hesitation, Darryl agreed to pay child support and set up a trust for the child. Paying the mother of the child was the least of his concerns. He had a firestorm brewing at home. His words would be like gasoline on a house that was already burning.

As Darryl pondered a way of relaying the news to his wife, she was already reading the story in the newspapers. When Darryl confessed to the allegations, Lisa exploded on him! She was beyond furious, and by May of that year, filed for divorce from her husband.

Darryl did not want to lose his family and pleaded with Lisa to give him another chance. He was in the last year of his contract with the Mets and had a shot of signing with the Los Angeles Dodgers within a year. If he could get the family back home to California, he believed he could save the marriage. He felt that if he played for the Dodgers, he could provide a more stable environment for her and the kids. He would have his immediate family back in his life and Lisa would have her mother back in her life as well.

Lisa listened to the proposition, but her trust for Darryl was irreparably damaged. Lisa packed her belongings and headed back to California without her husband. Darryl was heartbroken, but understood her decision. He begged, pleaded, and bribed her in every way possible, but Lisa was leaving and there was nothing he could do about it.

After the season concluded, Darryl rushed to California to see his children. Through hours of pleading, he finally convinced Lisa to move into their Encino home and give the marriage one last, final chance. She decided to move into the home if her mother was allowed to move into the house as well. Darryl agreed.

The Strawberry family was together again. It wasn't necessarily pleasant all the time, but in Darryl's mind, they were together. The arguments between Darryl and Lisa did not cease. Why would they? Lisa didn't trust Darryl as far she could pick him up and throw him. There was dissension in the ranks, and rage bubbled beneath the surface of Lisa's skin. She was like a volcano itching to erupt.

Darryl was still drinking and drugging. He tried to contain his habits as well as he could, but the addictions were alive and well within him. But, how could this be? He had everything he needed in life. He had money, family, fame—why couldn't he just drop his addictions at his feet and walk away? Darryl was imprisoned by his addictions.

Darryl's mental state was severely taxed. He was like two separate entities because of the addictions. He had his body, and he had his brain. His body (his heart) wanted what was best for him and his family. His brain was now diseased with the addictions. Drugs were much like his father. He didn't want them in his life, but felt vulnerable without them.

Darryl was in the same dark place in which Ronnie had been living. The difference between the two brother's lives were: Ronnie lived in a rat-infested death hole, while Darryl lived in a lush mansion. The two places were on opposite sides of the spectrum, but both places were equally dark inside. Darryl's brain now marched to the beat of a different drum. It was the same drumbeat that had hypnotized Ronnie for years prior.

Drugs are composed of chemicals. When taken, the chemicals of the drugs interfere with the communication systems of the brain. The brain is tricked into transmitting abnormal messages throughout the nerve network. In time, overstimulation of the brain leads to such euphoric releases that the brain demands a repeat performance. This is called addiction.

Escape, fear, sadness, and depression are just a few of the emotions that seek a euphoric release. Euphoria is pleasure. It is a wild ride that takes people far away from the troubles that plague them. Euphoria was the maestro behind the haunting drumbeats that lured Darryl off the straight and narrow.

Those alluring beats pulled at Darryl. They pulled him into the shadows.

NO MORE CHANCES

It was January 26th, 1990. Darryl had returned home from a long night of drinking. He was blitzed behind belief. When he arrived at his Encino home, he was shocked to find out that Lisa was out for the night as well. Darryl paced the living room floor like a madman as he impatiently awaited her return.

When the front door opened, Darryl flew into the greatest rage of his life. The combative Lisa was more than ready for the confrontation. Both Darryl and Lisa blew up like Roman candles. Their shouting shook the walls of the house. Darryl was out of his mind with rage, as Lisa's bubbling volcano finally erupted. Their arms flailed as their vicious words cut like knives. Darryl's fiery red eyes bulged from his head, as he clenched his giant fists.

THWACK!

Darryl punched his wife in the side of her head, sending her end over end across the living room floor. Lisa slowly gathered herself, shaking the cobwebs from her brain. She quickly grabbed a fireplace poker and with pure hatred in her veins, swung the iron bar into her husband's ribs. She would (or could) not stop! She struck Darryl over and over with the fireplace poker. Darryl blocked the blows with his arm before breaking away to the closet.

Lisa charged at Darryl with the fireplace poker. Before she could get one more swing at her husband, she was met with the barrel end of a .25 caliber pistol pointed directly between her eyes. Time stood still. The entire room was spinning as Lisa stared into the barrel of the gun. No words were spoken.

Lisa's mother opened her bedroom door to find Darryl pointing a pistol at her daughter. Her mouth quivered, but she could not speak. The room was eerily silent. The only sounds Darryl heard were the booming drumbeats ricocheting through his head.

As Lisa slowly backed away from the confrontation, Darryl stood silent. He had no intentions of using the firearm on his wife. He just wanted the madness to end. When his mother-in-law called the police, Darryl remained silent. He knew the authorities were coming for him.

When the drums stopped beating, Darryl stood alone in the darkness, the devilish ghoul standing directly before him. Darryl could not see the Monster, but he knew he was there. He could smell the liquor on his breath. When Darryl closed his eyes, he could see his father standing before him with the shotgun in his hands. His father was drunk and screaming, his arms wildly flailing.

Did he really want to shoot us? Or did he just want the madness to end?

FIRST INTERVENTION

After Darryl was released from jail, he was plagued with humiliation. He felt shame and sorrow for his actions. He was now forced to face his demons, whether he wanted to or not. Darryl's mother Ruby, as well as the New York Mets, wanted Darryl to pursue medical help. Ruby felt he had a behavior problem, while the Mets were more concerned with his alcohol consumption.

After speaking to the Mets' medical division, the team's psychiatrist recommended an eight-week stay for Darryl at a rehabilitation and detox center in New York. It was the same facility Dwight had entered years prior. The psychiatrist was convinced that Darryl needed to find sobriety in a clinical setting, and with haste.

Darryl reported to the facility, and did not drink a single drop of alcohol or pop a single pill during his two-month stay. At the conclusion of his time, Darryl felt much better. His head felt clear, his decision-making process had improved, and his moods were much more stable. But how long could these improved feelings last?

Darryl had entered the facility because of an alcohol addiction. However, he failed to mention anything about the amphetamines or cocaine he was routinely using. Darryl wanted to do his time in the center and get out as quickly as possible. He followed the orders of the Mets organization, but was not truthful to the facility regarding his drug addictions. He was not truthful to himself. No one can truly be healed without first speaking the truth.

When Darryl left the center, he was far from being cured. His drug addictions were deep-rooted, and the facility wasn't even privy to all facts. When Darryl left the center and reentered society, the Monster was there waiting. The dark traveler used his growling voice to taunt Darryl: "Welcome home, my son."

Shortly after Darryl's stint at the center, he started his 1990 season. Darryl was having a great year with the Mets, but it was quite apparent that the Mets had gone sour on Darryl and his mischievous ways. Darryl had maintained his sobriety for a while after his stay at the center, but the stresses of his job and personal life pushed his fragile psyche once again. Darryl Strawberry broke free from his sobriety and quickly shackled himself to a cell of despair. He was a prisoner once again.

Darryl's fall from grace was caused by several personal factors. He was distressed over the Mets' front office and their lack of interest in him. He was sinking into the old mind sets of "I am a failure," "I am a worthless father," "I am NOTHING!" He started drinking again to ease the pain. He started drugging again to mask the sorrow.

He wished he could go back in time and start over. He wished he could have a father figure in his life, someone he could confide in, talk to, and lean upon. He needed to truly face the demons of his life, but he needed to go back in time- to the root of his problems.

Darryl needed to find solace. He had to figure out a way to chase the deep-rooted feelings of rejection far from his brain. He needed to talk to his father. He needed to face the Monster.

* * * * *

DOCTOR'S NOTES AND COMMENTS TO CHAPTER 6

with Rich Capiola, MD

Anxiety was the true name of the game for Darryl during this period of his life. The combinations of his past-life memories, his present-day stresses, and his multiple addictions weighed heavily on his mind and body. His personal decisions and actions were out of control, and his future was crying for change. He had been arrested and placed in an intervention facility, but were these harsh consequences truly speaking to Darryl? Or was he just not listening?

The first item of discussion involves Darryl's first intervention. Why didn't the intervention work for him? He had the perfect opportunity to face all his fears and tackle every one of his addictions during his time at the detox facility. However, his mind was geared more to just "doing the time" and getting out of the detox center. He wanted to save face with his many fans and return to his work at the ball field. The intervention did not work for Darryl because he was not ready or willing to do the work.

Darryl was a celebrity who was bringing home enormously fat paychecks. He was harboring psychological baggage that caused him to avoid his own self-reflection. As I stated earlier, making changes in your life is hard work. The act of self-reflection can be extremely painful, because it exposes the truth of a person's inner-being. This process becomes even more challenging when the person attempting to make changes has millions of dollars in his or her bank account.

People with grand financial portfolios are not even close to hitting rock bottom in their lives. When individuals hit rock bottom, it means they have nothing else to lose in their life. Intervention can be difficult for individuals with significant wealth because they are not destitute or on the brink of starvation. Regardless, whether the addict is rich or poor, the person must be willing to do the work necessary if he is going to make the necessary changes required for an addiction-free life.

Addicts have been setting their brains up to receive pleasure for many years. People, places, and things support the culture of addiction and provide cues and triggers that fire up the brain's neurochemical responses. Once a person becomes an addict, this feeling or reaction to the triggers will never go away. This is why a person can seek out intervention, become sober for years, but will fall in an instant if a connection is made between the addict and his trigger source.

When an addict is exposed to the trigger and responds to its calling, one drink or one hit is all it takes to suck the addict right back into his world of addictions. When an addict falls, he falls very hard! This crash happens because the brain has been longing for this neurochemical release for months or years! Once the trigger has been activated, the ghost memory of his past addictions is activated. The ghost memory is a siren that alerts the brain of the intense pleasures awaiting the addict. In an instant, the dopamine is charged and released and the addict is engaged in his addiction once again.

The ghost memory provides an addict with a flowery depiction of the many pleasures received through the addictive substances. However, the ghost memory is a villainous prankster! The memories it provides are distorted views of the substance's magical powers. These recalled memories are based solely on the positive aspects of using the substance. It reminds the addict of the wonderful high or peaceful calm he received from the substance.

The addict reacts to the pleasures and totally forgets that these exact same substances have also caused him great pain and suffering. An addict's mind fails to connect the negative consequences of his prior actions. "I went to jail ... I lost my family ... I burned through my money." The addict's mindset does not factor these unfavorable happenings into the equation. The addict's thoughts are strictly centered on the epic highs and pleasures he received in years past.

Once the addict gets a taste of his past and that feeling of pleasure kicks in, he is captured once again. This happens because the brain has been primed for many years for this particular pleasure reward—it only takes one trigger to send the addict reeling. The trigger could be the Circle K that sells his favorite brand of vodka or it could happen when the recovering addict runs into his old drug dealer at a gas station. The addict receives an instantaneous dopamine charge when he comes into contact with a personal triggering mechanism.

* * * * *

The trigger response is alive and well in sober humans, as well as addicts. This theory can be illustrated by the connections between two former lovers. A man and woman shared incredible intimacy with one another, but the man was a filthy slob who drove the woman crazy because he did not have a job and spent all day playing "Tour of Duty" against a bunch of 14-year-olds. Although the woman thoroughly enjoyed the intimate moments with the man, she could not spend the rest of her life with a grown man wearing a head set, holding a joy stick, while eating Cheetos, and shooting down animated soldiers on a plasma screen.

The woman breaks up with the man. Three years later, she is out with friends at a gala when she sees a suave, handsome, and debonair man at the bar. She realizes it is her old flame, and before you know it, they are talking, laughing, and driving back to his place for a night cap. The woman could care less about the night cap because her mind is totally locked in on the memories of the amazing sex life they once shared. The dopamine reward system has been alerted and she is ready for action.

When she wakes up in his bedroom the next morning, she rubs her eyes and notices he is not in the bed. She walks out to the living room, where she finds him on his cluttered couch shooting down animated soldiers with his Cheeto-stained joy stick. Her ghost memory was based on the amazing sex life she shared with her former lover. But her brain had blocked out the rest of the ugly truths behind his lazy life of video games and orange-stained fingers.

The woman needed a barrier to block the pleasure reward system. She received that barrier when she saw the slovenly Johnny Joy Stick in his cluttered living room. This barrier instantly blocked the pleasure-reward system in her brain, and she was out the door in an instant.

* * * * *

Most addicts have a difficult time finding a barrier that can effectively block the triggers and diminish the pleasure-seeking actions of the limbic system.

Here is another example of blocking the brain's reward circuits. Let's say you are driving down the road and you see the Italian restaurant where you once had the most delicious calzone you had ever tasted. The thought of the rich, savory pizza pocket has your mouth watering. However, the calzone was not the trigger. In fact, the calzone would have never entered your mind had it not been for the trigger received by the restaurant's appearance. What was the trigger? Maybe it was the sight of the red, white, and green flag flapping in the wind near the roadside? Maybe it was the bright red shutters of the building?

Whatever the trigger happened to be, it was strong enough to make you turn your car around and make a beeline for the restaurant. The pleasure-reward system is now in full force and the ghost memory of the incredible calzone is all you can think about. You hurriedly park your car and speed-walk to the front door.

When you attempt to open restaurant's main door, you discover it is locked. The sign reads "CLOSED." Boom! The pathway is blocked and the stimulus raging in your brain is immediately shut down. You now have two options—get in your car and go to another Italian restaurant for a less appealing calzone or just continue driving home to leftovers.

*****

The pathway of an addict's mind is constantly searching for the next high. An addict needs to create a blockade or barrier against his or her addictions. An addict needs intervention, but more than anything, an addict needs a proper plan of attack to protect against the triggers of the addiction. It is vital that an addict has this plan activated before he or she is released from the detox or rehabilitation center.

Simple ideas to prevent or avoid triggers can be demonstrated in the following manner. Let's say an addict has bought his favorite brand of vodka from the same Circle K convenience store for years. This Circle K is convenient for the addict because it is located en route to his workplace. If the addict truly wants to stop drinking, he must engage in a plan to avoid the Circle K.

The addict rearranges his daily driving route to work and successfully bypasses the Circle K. He is doing the work! He is avoiding his trigger! In time, this person will be unable to avoid that particular Circle K, but by making a concerted effort to avoid the convenience store, the addict is able to soften the trigger mechanism.

Addicts need a solid plan to deal with their triggers, or they will inevitably fall again. In fact, an addict should create his or her own "trigger inventory" before they leave the intervention center. This trigger inventory will allow an addict to properly deal with, avoid, or manage addiction triggers that cause pleasure-seeking responses in his brain.

Addicts must also be honest in their interventions. They must be honest about each of their addictions. An addict must inform the intervention center about the depth and history of each addiction. Finally, an addict must reveal the many trigger mechanisms responsible for lighting up his brain chemistry.

"Cuing Mechanisms" are a very powerful and vital tool for human beings. Cuing occurs when a person is reminded of something based on a memorable signal or hint. We use cues

in our life to make intelligent decisions. These decisions are based on previous connections made in the brain. All humans rely on cuing mechanisms to solve problems, make quick choices, and avert dangers.

Here is an example of cuing: A club-toting caveman exits his cave and wanders down the mountain in search of his family's dinner. The caveman walks past a small lagoon as he heads toward a giant rock. As the caveman rounds the giant rock, he comes face to face with a ferocious saber-toothed tiger. The caveman had better possess solid cuing mechanisms or the encounter is going to turn real ugly, real fast.

The caveman quickly reverts to his cuing connections as his mind assesses the perilous situation at hand. He has personally witnessed a saber-toothed tiger rip another caveman in two. It was the talk of the village for months. His cues remind him that the saber-toothed tiger is afraid of water. Therefore, the cavemen uses his cues to make a split-second decision. The caveman slowly backs into the lagoon and submerges himself in the water. The big cat swats at the water like a cat does with a fish bowl. After a while, the saber-toothed tiger wanders off and the caveman is safe to hunt another day.

Treatment centers are designed as safe havens in which addicts can examine their lives and find ways to fight off their addictions. Intervention centers were designed to help addicts prepare for an inevitable face-to-face confrontation with the triggering mechanism of their addictions.

Treatment center staff cannot protect addicts once they leave the facility. That is why these professionals work to create various solutions that can be utilized to prevent a relapse when addicts depart. These professionals cannot live with the addict, drive with the addict, or oversee the addict on a daily basis. That said, intervention professionals can provide a support system, structure, and a battle plan against an addict's trigger mechanisms. Intervention professionals must redirect an addict's mindset from "How can I get high?" to "How can I stay sober and clean?"

Addictions are always in an addict's "Ready-Go!" state. This is because an addict's brain pathway is constantly primed for a pleasure-reward. It is vital that an addict eventually finds rewards in sobriety. An addict must understand that it takes constant work and a vigilant spirit to stare down the powers of a trigger. An addict must learn to utilize the cuing mechanisms instilled in his brain to avoid the saber-toothed tiger that is lying in wait to confront him by the giant rock.

Addiction is always in full force. Therefore, an addict must be on high alert and fully functional to battle his or her greatest foe. Addicts must be honest, truthful, and steadfast in their work if they are ever going to defeat this brain disease called addiction.

CHAPTER 7
THE BRAIN DISEASE

Based on an interview with Rich Capiola, MD

L et's make this simple. Addiction is a *brain disease!*
Now that we have that out of the way, let's discuss how
this is possible. Addiction is an uncontrollable need
for a substance that eventually becomes the most important
thing in a person's life. An addiction will negatively affect
mood, memory, personality, and most importantly, an addict's
perception of life. A skewed perception of life will lead an
addict to horrible choices, life-altering decisions, and increased
health-related issues.

The moment an addiction process becomes fully entrenched in a person, that person is officially dealing with a
brain disease. Addiction is found in our workplaces, our
schools, and our own families. When you recognize that a co-
worker smokes a cigarette every single work break, then you
are acknowledging that person has an addiction. When the
co-worker attaches the work break to smoking a cigarette, this
person is further entrenching his addiction.

If a person needs a cigarette and a cup of coffee every single morning to start the day, then that person is fully entrenched in an addiction. The anticipation and actual use of any addictive substance will provide an addict with his much-desired burst of dopamine. When a person relies on this burst of dopamine every day, and sometimes every hour of the day, he is suffering from the brain disease.

Alcohol and drugs are responsible for three addictive brain responses. These brain responses are the centerpiece of an addiction's stronghold. The first addictive brain response is *euphoria*, which is created when the pleasure-seeking neurochemicals flood the brain. The second addictive brain response *floods the brain with GABA and serotonin*, which results in a reduction of stress, anxiety, and fear. The final brain addiction response occurs when the addict has stopped using alcohol or drugs and the *brain chemistry bounces back and forth between pleasure and depression.*

These brain chemistry fluctuations cause radical mood shifts in those suffering from addiction. During these fluctuations, an addict is unable to properly lasso his or her emotions due to chemical spikes and drastic drops in the brain's chemistry. An addict's emotional state can swing from being diligent and functional to being agitated, depressed, and unmotivated within minutes. This is due to the intense brain chemistry responses that take place during drug and alcohol abuse.

When Darryl started using marijuana and alcohol as a teenager, he was using these substances in a casual, infrequent manner. This type of drug or alcohol use does not cause significant problems within an individual's brain chemistry. However, early substance use will begin the initial cementing process in the brain's reward circuits.

By the time Darryl made it to the Minor Leagues, he was using marijuana and alcohol to fight off the many stresses he was facing in his young life. This type of drug or alcohol use causes more of a euphoric response, which he needed to numb the painful thoughts he was enduring. When a person reaches this level of use, the euphoric state is actually dictating the frequency and quantity of the person's use. During this level of substance use, a person is beginning to create a tolerance towards the substances.

When Darryl reached the Major Leagues, his drug use had graduated to drug *abuse*. He was partying nearly every night of the week, and his drug use was starting to negatively affect the people around him. His late-night excursions were destroying his marriage and affecting his work production. But, most importantly, the heavier substance abuse was laying the tracks of his inevitable brain disease.

Once Darryl began his daily regimen of amphetamine abuse, his first viable addiction was in full force. Darryl had officially fallen prey to brain disease. The addiction was now a prominent fixture in Darryl's brain. He had permitted the addiction to take control of his brain with no chance of reversing the process.

According to multiple psychiatric publications, once a person is securely fastened to an addiction, he or she will journey through three levels of the disease: 1) Early Stage, 2) Middle Stage, and 3) Chronic or Late Stage.

The early stages of addiction are usually found in those addicts who habitually use drugs or alcohol, but are still able to function at high levels at their workplace or home. These addicts are often referred to as "functioning alcoholics" or "recreational drug users."

The middle stages of addiction can be found in those who drink until they black out, or become severely impaired in terms of their judgment and overall awareness. These are the addicts who will get drunk, jump in a lake, and have no recollection of their activities the following morning. The middle stage is also the onset of denial and rationalization among addicts. Defensive mechanisms are in full force with middle-stage addicts, because these addicts cannot and will not admit to the glaring complications of their addiction.

These addicts will mow down a line of mailboxes with their car during a late-night drinking binge, then make solemn vows they will never drive drunk again. The next night, the same alcoholic weaves down the road in a drunken stupor once again. These are the addicts who will provide bizarre reasoning to explain their repugnant behaviors. "I wouldn't have hit those mailboxes if it hadn't been so dark outside."

Most times, this type of addict will have no recollection of his intoxicated actions or his promises. The middle-stage addict lives in a world of denial to both the reality of his situation and the problems he and his addiction are creating for those around him. Brain disease and an addict's unconscious defense mechanisms are assiduously intertwined.

The chronic or late-stage level of addiction is the scariest of all levels. When an addict enters this stage, he is at the bottom of a deep, dark well and all he can do is frantically look upward to the faint light that once was his world. Such addicts are not the people we once knew. Their minds and bodies are deteriorating right before our very eyes. They are constantly struggling with legal, social, or financial predicaments. The synapses and biochemistry of their brains are chaotic and poorly functional, which in turn creates feelings of depression, paranoia, anger, guilt, and shame.

Once an addict reaches this stage of addiction, there are only four possible outcomes. They will either:

1. commit suicide,
2. die from an overdose,
3. go to prison, or
4. find a drug and alcohol recovery center.

You might be asking, "Is addiction treatable, let alone at this stage of the disease?"

The answer to this question is a resounding, YES! However, an addicted person has to be willing to put in the incredibly hard work necessary to make it happen. When people are diagnosed with diabetes or high blood pressure, they are required to avoid certain foods and drinks that could spike their blood sugar levels. These people have a disease that requires a thorough reconstruction of their current diet and lifestyle. It is imperative for diabetics to avoid certain foods that not only spike blood-sugar levels, but also trigger their brain's reward system. These lifestyle and nutritional changes require hard work, diligence, patience, and mental strength.

Diabetics understand the simple fact that they have no other choice in the matter. They must make changes in their dietary intake or they will surely die. Can a diabetic relapse? Yes, diabetics relapse all the time! However, once a diabetic relapse occurs, the individual must acknowledge his mistake, and formulate immediate revisions to his error in judgment. He has to "get back on the horse" to regain control of this important life-or-death scenario.

The diabetic must guard against the ghost memories of his past. He must develop a mental structure that can fight off certain food urges. He must also avoid the trigger mechanisms that can cause him to relapse. If this means the diabetic has to stop meeting with his "Donut Friend" on Wednesday mornings, then so be it. The "Donut Friend" will need to find another Krispy Kreme companion.

If someone is in a horrific car accident and loses his leg, he has no choice but to change his life to survive. If a person loses her eyesight, she needs to adapt to a completely different way of living. It takes work! It takes tears! Individuals have two choices: make the changes and live, or fail to make the changes and die.

If a recovering drug addict has to get a root canal, he must be able to converse with the dentist about the proper mode of pain management. Should he receive opiates? If he does receive opiates, should he be required to pick up his dosage on a daily basis instead of receiving a ten-day supply from the pharmacy? Such a proactive measure is an absolute requirement for addicts! Recovering addicts must protect themselves from their triggers.

Interventions are difficult for addicts, because these individuals do not want to admit they have a problem, and once they do admit a problem, then they do not want to admit the severity of the problem. It takes hard work! It takes real changes! It means sacrifice!

Do you know how long it takes to become addicted to a substance? In World War II, young soldiers received cigarettes in their C-Rations. Many of these soldiers had never smoked a cigarette in their lives, but due to the stresses of war and their disturbed sleep patterns, many young men began smoking the cigarettes. The soldiers became addicted to the cigarettes within a week of their first puffs.

Becoming addicted is easy. Rescuing yourself from the addiction is extremely difficult! When an addict is willing to do the work, he will not only defeat his addictions, he will regain his life. For addicts and for their loved ones, always remember these words of advice:

"Do the work!
Make the changes!
And take your life back!
You can do it!"

* * * * *

DARRYL'S STORY

HIDING AWAY

"A father is neither an anchor to hold us back, nor a sail to take us there, but a guiding light whose love shows us the way." This anonymous quote perfectly exemplifies the role of a father.

A mother's love for her child begins nine months before the baby is even born. The gestation period is a process that men cannot comprehend. A child relies on its mother for nourishment inside the womb. The baby grows and changes deep inside her, creating a bond that is unparalleled. Life is not possible without the sustenance provided by the mother.

A father's love is different. He loves the idea of the unborn child, but the bond between father and child is more apparent once the baby is delivered into the world. The sight of the precious baby's face and its tiny fingers and toes, strikes a deep accord with the father. Men are visual creatures, and when that baby's eyes focus on a brand-new world, so does a father's. The love of a father is shown through his protective nature and his acts of reinforced love through the acts of provision and guidance.

Ruby was a brave woman who breathed life into five people. She provided unconditional love to her children, even during the darkest days of their lives. She showed courage in the toughest of moments, and was a strong protector of her five babies. She gave balance to Darry's life, and was always there for him with words of advice or encouragement when he was falling. She also questioned his choices when he was faltering.

Henry was a man who could not truly love. He was a damaged soul from years gone by. The abuse he had endured carried into his own life as a father. He could not love, and his children felt the cold, indifferent spirit he exuded. Henry was devoid of happiness, and he passed on that trait to his two youngest sons. The question remained. Why would someone who felt unloved as a child become unloving as an adult? Why did Henry reject Darryl and Ronnie, but feel something different with his other three children?

Darryl and Ronnie definitely felt rejected by their father. Henry made them feel unloved and unworthy of love. When a person feels unloved, it is difficult for that person to love himself, let alone anyone else in his or her life. Individuals who do not feel love in their hearts will also struggle with the concept of love later in their lives.

Although, Darryl and Ronnie had two different personalities, they were both victims of the same abusive parental figure. They lived through the horrors of their childhood home, and were now forced to make choices without the guidance of the man who was supposed to love them and protect them. Where was the man who was supposed to guide them along their journeys?

Darryl needed to talk to his father. He needed to find some source of solace for his heart. He needed advice and encouragement. He needed a strong voice to calm his spirt. He needed a protector. He needed an apology.

It took every ounce of strength for Darryl to make the phone call to his father. His words were brief and so were those of his father. The call proved uneventful. Darryl did not know what he could have expected from a conversation with his father, but he was hoping it would give him some explanation for his father's abusive actions.

In fact, the call was cold and empty. There was no sense of sorrow or any type of remorseful apology for his horrible actions. The Monster remained stoic and unmoved by Darryl's courageous attempt to reach out and talk to his father.

Once again, Darryl turned to his mother, Ruby, for the much-needed advice he was seeking. Ruby had always felt that Darryl's behavior was the primary reason for his actions. Years later, Darryl connected with his mother's theories. Her thoughts were simple—"Son, if you stop going to bars where these promiscuous women congregate, then you will be less likely to drink and pursue your sexual cravings." This was logical thinking from a sensible woman.

Darryl had become a major womanizer in his adult life. He was a hunter who relished the excitement of the chase. He thoroughly enjoyed the instantaneous satisfaction of being wanted and desired. When a woman showed him attention, it filled a void deep inside him. He had no fears of being rejected when he was tracking down female companionship.

Ruby wanted Darryl to curb his carnal urges and concentrate on his work and his children. She told him to stop going into places where temptations were prevalent. Ruby preached and pleaded with her youngest son. She told him these two simple words: **"Stay focused!"**

Darryl had heard these words of advice before. It seemed to be a recurring theme for his life: "Stay focused." But, could he stay focused without the assistance of his "old friends"—the amphetamines, other stimulants, and alcohol?

He was open-minded with regard to his mother's sentiments. He too believed that if he could stop chasing women, then maybe his drinking would lessen and his addictions to drugs would decrease. Actually, Ruby was unaware of Darryl's drug use. Cocaine and amphetamines were a huge part of his life, but he had never told his mother the true seriousness of his drug abuse.

Ruby also never truly understood the depths of Darryl's self-loathing, just like she was never privy to the numerous times he and Ronnie were actually beaten by her husband. She had no idea of the levels of self-affliction her son was enduring, because Darryl was a master at hiding his pain. He could not talk about his life and his feelings, because he didn't want to share such darkness with his mother, or anyone else for that matter.

So, he hid behind the addictions. If a person cannot talk about his pain, he will consume himself with something that will surely hide the pain away. Darryl was hiding behind his booze, his pills, and the comforts of women.

As long as the Monster breathes, Darryl will just keep hiding away.

HOMETOWN HERO

After eleven years in the New York Mets organization, Darryl now found himself back in his hometown of Los Angeles. Darryl signed with the Dodgers and was excited about the change in scenery. By moving home, Darryl would be renewing old friendships and reconnecting with family members in the area.

The downfall to his move back home would be the revival of his underworld connections. Drugs, drinks, and more drugs would be available upon his command, and drug dealers knew that Darryl was always good for the money. He was a favorite target.

The Hometown Hero returns! This was a common saying around the L.A. party scene, when the 6-foot-6 Darryl Strawberry entered a room. His great height allowed him to stand out in a crowd, and his grand celebrity status provided him free access to anything he desired. His "old friends" were in his possession at the snap of his fingers.

It was at one of these chic soirees when Darryl was introduced to his future nemesis, crack cocaine. This particular poison was the new heavy-hitter among drug dealers and users. When Darryl smoked crack for the first time, he was immediately hooked. The high was intense! The results were phenomenal! And the addiction to crack would be the strongest of all the drugs he had ever tried.

The old adage, "Money can't buy you happiness," had never been more apropos when it applied to the life of Darryl Strawberry. He had everything! He had millions of dollars, celebrity fame, and incredible success in the game of baseball. He was a living legend who lived in a world devoid of genuine happiness and self-admiration. Darryl was lost, but his newest friend, crack cocaine, would surely show him the way to a better existence, right?

Crack to humans is what Kryptonite is to Superman. So how could this be the drug of choice for anyone? Darryl was completely sucked in by the drug. It offered an escape that he was unable to find anywhere else. When he was flying on this drug, the Monster was nowhere to be found.

Crack cocaine is a powerful stimulant that dwarfs the effects created by cocaine. Crack provides intense euphoria in a quicker amount of time, which is the main selling point of the drug. However, the horrific side effects following chronic crack-cocaine usage are some of the ugliest a person could ever endure.

The side effects of ongoing crack cocaine highs include the following:

- Disturbed sleep patterns
- High levels of anxiety
- High levels of paranoia
- Bizarre, erratic, violent behaviors
- Panic and psychosis
- Depression
- Convulsions and seizures
- Irritability
- Nausea
- *An intense craving for the drug!!!*

Crack cocaine is the gift that keeps on giving. A person gets hooked on the first toke of crack, then battles through the ugliest side effects possible, only to be summoned once again by the drug. Coming down from a crack-cocaine high gets tougher and tougher with each use. As the person becomes increasingly depressed, he seeks the drug more often. The drug also interferes with the normal way a person's brain processes chemicals and transfers messages.

Drugs like crack cocaine also affect the way our brain's pleasure or reward circuit is activated. Our brains are wired to associate self-sustaining activities with a feeling of pleasure or reward. When the reward circuit is activated, the brain makes notes of the pleasure associated with the activation. The brain then remembers the special feelings, and activates our body to repeat the activity, again and again, without hesitation.

Drug use also stimulates the same reward circuit in humans, which leads to the abuse of the drug. Combining a drug addiction with the reward circuit is a highly dangerous situation! The effects of a potent pleasure-reward strongly motivate a person to take more and more drugs. The potency of crack cocaine and its impact on the reward circuit is incomparable.

Crack cocaine became Darryl's new "best bud," and with friends like crack, who needs enemies? Crack cocaine is not a gift at all—it is the Devil's cigarette.

MORE INTRODUCTIONS

As Darryl plunged lower and lower into the L.A. drug scene, he remained in constant search for an escape hatch to flee the clutches of his addiction's imprisonment. He would claw and fight his way through the temptations, but would always fall prey to the addiction's powerful grip. Every time he smoked crack, he was pulled into a deeper portion of Hell.

Darryl was confused and his heart was torn with pain. His search for inner peace took him to a spiritual revival held in Anaheim. The speaker's remarks moved Darryl to tears, but the words were still not enough to free him from the clutches of his "old friends." Darryl remained trapped in the dungeons of his addictions.

To properly live in the Word of God, one must walk with the truth in the word. In plain English, a person must become steadfast in the teachings of the Word and defy the temptations that are laid before him. This is a tough proposition, when one's soul is already possessed by the Monster, and his arsenal of drugs and alcohol.

Darryl had always known the teachings of Christianity, but keeping the faith through his recent baseball injuries and personal problems, kept his belief systems at arm's length. Thus, Darryl continued his journey onward with his traveling companions— crack cocaine, alcohol, and amphetamines, while his Bible collected dust on the end table of his apartment. He believed in the word of God, but the shackles that bound him had become embedded around his wrists.

As Darryl's baseball-related injuries mounted, he started sliding deeper into his own prison. He failed to follow his mother's sage words of advice to stay focused as a Dodgers outfielder and tending to his two children.

Instead, Darryl leaped like a sex-crazed frog from one lily pad to the other, conquering as many females as possible. And just when he thought his legs couldn't jump again, he would sail through the air and land upon another pad. Darryl's bad behaviors were at an all-time high!

During an L.A. gala, Darryl was introduced to another key figure in his life—Charisse Simon. Darryl put the full-court press on Charisse, asking for her number and playing on his celebrity status. Charisse did not buy into his pathetic game, and avoided him like the Plague. In fact, she gave Darryl her girlfriend's phone number, instead of hers.

Bugles blared! Dogs barked! And the horses bucked! The hunt was on for Darryl! He didn't think of another woman during the next few weeks; he only thought of Charisse. Weeks after their first introduction, Charisse gave into Darryl's date requests, and the two began seeing one another.

Although Darryl was not yet officially divorced, he and Charisse began a friendship. He shared everything with Charisse. He told her of his drugging, drinking, and his divorce. He told her of the horrible things he had done to Lisa in his first marriage. He even told her some portions of his life with the Monster, but he did not reveal it all. No one knew everything about the Monster except Darryl and his brother Ronnie.

As it turned out, Charisse loved Darryl more than Darryl loved himself. She helped Darryl battle through his divorce, and was a strong influence on Darryl's spiritual needs. Charisse was well aware of the relationship she was bravely entering. She knew she would have steep mountains to climb and deep, dark holes to blindly venture into if she wanted to help him. She saw a good man with a dark cloak of pain wrapped tightly around his lanky frame.

Charisse tried to motivate Darryl to rise above his on-field issues and nagging injuries, and find joy instead of bitterness. Darryl had trouble buying into that mindset and would continue relying on his "old friends" to sidestep issues. As far as happiness went, Darryl had no ideas on how to find it.

Charisse tried to provide him a loving relationship that would provoke a positive, self-image for Darryl. He defied her loving attempts. In his eyes, his mirrored image was like a twisted reflection from a fun-house mirror.

His drugging, drinking, and womanizing continued to plague his life. He was slipping deeper and deeper into the party scene, despite Charisse's loving support. Darryl felt like a failure as a father and the crack was a constant reminder that he would always be a failure. The moment the hit lit up, he felt free. The moment the high came crashing down, he would plummet to an all-time low. It was a vicious cycle.

Within months, the divorce documents were signed and his marriage to Lisa Andrews-Strawberry was finally dead and buried. Darryl and Charisse were free to pursue a life together, especially since she was now pregnant. However, just months into the pregnancy, Charisse and Darryl had a terrible argument that would forever haunt their relationship.

SAY IT ISN'T SO

A stunned and silent Darryl sat in the back of a squad car as he was once again taken into custody for assault and battery. He had struck the one person who had proven to be the rock he had always longed for in his life. He had struck his beautiful girlfriend, the mother of his unborn child.

Darryl slipped into an even darker place. He was beyond mortified by his actions, and had no one to blame but himself. When he stared into the backseat window of the police cruiser, he could see the faint reflection of his tear-streaked face. He could see the Monster appearing through the fogged glass. He could see the dark, red eyes staring back him. He could smell the liquor on his breath and the bitter, burning plastic fumes from the crack pipe.

The Monster was alive in Darryl. He could feel the Monster's claws scraping its sharp nails beneath the surface of his skin. He could feel the Monster's blood coursing through his veins. He despised the person staring back at him. His mind blankly wandered as his best friend, crack cocaine, called out to him!

"DARRYL!"   "DARRYL!"

As the saying goes, "A father is neither an anchor to hold us back, nor a sail to take us there, but a guiding light whose love shows us the way." Darryl's light was hiding away.

DOCTOR'S NOTES AND COMMENTS TO CHAPTER 7

with Rich Capiola, MD

When Darryl reached out to his father, the response he received was as cold as his upbringing. As stated earlier, Darryl was a survivor of verbal and physical abuse. Darryl's mother and his brother Ronnie were also survivors of the same abusive environment. Even after the three Strawberry brothers chased their abusive father from their home, the two younger boys were still left with the constant replay of the horrors they endured during their childhoods.

Many women who are assaulted by their husbands will continue to stay in their abusive relationship because they have a greater fear of the unknown. Many thoughts race through a woman's mind: "Where will I go? How will I feed my kids? What if he chases me down and beats me again?" Sometimes the fears of the unknown are worse than the physical beatings they are receiving at home.

When the abuser is a drug addict or alcoholic, the levels of abuse are taken to an even higher level. This is because addicts lack both impulse control and logical thinking when they are high or seeking a high. The severity of abuse can be indicated by an addict's level or stage of addiction. If an addict is in the middle or chronic stages of addiction, he or she will be at a heightened state of agitation, anger, and paranoia. It is at these times all impulse control is lost, and the addicts have trouble loving themselves, let alone anyone else.

A victim of abuse is usually unable to fight back. Because the victim is weaker, she or he becomes an easy target for the victimizer. The victim is not only exposed to the violent acts of the abuser, he or she is also left with a broken mind, body, and spirit. It takes a lot of work to leave an abusive home and unfortunately, most abused spouses will not leave unless a drastic act or tragedy is committed. When the abused spouse fails to leave the abusive home, the children become targets of abuse as well.

Many addicts have spent their entire lives formalizing a way to escape the many injustices that befell them as children. "Why did my father treat me so badly?" and "How could she have done this to me?" These are normal feelings that are righteously justified in a victim's mind. However, the victims of these horrible wrongdoings must understand that the abuse they endured was out of their control, and they are not responsible for the brutality they sustained. They must learn to remove any personal guilt they have attached to the situation.

The victims must also understand that there was nothing they could have done to deserve such inexcusable treatment. The victims must understand these acts of violence cannot gain control of the victim's mind, body, or spirit. The victims cannot allow their past fears to dictate their future lives. These are bold statements that are difficult to conceive by those who are haunted by abusive scenarios.

However, victims must, in addition, comprehend that the abusive situations they endured as children are but a small portion of their lives. The abuse cannot be allowed to dictate a victim's future actions or sentiments. Victims must realize that the abuse is not a reflection of who they are, but a horrible breach of love and trust between a victim and his or her assailant. Hopefully, the abuser has been incarcerated for his or her atrocious wrongdoings.

But how can victims dismiss or hide the memories of their past? This statement sounds cold and unsympathetic, so let's break it down into simpler terms. No one can be expected to forget the injustices that were perpetrated against that individual. No one can be expected to forgive the abusers for their heinous acts.

However, if a victim can somehow learn to shrink the intensity of the horrible memory, he or she will ultimately decrease the importance of its existence. No one can make the memories vanish, but by lessening the significance of the memory, a victim will be less likely to rely on addictions as a method of inner-healing. The basis of this theory can be found in the following examples.

Military personnel in war-torn countries are witnesses to numerous atrocities. Young soldiers have watched as their friends were mowed down by enemy fire. They have been tortured as prisoners of war and have observed the gruesome deaths of men, women, and children. If these soldiers are unable to shrink the significance of these memories, they will have difficulties adjusting to their own future lives. These soldiers must be able to minimize the effects of their horrific memories if they are ever going to trust and love again.

During Adolf Hitler's European reign of terror in the 1930s and 1940s, Nazi concentration camps were located throughout central and eastern Europe. Within the walls of these despicable houses of horror, Jewish men, women, and children were beaten, poisoned, and slaughtered by the thousands, along with many other who were deemed threats to the Nazi regime. But did these violent acts create an entire generation of Jewish drug addicts and alcoholics? No! The survivors of the Holocaust, with time, learned to shrink the power of the memories to minimize the effects of the evils they witnessed. This step was vital to their mental survival.

Does trauma automatically lead to addictions? No, not in everyone, but childhood abuse is a colossal risk factor for future addiction. Victims who receive proper psychological guidance and therapy can successfully contain, shrink, and minimize the negative effects of their past. If individuals complete the work and are truthful with their reveal, then they will have a better chance of living a life free of addictions.

As stated above, addicts and alcoholics deal with trigger mechanisms on a daily basis. Recovering addicts learn to avoid triggers, but that is not a simple solution, because triggers exist on every corner. Therefore, recovering addicts must practice to properly reduce the powers of these triggers, while also decreasing the importance of addictive substances in their lives. This is not a life choice—it is a survival choice.

Victims of abuse also have trigger mechanisms that can take them back to painful recollections. These cuing mechanisms are very similar to the triggers of the alcoholic who associates his favorite brand of vodka to the Circle K convenience store. This happens because our brains are constantly searching for connections in life. Whether the connections are good or bad, people always strive to connect dots in their daily walk.

"Connecting Dots" is the effect of one object or person reminding you of another object or person. Here is an example: A young altar boy was sexually abused by a priest in St. Mary's Catholic Church. The priest was eventually apprehended, charged, and imprisoned for his horrific acts upon the young boy. Twenty years later, the abused altar boy is now a man in his thirties. The man has dealt with his alcoholism, but is currently in the recovery process of his addiction.

One day, the man receives a beautiful card, inviting him to the 30th annual St. Mary's Church Christmas Cantata. The man's hands tremble as he stares at the photograph of the church on the front of the card. His mind races back to his days as the altar boy of that church.

The card is a trigger for not only his abuse, but also for his addictions. He sees the sexual abuse he endured in the photograph of the church. He sees the church as the victimizer of his life. He has two choices in this situation: 1) Begin drinking *again or 2) Shrink the memory, reduce the power of the memory, minimize the effects of the memory, and ultimately own the addiction. He must also develop a plan of attack when it comes to properly managing triggers when they arise.*

Victims need to shrink their negative memories into the smallest piece of their life's puzzle. They must understand that the abuse they endured is not a symbol of their existence. They must change their mindset from victim to survivor! They must learn or remember that torture and abuse of any kind can never take their souls!

If you are a victim, find a psychological professional who can help you create a plan of attack against the negative images and memories of your past. Find a way to diffuse the triggers that beckon you. Those who have successfully conquered their addictions and enjoyed continuous years of sobriety have found a way to reduce the significance of their addictions on a daily basis, and in doing so, have ultimately reduced the power of the unresolved traumas that remain affixed in the backgrounds of their minds.

If you can accept and understand your addiction as it belongs to you, you will have a better chance of defeating this brain disease.

CHAPTER 8

ADDICTIVE SUBSTANCES

Based on an interview with Rich Capiola, MD

Do addicts normally stick with one addictive substance, or do they continue to search for the greater high with other substances? As stated earlier, an addict is always in search of the greater high! The novel feeling of receiving something new and exciting always plays in the forefront of an addict's mind. Most addicts have their "back-pocket" addiction, but when they are in the middle of a fix, and are told that they can receive a greater high from a new source, the addict is more than willing to take a chance on the exciting premise of the "greater high."

When Darryl smoked marijuana as a teenager, that drug primed him for later drug use as an adult. His drug use eventually graduated to amphetamines and cocaine. The amphetamines were primarily used for performance-enhancing reasons. The cocaine was a stimulant that provided powerful feelings of invincibility and renewed energy.

Then, however, Darryl was introduced to a newer, faster-acting drug source. He was promised a drug that would create the same dynamic effects of cocaine, but would be delivered in a much shorter time period. This drug was called "crack" or "crack cocaine," and the promises made about this drug, were right on the money!

Cocaine is normally snorted. When the cocaine powder enters the nasal passage, it is absorbed into the mucus membranes inside the nasal cavity. The capillaries inside the nasal cavity absorb the cocaine powder and deliver it to the bloodstream. The effects of the drug are normally felt within two minutes, with the high lasting 20 to 40 minutes.

Crack cocaine is the freebase form of cocaine, and can be smoked. ("Freebase" is a method of inhaling drugs by holding a flame under a metal spoon filled with cocaine or any crushed pill.) Smoking the drug delivers it directly into the lungs. This delivery system is a very effective way of entering the blood stream and is extremely addictive. This is the same reason cigarettes become so addicting. The effects of crack are felt within a few seconds of its use. This high is extraordinarily intense and the effects are ten times more rapid than snorting cocaine powder.

Any form of cocaine will flood the brain with a surge of dopamine upon its initial use, but the high will only last for a short period of time. These dopamine surges result in a fulfilled reward system within the brain, but the brain wants to turn off the surge because it knows the feeling is unnatural. The most significant problem associated with cocaine and crack is the tolerance that develops within the brain's pathway against the drug's potency. Through it all, the user wants to keep trying the drug over and over as he searches and longs for that initial high created by the drug. The user battles hard to overcome the brain's mechanism of stopping an abnormal process.

In time, the brain adapts to the drugs, causing the dopamine responses to become weaker and weaker with each use. These weaker responses result in a less pleasurable experience for the user. When addictive drugs attack the brain, the dopamine system is flooded and the brain has a difficult time managing the blitzing action of the drugs. When addicts use drugs, their initial substance-inspired dopamine releases are ten to twelve times greater than a normal dopamine release.

In time, the brain's receptors manufacture less and less dopamine. This action can be best described in the following comparison: Let's say you are watching an action movie on your plasma screen and the surround-sound volume is set at a perfect level. As the movie progresses, the first action sequence takes place with explosions filling the screen and gunfire erupting around you! The sound blaring from the speakers is deafening! You hurriedly grab your television remote and quickly turn down the sound during every action sequence in the movie.

The brain's receptors are completing the same, exact action! The receptors are basically turning down the release of dopamine inside the brain, because the drugs are too intense to handle properly. When the dopamine releases continue to decrease, the addict receives less pleasure from the drug. This is referred to as a "tolerance" to the drug. The brain has basically reacted to the drug use by reducing the number of receptors, so the brain can properly regulate the release of dopamine. The end result is the regulation of receptors and a decreased high from the drug being used.

A drug tolerance sounds like a tremendous physiological occurrence for a drug addict. But, unfortunately, this brain receptor reaction not only fails to decrease an addict's use, it actually causes the addict to either search for a bigger, better drug source or he increases the quantity and frequency of using his specific drug of choice. An addict will search high and low for a greater source of reward.

When Darryl began his crack cocaine use, he had no idea of the serious repercussions that would ensue. A crack addiction is unlike any other drug addiction. A person can buy a dime bag of marijuana and casually smoke the contents of the bag in a week's time. A person who is hooked on crack will never put the substance down until it has been completely exhausted. There is no such thing as "I will save some for later" mentality.

When lab rats are given the choice of a crack pellet or food, the rats will choose the crack pellet every time. By choosing the crack pellet, their reward circuit is stimulated to the maximum. The rats become so content by the dopamine-releasing actions in their brains that they do not desire food or water. The rats will continue this reward-seeking process until they die of starvation or dehydration.

Crack cocaine would become a powerful force in Darryl's future life. He had fallen prey to the beast, and was in dire need of psychological assistance; he just didn't know it. He was becoming an addict for another drug, and this one would eventually become the toughest opponent of his life.

Addiction is attached to a greater purpose for each individual addict. Some people use the drugs to escape their past. Some need their addiction to calm their nerves and give them peace. Some addicts need their addiction to gain an edge in their profession or with a particular sport. Darryl was using his addictions for every reason listed. The following addictions may be found in the people of your life:

Amphetamines or Steroids: These addictions are tied to the brain's reward system in two different ways:

1. The drugs release dopamine, which provides increased focus and energy;

2. The results of their drug use may result in better performance in their work or on in their particular sporting endeavor. Better performance may result in team championships or individual awards, which will consequently create an additional dopamine release in the brain.

If an individual performs at higher levels while taking a particular drug or supplement, the individual may create a faulty connection between the drugs and his own personal accomplishments. An amphetamine or steroid addict will entrench himself into the false theorization that "more is better." In the mind of a sports figure, "If I hit 20 home runs taking 10 mg of Androstenedione, then I can probably hit 30 home runs if I take 20 mg of Androstenedione!" Such a mindset runs rampant in today's competitive sports leagues.

This porous mode of thinking encourages a more repetitive process in the individual's performance-enhancing drug use, leading to an addiction for these substances. When people stop using amphetamines and steroids, they go through withdrawal. An amphetamine or steroid addict will suffer from decreased motivation, energy, and mental alertness.

Darryl dealt with the effects of amphetamine use and withdrawal. When he was unable to use amphetamines, he replaced its use with anything that would stimulate mental clarity. The new world of stimulants is now found in Adderall, ephedra, and caffeine products.

In the world of hardcore drugs, two drugs have rivaled the potency of cocaine and crack cocaine. Methamphetamines and heroin have been the most popular drugs of choice for addicts in the past ten years. These drugs come in various forms of delivery and can be inhaled, injected, snorted, or eaten.

Methamphetamine is a cousin to cocaine and crack. Meth became popular in the early 2000s because people could save money by making it themselves. "Meth houses" started popping up all over the country, as their cooks used basements, sheds, or their own run-down homes to create their poisonous concoctions. Meth is a very popular drug source in rural America. The most dangerous aspect of this drug is the variety of poisonous chemicals used to create the drug.

Heroin is a long-acting, homemade opiate that creates an immediate euphoric feeling. Most pharmacy-grade opiates are taken orally, therefore their properties are weakened in the delivery system of the drug because it is ingested, rather than being inhaled or injected. Heroin is injected directly into the bloodstream, which causes an instant response in the brain.

Heroin lost its popularity for many years because of the various illegal "pill mills" that were providing pain killers to people like they were Tic-Tacs. Now that pharmacy-grade opiates are managed in a more restricted environment, pain pills are much more difficult to come by without a doctor's prescription. Therefore, heroin has become a cheap replacement for opiates.

DARRYL'S STORY

WHAT'S UP WITH YOUR BROTHER?

A dark cloud was following Darryl Strawberry. He had battled through much adversity for a 30-year old man. His behaviors had triggered addictions and his addictions had, in turn, created his terrible behaviors. Life is made of choices, and Darryl's track record with decision-making was far from good. He would fall upon his face, then scramble up to his feet, just to fall again. Darryl was running out of places to hide, and unknown to him, wicked storms were headed his way.

Darryl and his new wife Charisse's relationship was practically destroyed because of his fits of anger and continued drug and alcohol abuse. His "over-the-top" partying was also affecting his play on the field, and the Dodgers were losing patience with him and his wild antics. He had purposely skipped an exhibition game in Anaheim because of a severe hangover, which further infuriated the Dodgers' front office.

On top of it all, the IRS was investigating him for tax fraud to the tune of $350,000. His head was blurry from all the money woes he was experiencing. He had just settled with his ex-wife for millions of dollars, and now he was going to be receiving another enormous financial hit if he was found guilty of the IRS' claims.

Darryl was exhausted and totally ashamed of his actions. Yet, he continued to wreck himself night after night, hiding behind the masks provided by his "old friends." Darryl's actions were completely out of control. In fact, Mike's fellow law enforcement officers bombarded Darryl's oldest brother with the same recurring question: "Mike, *what's up with your brother?*"

Mike heard it all. "He has everything. Why can't he get his life together?" and "He's going to end up divorced again if he doesn't watch himself!" Mike had no answer for them. He understood their sentiments, but was torn between agreeing with his co-workers and protecting his youngest brother. He usually just told them to mind their own business. Nevertheless, Mike knew his brother was headed for deep waters. He knew he had to act soon.

Mike's chance to intervene into Darryl's life came at the beginning of his 1993 season. The Dodgers organization and Charisse convinced Darryl to admit himself to the Betty Ford Center in Rancho Mirage, California, for a month of rehabilitation and detox. Darryl felt remorse and humiliation. He did not want to be at the Center. The press would have a field day on his admitted failures.

He reflected on his previous detox stint at the rehabilitation center in New York. The facility had helped him dry out, but it did not attack the core issue he was suffering from—his addiction to drugs. Darryl knew he was a drug addict and if he was ever going to find relief from the disease, he would have to comply with the orders of his organization and his wife.

During his time at the Betty Ford Center, Darryl met with several rehabilitation specialists. The most important healing moment he received, however, was not conducted by a rehabilitation professional or physician in the Center. This particular session allowed Darryl to reveal the deepest pains that ruled his heart and mind. This poignant moment happened during a session called "Family Day."

Seated in the "Family Day" session room were Darryl, his mother Ruby, his two sisters, his brother Mike, and one other person. Darryl's shame turned to anger as his eyes focused on the final member in the room.

Darryl's eyes bulged with fury as he looked upon the Monster.

FACE TO FACE

Imagine the anguish on Darryl's face when he was seated directly across from the man who had so terrorized him as a child. It was the same man who had beaten him, his dreadful cries drifting through the emptiness of the cold dungeon he knew as home. This was the man who abandoned him when he was eleven years old. This was the same man who shadowed his every step, his every drink, his every toke, and his every breath as an adult. This was the same man who haunted his dreams!

It was the first time in Darryl's life that he was able to look his father in his eyes, and unleash the poisonous bile absorbed deep inside his core. He berated his father without hesitation! He nailed the older man for his physical abuse, his neglect, the abandonment, but most of all, he reprimanded him on the absence of a father's love.

"Where were you? How could you? Why couldn't you love us?"

No children should ever walk this earth feeling that they are unloved and unwanted. That is exactly what Darryl had grappled with his entire life. He was filled with self-doubt and lacked self-esteem. He felt unworthy and unloved. He needed a father figure in the worst way, but instead, had been shoved out into the world with nothing but a negative self-image and a band of scars that wrapped around his back and through his heart.

The Monster's red eyes faded, as his cold, stone face thawed in the heat of the moment. Henry dropped his head in shame, for he knew the words from his son were true. He was well aware of his guilt, and seemed sorrowful for his actions. However, he was unable to convey such feelings to Darryl or his other children. He could only murmur these few words: "I don't know what to say. I don't know what to say. I wish I could've done better."

As Darryl stared at his father, he saw something he had never seen before. He saw a damaged man. He saw a man who had also been terrorized, beaten, abandoned, and unloved. He saw a man unable to love, because he himself felt unworthy of the notion. He saw an abusive man, who had also been severely beaten as a child, by a man who was supposed to be his guardian and protector.

Darryl was realizing that the Monster he had known for so many years was not his father, but rather, the alcoholism that dominated and controlled Henry's mind, spirit, and soul. The true monster lived inside a whiskey bottle and was summoned like a despicably abusive genie when the bottle was empty. Darryl's father made terrible decisions. He made awful choices. Henry's biggest mistake, however, was allowing the real Monster—his addictions—to continually dictate his abusive actions.

Genetics play a huge role in an individual's makeup. Alcoholism and drug addiction are a curse that can be generational, if an addict allows it to happen. Darryl did not see himself in his father, but he knew of his pain. He understood the effects of abuse and only wished it could have been different for them both.

Darryl's ability to release the pain was a monumental step in his rehabilitation process. He knew that he would never have a relationship with his father, but he also knew that he would never physically abuse his children, because of what his father had done to him and Ronnie. Darryl made a vow to himself that his father would be the last generational abuser of the Strawberry blood line. The act of physical abuse would no longer be passed down through his generations.

Even with these promises, a major concern still loomed over Darryl. Was he dealing with a cycle of generational abuse or was he dealing with an episodic abuse cycle? "Generational abuse" is the day-to-day physical, sexual, or verbal abuse that is a learned trait from one or both of the parents. "Episodic abuse" happens much more infrequently, but when it does occur, the fits of rage or abuse are extremely intense.

A post-reaction for an episodic abuser is to become passionately apologetic. Following a sincere and heartfelt apology for his or her violent acts, the abuser is calm and loving for extended periods of time. But in time, another episodic abuse moment will rear its ugly head, and the pattern of remorse and repentance will closely follow. It is a disturbing cycle.

Would Darryl be able to control his abusive nature? He had already been physically aggressive with both of his wives. Could he control his temper with his children? Could he make such a vow as a man, let alone a drug addict and alcoholic?

Children of addicts are eight times more likely to become addicts, compared to those who are born free from generational addictive behavior. Genetic addictions are real. In fact, this truth not only applies to humans, it also applies to the animal kingdom.

Have you ever wondered why certain animals eat definitive types of foods? This happens because their food choices have already been established by prior generations of their species.

If this is the case, however, why did Darryl and Ronnie become hooked on drugs and alcohol while their three older siblings lived their lives drug- and alcohol-free? Why did Ronnie accept his life as a crackhead and choose to live in a rat-infested hovel? Why did Darryl choose to follow the path to destruction when he had it all?

Who and what were to blame for the fall of Darryl Strawberry?

THE BLAME GAME

Darryl blamed everything and everyone for his lifelong transgressions. He blamed his wives for their lack of compassion and understanding during his two marriages. Meanwhile, he was relieving his stresses and frustrations by getting high, drinking, and receiving sexual pleasures outside of his home. His sordid acts were a twisted means of justification.

He blamed his financial woes on his divorce settlement and the IRS investigations. He blamed his decreased baseball production on his nagging injuries and his tormenting fans. But most of all, he blamed his lifelong unhappiness on his father and the the Monster that controlled the elder Strawberry. Yes, it was the same Monster that haunted Darryl's every step.

Why was Darryl unable to shake the memories of his father? Why was he unable to move forward and concentrate on the many blessings that had been bestowed upon him?

The rejection he endured from his father ultimately parlayed into a bitter disposition that was carried around like a briefcase. Everywhere Darryl ventured, he had the briefcase shackled to his wrist. Every time he opened the case, the "ghosts of Darryl's past" were set free to cling upon his being and roam wildly about his mind.

While staying at the Betty Ford Center, Darryl searched for answers. He searched his mind to find relief from the scarring images that haunted his every thought. He was desperately searching, but missing the evident clues before him. He could not see the forest for the trees.

Darryl needed to pause. He needed to look into the mirror and stare deeply at his own reflection, where he would find the real truth of his incessant "Blame Game." Throughout each and every period of his life, there had been one common denominator to his struggles. There was always one person who was directly involved with every aspect of his life. There was always one person tied to the struggles he had endured.

Darryl Strawberry himself was the common denominator.

Darryl needed to fully grasp this revelation. He could spend the rest of his days at drug rehabilitation facilities, but he would never truly find solace to his problems until he could finally admit, that he was the recurring theme to every painful scene that played out in his life. Darryl needed to realize that he was the one creating the chaos and adding the undo strife in his life. He was the common thread to every one of his transgressions.

Darryl needed to open the briefcase and purge its contents. It was the only way he could heal the jagged memories that sliced his heart wide open with every flashback to his youth. It was time for him to put away the masks and turn away from his "old friends" once and for all. It was time for Darryl, to be cured of this madness.

The only way Darryl could achieve such a plan was to tackle the real issues of his life head on! He needed to search deep inside his heart for the strength required to make such drastic changes in his life. He needed to find the truth, embrace it, and then destroy it! Sadly, this plan of attack would not come to fruition for many years. Darryl was still not ready for such an intense battle.

Darryl understood the game plan, but he also knew he had to get back to the playing field, and to his wife and family. He was well aware of the "shelf-life" of a professional ball player, and he knew his time was limited.

After his brief admission to Betty Ford, Darryl left the facility feeling he was clean and sober. He felt much better than he had before, and that was all that truly mattered to him. He wanted to be a better person, a better father, and a better husband. He would try his very best to accomplish these goals. That said, he could not spend his time locked into a psychological battle with the demons when his playing days were quickly shrinking.

Darryl would continue masking his feelings and moving forward in his life—he had no other choice. Would he allow his "old friends" back into his life? Would the shadows of the Monster push him toward the dark path again? Only time could provide the answers to these questions, especially since the Los Angeles Dodgers had just released Darryl Strawberry of his duties.

NEW BEGINNINGS

After Darryl was dismissed from the Betty Ford Center, Charisse and Mike were determined to protect Darryl from the worldly temptations that had cast a spell on him. Fortunately, the San Francisco Giants and Manager Dusty Baker signed Darryl after he was released by the Dodgers. Baker considered the past life of Darryl Strawberry as water under the bridge, and he looked forward to the All-Star outfielder's offensive contributions at Candlestick Park.

Mike sacrificed his own career with the Los Angeles Police Department to travel with Darryl throughout the remainder of the baseball season. Mike would become Darryl's official chaperone. He accompanied Darryl to and from the field, and they would share residence wherever the team traveled. Mike did not allow Darryl to leave his sight.

Darryl was signed by the Giants in July 1994, and made an immediate impact with the team. With Darryl's stick in the lineup, the Giants went on a ten-game winning streak. Darryl was scorching the ball and blasting home runs wherever the Giants played. He was stealing bases and making outstanding grabs in the outfield. It was like he was a 21-year old rookie again! Darryl felt fresh and full of energy, and his offensive numbers correlated with the youthful spring in his step.

Mike was a breath of fresh air for Darryl. They shared a room, ate together, and prayed together. Darryl was excelling for the Giants, and his brother was an integral part of his new approach to the game, and his life. Mike was the guiding light that illuminated Darryl's darkened path. And for a brief moment in time, the Monster was hidden away.

As Darryl pounded his opposition on a nightly basis, rumors of a disturbing possibility was circulating throughout the Giants' clubhouse. A player's strike was an ominous probability. Darryl could not worry about the likelihood of this situation; he needed to stay focused on his task at hand and stay true to the game and to Mike's guidance.

However, within 30 games, the season was officially halted due to the player's strike. The stoppage in play would not only extend throughout the remaining regular season, it also eliminated the playoffs and World Series for the first time in baseball history. Darryl's season was complete.

Darryl and Mike returned to Los Angeles. Darryl was exceedingly grateful to his older brother for the love and support he exhibited through the 30 days. And although the season might have come to an abrupt end, the positive gains made by Darryl during this period were incomparable.

Darryl returned to his home in Palm Springs with a renewed spirit. He was thankful for his brother's intervention, and felt remarkably positive about his future in the game and with his personal matters. He knew he had some hurdles to clear in the near future, with the Internal Revenue Service pounding on his door, but he felt stronger and better equipped for the battles to come.

In years past, Darryl had learned how to live in the public eye while feeding his addictions. He was able to hide the fact that he was high or hungover, and blended into society like a chameleon. He had lived a life of addiction to drugs, alcohol, and sex, with very few people realizing the full extent of his depravity. Mike's constant vigilance was a major factor in Darryl's ability to stay clean and avoid the temptations.

Addiction has no boundaries. The richest of the rich and the poorest of the poor can be equally hooked on any and all types of addictive substances. A teacher, preacher, police officer, and professional baseball player are all targets of the seductive sirens of the underworld.

Darryl's path was remarkably brighter. He could now walk the path without hesitation, without fearing the unseen twists and turns that lay before him.

Darryl Strawberry was on his way, or was he?

LIFE = PAIN

Darryl Strawberry had lived through much pain and heartache in his young life. His heart had been bruised by many excruciating circumstances. When one has been a victim of abuse and has suffered through the ongoing agonies of substance abuse, it is hard to imagine anything more emotionally torturous.

Weeks after the end of the 1994 baseball season, Darryl received word that his mother, Ruby, had been diagnosed with breast cancer. Ruby was the rock of the Strawberry family. She was the centerpiece. Her strength and humble spirit were the bond that connected each of her children.

When Ruby was diagnosed, Darryl collapsed. He wanted to be strong for her. He longed to be the pillar of strength that she had been for him through the years. Instead, Darryl retreated to the shadows. He sought out the companionship of his "old friends" to cope with the situation at hand. Darryl was once again smoking crack and drinking heavily.

All the progress achieved by Darryl, Mike, Charisse, and the Betty Ford Clinic was now a plume of smoke, dissipating in the night sky. Darryl's brightened path was now filled with a gloomy shade as dusk evolved to darkness. Darryl relied on his "old friends" to lead him around the dim corners of his path, his footsteps undetectable. The oncoming pitfalls of his life were unforeseeable.

Darryl stumbled mightily in the next months. He was indicted for tax evasion to the tune of $350,000. He then failed the Giants' drug test and was released from his contract. Darryl had not only lost his job, so had his brother. Mike had sacrificed his police career to help his younger sibling, but now, he was not only unemployed with the Giants, he had no job with the LAPD.

Darryl felt horrible about his brother's job situation. He knew he was the reason for his brother's dilemma. Mike's fellow officers were infuriated by the entire situation and asked Mike, once again: "What's up with your brother?"

Darryl knew it was all his fault. He was now dealing with the guilt of his brother's losses, his unemployment status, his federal indictment, and his mother's upgraded cancer status, which was now determined to be terminal. Darryl no longer worried about the Monster; he had his own demons and painful truths to combat.

Time passed for Darryl. He was left alone with his thoughts, his guilt, and his fears. Being idle was chewing him up. He battled onward, but faced many dark nights and temptations. He was taking life one tiny step at a time.

Six months later, Darryl's agent Bill Goodstein met with New York Yankees owner, George Steinbrenner. The brash Yankees owner agreed to a contract—if and only if Darryl was drug-free. Steinbrenner was a tough negotiator, but he knew the value of Darryl Strawberry in New York. Steinbrenner's contract offer and personal demands were fair, and his expectations of Darryl were to be reciprocated. Darryl agreed.

Once Darryl signed on the dotted line with the Yankees, Steinbrenner immediately assigned him to Ron Dock, the Yankees' drug addiction counselor. Dock was a recovering drug addict who had assisted several other young athletes in the Yankees' organization. Dock would be at Darryl's beck and call, and would assist him with any issues that may arise during Darryl's time with the Yanks.

In June, Darryl reported to New York and played sparingly throughout the remaining games of the 1995 season. Although, Darryl's playing time was minimal, his main focus was staying clean throughout the season. The Big Apple was a temptress, and her haunting drumbeats of euphoria were a constant allure to Darryl and his limbic system needs.

Darryl had already lived the NYC lifestyle and knew of its hidden pleasures. He did everything he could to avoid the Sirens of the City! He moved his family to Fort Lee, New Jersey, and drove straight home after every home game. He heard the words of his dear mother and his old coach, Jim Frey: "**Stay focused!**"

Darryl wanted his mother to know that he was controlling his bad behavior and remaining drug-free. Darryl wanted to make amends to his brother Mike by staying clean. He wanted to be the best person possible for his wife, Charisse. In addition, Darryl had increased motivation to keep his nose clean—that motivation was George Steinbrenner.

Darryl finished the season with the Yankees, clean and sober. He had accomplished every goal he had set out to achieve. He was looking forward to a return to New York the following year, so he could make a bigger impact on the team's drive to an American League pennant and possible World Series berth.

Unfortunately, Darryl's aspirations were not on the same page as the Yankees' front office. Darryl was not given another contract. In fact, Darryl was not offered a contract by any Major League team the entire baseball off-season.

Darryl was devastated. Was this the end of his playing career?

PAINFUL GOODBYES

In January of 1996, Darryl lost a dear friend when his agent, Bill Goodstein, passed away from a heart attack. Darryl was broken. One month later, in February of 1996, Darryl's heart was beyond broken; it crumbled into a million pieces with the passing of his beloved mother, Ruby Strawberry. Her death stung Darryl's heart with a pain he could have never comprehended. He yelled at God. "Why Mom?!" Why not me?!!"

Darryl had lost the one and only person of his life who had showed him unconditional love. He lost the one person who was not afraid to voice her opinion about his actions—good or bad. He had a tremendous, aching hole in heart and had no earthly idea how to fill it. Darryl wanted to leave this world behind! He was trying to make sense of it all, but struggled to maintain his faith in God or any other higher power responsible for such actions.

The brain's limbic system contains the brain's reward structure. This system motivates the brain to repeat behaviors that provide pleasure. This system also provides the perceptions of other emotions, especially negative ones. When the brain is already diseased with the critical responses to addictions, the limbic system can trigger negative actions by those who are stimulated by a negative emotion.

Darryl would have to fight with every fiber of his being to chase off the demons that were congregating inside his mind. His sadness was unbearable! He had no job, he had lost a dear friend, and his mother was no longer walking beside him on this Earth. He was an emotional wreck, his heart was a ticking time bomb!

Ruby had always been there for her children. Even when Ronnie was consumed with drugs and walking the streets with TV sets hoisted on his naked shoulder as he peddled them for drug money. Even when Ronnie was in and out of jail, strung out beyond recognition—she was there for him. It was no different for her baby boy, Darryl. She was always there for him through thick and thin. She was his earthly angel.

Some people may believe that Ruby was an enabler to her son's drug addictions. In fact, she was a staunch believer that bad behaviors dictate actions which, in turn, activate the needs for one's addictions. She provided sound advice to her sons, but it was up to them to follow the guidance. Ronnie chose to live the life he had created for himself.

She had asked Ronnie to stop using drugs, and to stop selling stolen television sets, and to wear a shirt when walking the streets of the neighborhood. She gave Ronnie proper guidance, but it was up to Ronnie to follow through with the logical advice she provided. She maintained her strength, despite her constant fears of Ronnie's possible demise. Ronnie was his own man, and she had to let him go.

Darryl was proud of the way his mother had handled their family. There are so many people and families who live two-separate lives. They live one life in public, where they pretend everything is peachy keen. But, behind closed doors, they are in financial ruin, possess addiction(s), are abusive, or possibly all three.

People provide skewed perceptions of themselves. People want to be liked, so they tell you what you want to hear. People want to be considered perfect in other people's eyes, so they tell them what they wish they had become. These people will avoid the truth, lie to protect, and create all types of smokescreens to make others perceive them as perfect.

There is no such thing as a perfect individual. We all have shortcomings, and unfortunately, many people rely on addictions to mask their pain, hide their true identities, or create a false reality. People are addicted to the perception of perfection and personal success. People need to feel they are special, so they hide behind their masks and untruths so they can feel better about themselves.

Ruby Strawberry was not one of those people. She was a humble woman who did not dictate her sons' choices, nor did she accept their choices. She was a home to her children when they needed her. She did not pretend their family was free of sin or perfect in any way. She was not addicted to perceptions. She was a loving woman who wanted her children to love themselves as much as she loved them. She wanted them to believe in themselves, as she believed in them.

Darryl's heart was crushed by his mother's passing. He wondered if he had let her down with his selfish actions over the years. He wondered if he paid too much attention to the lack of love provided by his father, and not enough attention to the love of his mother.

Darryl wanted to make his mother proud. He needed to heed the words she had preached to him: "Stay focused!"

As Darryl said his final goodbyes to his mother, he made one last request of her: "**Don't give up on me.**"

To her dying day, she never did.

Doctor's Notes and Comments to Chapter 8

with Rich Capiola, MD

Is addiction caused by a genetic predisposition? According to most psychologists and psychiatrists, the answer is, "Yes and No." Does a human being possess a specific gene that will automatically turn an individual into an alcoholic or make that person a cocaine addict? The answer is "No." However, genetic studies do indicate elevated risk factors and a strong disposition for substance dependence in certain family trees. Would a person have a much greater chance of becoming an alcoholic or addict if his father and grandfather were alcoholics/addicts, even if that person had not been raised by them? The answer is "Yes."

Humans may possess a variety of behavior genetics that, when combined with psychological trauma and familial or environmental influences, may indeed promote future addictions in a predisposed child or adult. This statement is a perfect correlation to Dr. Miller's "hardware/software" analogy, mentioned earlier.

Does this then mean that children are doomed to become drug addicts and alcoholics the moment they are born? The answer is once again, "No." An individual may possess a genetic predisposition to diabetes, but if the person maintains healthy eating habits throughout his childhood years, his ability to prevent acquiring this disease is more likely. This theory also applies to those who are exposed to drugs, trauma, and negative environmental influences.

Early childhood abuse is a strong indicator of future addictions. When children watch their parents getting drunk or their neighbors getting high, their brains are being rewired to believe alcohol and drugs are the only pathways to happiness. That said, no matter what a child has experienced, the decision to use addictive substances is a personal choice.

Although there are several factors that lead to a person's addiction, everyone has the ability to say, "No, thank you" to anything he or she is unwilling to consume or ingest. "If you don't want to eat an orange, you will not eat an orange."

Drug use is a choice.

If a child or teenager decides to take drugs or drink alcohol at a young age, the chances of that individual becoming an alcoholic or a drug addict is much greater due to generational or behavioral genetic connections. These behavioral genetic connections include a child's temperament, emotionality, sociability, and adaptability.

When addicts enter or reenter rehabilitation at a recovery center, one of the most common scenarios experienced by psychological professionals is "The Blame Game." Dr. Capiola refers to this type of blaming response as "Stinking Thinking." The "Blame Game" begins the moment a person decides to take drugs, drink alcohol, or behave poorly in our society. People blame their upbringing, life stresses, and other people for their addictions.

Blame is a common denial feature in an addict's defensive arsenal, and "Stinking Thinking" is a common denial response by individuals in recovery. "I am an addict because people were mean to me!" or "I am an addict because my cousin gave me my first beer." The terrible atrocities of a person's childhood should never be downplayed. These violent attackers should be imprisoned for their vile acts against innocent children! However, there comes a time, when an addict must stand up and take responsibility for his or her decision to keep using a drug.

The first step to recovery is admitting you are an addict. An addict never asked to be abused or neglected as a child. The terrible acts of abuse cannot be reversed. But, the choice of becoming an addict or continuing an addiction can be avoided. When a person suffers from high blood pressure, the doctor gives his patient medicine and advice. If the advice is followed and the medication is properly administered, the high blood *pressure will eventually decline. If the patient fails to follow these steps, however, he or she will become sicker, and will ultimately die.*

People make excuses for many things in life. Have you ever noticed that there is one person in your life who is mysteriously unemployed every time you speak to him? He has a million excuses for his inability to find or keep a job. "The boss was crazy!" or "They only want to pay me 15 dollars an hour." Addicts in recovery use these same excuses during their drug recovery treatment. "I didn't like the way the doctor talked to me" or "I don't like the feeling of being held captive." These types of excuses justify a person's illogical mindset and actions and ultimately sabotage his or her chances of recovery. Such excuses are defense mechanisms (often unconscious and unknown to the addict) that are used by the addict to support his addiction.

Addicts must understand the importance of active recovery work. They must work hard and continue shrinking and minimizing the importance of their past tragedies. Addicts need encouragement during their rehabilitation, but most importantly, they need to take blame totally out of the equation. By the time an addict has reached the recovery phase, the damaging events given power sit far back in his past. If a recovering addict is to become healthy once again, the individual must release the pain, let go of the blame, and restart his life free of negativity. A recovering addict needs to hit the

"Reset" button of his life, and any excuses given for his addictions must be discarded!

Caregivers must show understanding and compassion, while providing strength and confidence to those suffering from this brain disease. Boundaries must be established to maintain compliance within an individual's recovery needs. It is much easier for a recovering addict to relapse than it is to do the work! That is why it is imperative for a caregiver to provide motivation and encouragement. Addicts need to hit the "Reset" button, and so must the caregiver.

When Darryl confronted his father, he was beginning the process of true recovery. Life is unpredictable, and the losses he endured were great. He would be faced with many more challenges in his recovery process. He was slowly relinquishing the blame, which would become a vital cog in his chances of a healthy recovery. His work was just beginning.

CHAPTER 9

TAKING CHARGE

Based on an interview with Rich Capiola, MD

Have you ever wondered why so many addicts relapse after recovery work? The triggers in the outside world are the subconscious snipers of a failed recovery. Recovering addicts who are unable to relinquish blame will continue using blame as a crutch or defense mechanism against the real issues and reasons for their addictions.

When it comes to relapse, addicts fail because they are not properly prepared for the multiple trigger mechanisms awaiting them in the outside world. Addicts are affected by sight, smell, conversation, and innuendo. A cocaine addict's mind will start spinning at the sight of spilled baby powder on a changing table. It does not take much to trigger addicts' emotional memory cues of the addictive substances that once controlled their thoughts and desires.

Recovering addicts must construct a durable force field that protects them from the temptations of their past. A successfully recovered addict is someone who can see or think about a trigger, but will not act upon the temptations of that particular trigger mechanism. However, if recovering addicts are not in a healthy place in their recovery process, they will continue to be vulnerable to specific triggers.

As stated earlier, recovering addicts need to set barriers and blockades in their brains' pathway systems to avoid being lured back into the controlling powers of their addiction. By setting up these barriers, an addict is more capable of owning his addiction.

What does it mean to own your addiction?

The whole premise of owning an addiction is the creation of thought processes or actions that are more powerful than the addiction. When an addict owns his addiction, he is making sobriety the most important thing in his life. When an individual finds something that is more important than his drug use, he has a better chance of avoiding the temptations of his specific addiction. A perfect illustration of this type of behavioral action can be found in the following manner:

A drug-addicted young woman has been hooked on heroin for the past four years of her life. She has gone through interventions and has relapsed. She has been arrested, but continued her heroin use within minutes of her release. One day, the young woman becomes pregnant. Many people are concerned that her drug abuse will affect her unborn child.

When asked if she is taking drugs during her pregnancy, she replies, "Are you kidding me? I would never harm my baby!" The young woman remains drug-free throughout her pregnancy and her child is born without complications. The woman needed something bigger than her addiction! By creating a safe haven for her unborn child, she made sobriety the most important aspect of her life. This story is a perfect illustration of an addict owning her addiction.

This happens with other addictions as well. How many times have you watched as your unfit, obese friend hammers down three cheeseburgers and a plate of onion rings? You care about your friend, so you speak to him about his unhealthy diet, and the possible repercussions of his sedentary lifestyle and grease-laden food choices.

The obese friend shrugs it off because the onion rings are so darned delicious. Then one day, the obese friend has a heart attack and is rushed to the hospital emergency room. His life is spared, but he is left weak and afraid. He is reprimanded for his unhealthy lifestyle and warned of his impending doom by physicians and friends.

Within a year, your obese friend is in the best shape of his life. He is exercising, eating healthy, and has lost over 97 pounds! This man was suffering from a food addiction, and he needed something bigger than his addiction to keep himself alive. He needed a powerful reason to not only make changes in his life, but to stay true to those changes. He made a commitment to hard work and the creation of barriers against his trigger mechanisms. In time, he became the proud owner of his addictions.

These two stories are further proof that addicts from every walk of life have the ability to rise up and face their challenges. They have the ability to make wiser choices for themselves and their loved ones.

To properly own an addiction, people must retrain their brains. If this sounds like a science fiction movie plot, then you are watching too many sci-fi movies. Retraining the brain begins by believing in oneself, building one's self-esteem, and eliminating negative thoughts that can promote negative self-worth. These exercises in self-promotion must be practiced over and over along one's journey to recovery. Once individuals establish this mental groundwork, they will eventually create a better self-image.

The brain's limbic system is constantly searching for pleasure and joy. This system is also responsible for the neurochemical releases attached to addiction—drugs, alcohol, gambling, and sex. When addicts receive proper recovery treatment, they are able to properly manage the brain pathways that led to their addictions.

An important step in this managing process is the addict's willingness to retrain his brain and open new, natural doors that create pleasure within the reward system without their addictions.

These "Barricades to Addictions" may be found in new or past endeavors or activities such as hobbies, sports, fitness, or religion. The creation of new personal goals or an inner purpose can also lead to a much-needed blockade to the addictions.

The act of retraining one's brain can be difficult for those who are suffering from addiction. Addicts already live in a world that revolves around negative self-images and self-worth. Recovering addicts must learn to love themselves, believe in the greater good, and make a substance-free life for themselves.

Caregivers can play a significant role in their loved one's retraining process. Caregivers can help establish barriers to addictions by promoting self-esteem with words of encouragement for the addict.

A recovering addict must retrain his mindset if he is going to fight the good fight against addiction. Let's say a recovering addict is hired to build a house. The job is going well until the day he accidentally backs the forklift into the framework of the home. As the man watches the left wing of the house collapse to the ground, he becomes extremely agitated and anxious.

His brain is shouting out one expletive after another! The limbic system in his brain is firing up and the pathways to his addiction are lighting up like a Christmas tree. He is connecting the accident to his already damaged self-esteem issues. "You are so stupid! You can't do anything right! You are a loser!" His limbic system is now running on high! Images of drinking, drugging, and gambling begin filling the man's brain.

The foreman of the construction company reprimands the man for the accident. But instead of accepting the lecture, the unhealthy addict responds, "Oh, yeah! Well, if you think you can do any better, then you do it! I don't need this job! Screw this job! And screw you!" The man leaves the construction site in search of a mental stress release.

The man's limbic system is completely overwhelmed and his impulse control is now gone. The thoughts of drinking and escaping have tapped into his brain's reward system. He will seek out a bar if it takes all night. The frantic search for a bar is further activating the dopamine rush, which has now depleted his mind of logical thought.

The man will continue to drive around until he finds a bar! Why do you think dive bars exist in our culture? Such establishments prey on those struggling from this type of situation. Go to a dive bar in the middle of a sunny day. When you walk into the bar, it is dark, smelly, and downright disgusting. A person would never step foot in this place unless he was desperate to satisfy his needs. The dive bar provides product, socialization, and instantaneous relief from the stresses consuming the addict's mind. When the brain's reward system is triggered, people will do anything to alleviate the desire.

A recovered addict who has applied proper retraining techniques to his life will respond differently than the unhealthy addict. The limbic system of his brain will light up in the same fashion, but his response will be calmer and more collected. He will accept the lecture from the foreman as part of his job, and will help in the cleanup process, rather than exploding and losing his job.

What is the difference between the two men?

The first man allowed his limbic system to control his actions. The term "going postal" is a term linked to radical decisions that are emotionally based on the limbic system's response to a situation. The flooding response in his brain needed to be resolved and the first man did so with a dose of self-hatred, followed by quitting and ultimately drinking.

The second man took a deep breath and let his mind run its course before reacting. He created a barrier or a stopgap in his mind to remind him to stay cool under pressure. Maybe he thought about his children going hungry, or he knew he would not be able to buy the new Silverado truck if he loses his job. He recognized the bigger problems that could ensue if he allowed the problem to fester. He changed what once had been "stinking thinking" and resolved the matter with a positive thought process.

The biggest difference between the two recovering addicts in this scenario can be explained in much simpler terms. The second man was ready to make changes in his life. He completed the work and was truthful to himself in the intervention process. The second man understood that he had no other choice in the matter. He had to change his life or die.

DARRYL'S STORY

A SECOND CHANCE

"Don't give up on me!"

These are five very powerful words. Ruby Strawberry never gave up on her children. She could have been embarrassed by her son's actions. One was a druggie living in a rat-infested hovel and the other was a rich, powerful sports star being arrested for beating his wives. She did not give up on them. She was always the bright beacon shining out from the darkest of nights. She was the forever home for her prodigal sons.

Darryl was trying hard to stay strong through these agonizing times. He did not want to give up on himself or his mother's wishes. He understood that he had been given multiple chances to redeem himself over the years, but had failed multiple times in the process. The weight of those failures, coupled with his already stained self-esteem issues, bore down on his soul.

Darryl was now facing a mountain he had never climbed— the possible end to his storied baseball career. Not one Major League team wanted or required his services. Was it because his baseball abilities were no longer worthy of the Big Leagues, or was it because teams did not want to deal with his off-the-field antics?

After weeks of searching for a roster spot, Darryl was informed of a team that was inquiring about his availability. The team was the St. Paul Saints, an Independent team from the Northern League. Darryl was distraught. "How could this be? How could I go from Yankee Stadium to the tiny ballparks in South Dakota and Northern Minnesota?"

Darryl had no other choice. He had to suit up for the Saints, and make one more last ditch effort to make it back to the Big Leagues. He had to push pride to the side and accept the challenge. He had to stay focused!

When Darryl made his first road trip with the Saints, he felt as if he were back in Kingsport, Tennessee. He was not riding in chartered planes or sleeping in 5-star hotels. He rode in vans and buses, and stayed in road-side motels. He did not have room service—he had vending machines filled with soda, chips and Zagnut bars.

As the season progressed, so did Darryl's stat line. He was playing baseball again, but this time without the pressures from big-city media and boo-happy fans of the National League. He was enjoying his time in St. Paul, and he was drug-free and alcohol-free. He and his family enjoyed the small-town atmosphere, and the league proved to be a positive experience.

Darryl was swinging the bat well, driving balls well beyond the fences of every town he played in. His mind was clear and his heart was mending, and then it happened. Darryl got a second chance with the New York Yankees. The Bronx Bombers wanted Darryl back on the team, and Darryl did not hesitate to say "yes"!

George Steinbrenner, Manager Joe Torre, and the rest of the 1996 Yankees welcomed Darryl back with open arms. His allegiance to Steinbrenner was strong! The Boss believed in him and he was thankful for George's loyalty. Steinbrenner had not only given Darryl a second chance in life, he had also given Dwight Gooden, Steve Howe, and several other players and coaches a second chance in life after their challenges with addictions as well. George Steinbrenner was a true humanitarian.

Darryl finished up the 1996 season with great numbers and a World Series ring, as the Yanks defeated the Atlanta Braves in six games. Darryl was on a good path once again, and it carried over to the off-season, when he started working with St. Stephen Church. Darryl was on the mend, and his gratitude radiated brightly from his smile.

As a member of St. Stephen Church, Darryl volunteered his services by delivering meals to the homeless in downtown Los Angeles. The work was extremely rewarding for Darryl. The experience was sobering when he looked upon the swarms of homeless people gathering around the food trucks. Some of the people were covered in grime from head to toe, others did not seem homeless at all. Some were aggressive, others were meek and mild.

Darryl knew that most of these destitute men and women were battling addictions, just like him. He knew there were several crackheads and alcoholics among the group. These were men and women who had ruined their lives by falling prey to the powers of addictions. He could see the humiliation and suffering in their disheartened frowns.

He knew their brains were fried as they scrounged meals from dumpsters and garbage cans in the alleyways of the city. He could tell which person was "Jonesing" for his next fix, and which one had just finished smoking a crack pipe. These people were no different than him, other than that he was a famous baseball player. Darryl was appreciative for the blessings he had received in his life. He was thankful for his second chance.

Darryl thought of Ronnie, knowing his brother lived the same existence as these poor, unfortunate souls. As Darryl stared into the eyes of the discarded individuals, he could hear the gratitude cracking from their voices. As he peered upon their shadowy silhouettes, he could sense the unsettled spirits longing to escape the prisons that held them captive.

Darryl thought of his own life. He could never let his addictions drag him down to such depths. He could not fathom a path so bereft of light. Who were these people and where did they come from? He wondered how tough their lives must have been to find nourishment from the depths of a trash can.

These people were daughters, sons, fathers, and mothers. They were teachers, preachers, and executives. Mental anguish and self-inflicted torture had overtaken their spirits—he could see this in their trembling hands. How many of them had a Monster in their lives? How many of them lacked self-worth and felt unloved and unwanted? Darryl could feel their pain. He knew it all too well. He could hear their pleas, without actually receiving a single word from their mouths.

"DON'T GIVE UP ON ME!"

Darryl had to continue his march forward. He could not leave the lighted path before him. He had to summon every ounce of faith from within to combat the urges of his past. For he did not want to share the same tragedies as those broken individuals, abandoned by their peers and families. He was not a piece of garbage, waiting to be swept away and buried in the cold, dark earth. Darryl needed to remain steadfast upon his journey.

Darryl needed to focus on those who had never given up on him during the low moments of his life. He had offered too much time and thought to the Monster and the negative people who maintained strongholds on his psyche. He knew he had to focus on positive images, inspirational people, and those who appeared in his life when he needed them the most.

He had to focus on the words of his mother Ruby and the many sacrifices made by his brother Mike. He was beholden to Lloyd Mc Clendon, Bill Goodstein, Ron Dock, George Steinbrenner, and the many others who were part of his life while he was crashing.

Darryl Strawberry was turning the corner to recovery! He had to make the turn; he had no other options.

AN UNEXPECTED VISITOR

Darryl remained drug-free throughout the entire 1997 baseball season. Unfortunately, he was plagued with a knee injury that shelved him for most of the season. He worked hard throughout the 1997 off-season and would be ready for action the following year.

In 1998, Darryl had a solid comeback season with the Yanks, hitting 24 home runs for the one of the greatest teams in Major

League baseball history. The Yankees finished the regular season with a record-breaking 114 wins! The Yanks went on to sweep the San Diego Padres in four straight to capture their 24th World Championship. Darryl was an integral part of this outstanding baseball squad.

Darryl competed every night for the Yankees! He played hard and stayed clean throughout the entire championship season. By mid-summer of that season, though, Darryl started feeling odd. He was losing weight and had lost his appetite. He was also experiencing various stomach ailments throughout the latter part of the season. Violent stomach cramps kept him up throughout the night.

During the team's first post-season match-up with the Texas Rangers, Darryl told the team physician about his symptoms. Then Darryl and Charisse reported to Columbia Presbyterian Hospital in New York, where he was given multiple tests. The initial medical speculation was diverticulitis, but upon further review, Darryl was diagnosed with a malignant tumor in his colon.

Darryl Strawberry had colon cancer.

"How could I have cancer? I am 36 years old! How could this be? I have been living clean and I am sober and for the first time in a long time. I am content. How could this be? Am I going to die?"

These were just a few of the sentiments that wildly flashed through Darry's mind as he attempted to make sense of the diagnosis. Darryl instantly thought of his mother, who had died of cancer, and Bill Goodstein, who had vanished from his life without warning. He was numb and his mind was spinning. He knew his season was finished, but would his life be over too?

Darryl had worked diligently at staying clean and sober. Every day was a cage battle between him and his addictions. He continued to stave off the urges and walked steadfastly within the wishes of his late mother. Emotions tore at Darryl. He was at the crossroads of his life, wondering if he should succumb to the disease or continue the battles, as his mother and family would have wanted.

Maybe this illness was a sign from God? Maybe the diagnosis was the consequence to his many transgressions? Maybe he should let the cancer devour him, so the world is finally rid of his troubling presence? Or maybe this is just a test from God!? These were the thoughts that raced through Darryl's mind as he decided to have a surgical procedure that could possibly sustain his life.

He thought about the homeless people he had helped feed through the great works of St. Stephen Church. Would they give up if they were in his shoes? Would they battle onward? Would they realize their lives were gifts and worthy of the fight? Or would they just give up, allowing themselves to be swept away and buried in the cold, dark earth?

Darryl pondered these troubling images. He did not want people to give up on him, and he knew that he could not give up on himself. He could not allow himself to be a tragedy. He had to fight!

Darryl took up the sword in his left hand. He was determined to go to war! He would fight for his life and defeat the disease that was choking him. Darryl had already fought many battles in his life, but never had he obtained such support in doing so. He received love and support from his wife and family. He drew strength from his Yankees' teammates. He received well wishes from friends and fans of baseball. The greatest impact on Darryl were the cards and letters from children who were also suffering from cancer.

These little children were located down the hallway from Darryl's hospital room. These little children had no business being in a cancer ward. These little children had no business fighting a war at such tender ages. These were little children devoid of hair from their many bouts of chemotherapy. These were little children fighting for just one more day, just one more breath.

Darryl gathered true courage from these little children. His eyes welled with tears as he took his place upon the surgical table. These little children were his focus when the tumor and lymph nodes were extracted from his body. These little children were his focus as his body absorbed the poisonous chemicals used to destroy the cancerous cells inside his body. These little children were his focus. He had to fight, if not for himself—for them.

Darryl was confined to the cancer ward for two weeks. In this time, his Yankee teammates went on to win the World Series over the Padres. Darryl received a call from Derek Jeter during the team's clubhouse celebration. It was a noble gesture from a noble man. Derek wanted Darryl to know the team was thinking and praying for him. Derek also wanted Darryl to be a part of the Victory Parade in New York City!

Darryl wanted nothing more than to be with his team. Two days after receiving permission from the medical staff, Darryl and Charisse joined the Yankee caravan as it motored down the majestic streets of New York City. The day was absolutely perfect! Clear skies and a cool, refreshing breeze caressed Darryl's face as the motorcade made its way through the raucous crowd of the Yankee faithful.

Darryl leaned his head back and stared up at the clouds above. All he could see was a downpour of confetti. He closed his eyes and breathed in the celebration. This victory parade was much different than the Mets victory parade ten years earlier. This time, Darryl was drug-free and alcohol-free. He could truly feel the electricity of the crowd and the appreciation in the city's cheers.

Two weeks prior to this glorious occasion, Darryl Strawberry had been diagnosed with colon cancer. He had surgery to have a tumor removed from his colon and had been bedridden from that day forward. Despite all the mental and physical afflictions he was currently facing, Darryl felt alive! He had never felt such love in his life.

The crowd's cheers were healing. He thought of his mother. He thought of Bill Goodstein. He thought of his family and the children in the cancer ward. He could hear the fans chanting his name.

"DAR-RYL! DAR-RYL! DAR-RYL!"

Darryl Strawberry was a world champion. He and his Yankee teammates stood taller than the buildings of the city. The Mighty Thor with his powerful thunder stick was grateful for the opportunities George Steinbrenner had afforded him. The Boss had given him something he had never received before—a true second chance.

Steinbrenner had never judged Darryl, and he never expected more than Darryl could give. His gift was just that—a gift. He never expected a return—he just wanted Darryl to get better.

The Bronx Bombers were a family who worked together and played like champions! There were no spoils to the victors, because this group of men shared their wins and their World Championship trophy with the entire city.

"DAR-RYL! DAR-RYL! DAR-RYL!"

As Darryl squinted upward toward the thousands of exuberant fans waving their arms and cheering his name, he listened as the screaming voices faded into an odd, muted whisper.

Darryl could feel the cool breeze gently grazing his slender face, the confetti dancing upon his thin, weakened arms. He reveled in the beautiful silence of the moment. He was here. He was alive. The encouraging words of his mother were poignant and powerful. And as he looked upon the heavenly skies, he was reminded of these five words:

"Don't give up on me."

Darryl smiled, for the Monster had nothing more to say.

Doctor's Notes and Comments to Chapter 9

With Rich Capiola, MD & John Picciano, LCSW, MSW

Addiction recovery is an extremely difficult procedure that involves several stages of medical and psychiatric treatment. Recovering addicts will go through extreme highs and lows during their treatments. They will feel empty, angry, weak, and highly emotional. The intervention or rehabilitation process is designed to provide tough love to its clientele by demonstrating compassion through confrontation.

A treatment center provides a recovering addict a sense of security while living in a drug-free, therapeutic environment. A treatment center is a safe haven for those in need of medical attention, psychological or psychiatric therapy, or protection from the addictions that have stolen their lives. A treatment center provides physicians, psychologists and psychiatrists, drug counselors, nurses, and sponsors. These intervention professionals are better known as, "the Treatment Team".

When addicts attempt to treat their addictions without the assistance of intervention professionals, they are setting themselves up for complete failure. Addicts are at a severe disadvantage against the great powers of their particular addictions. They must realize they are facing a life-threatening predicament that requires professional assistance. An addict dealing with his own addictions is like putting a Band-Aid on a shark bite.

People suffering from addictions are unable to effectively peel away the numerous layers of guilt, shame, and denial they have incurred throughout their lives. Addicts in the moderate to severe stage of addiction are totally incapable of recognizing the imminent threats upon their livelihood, health, and families. They are constantly searching for temporary solutions to their deep-rooted issues. Addicts address these issues by self-medicating with excess drinking and drugging so they do not have to let the reality of their lives surface.

One of the most critical functions of a treatment or recovery center is relieving the withdrawal symptoms involved in detox or the detoxification process. Detox is the first crucial step taken in the fight against addiction. Detox can be compared to a boxer stepping through the ropes and into the ring for his match. Detox is the removal of all toxins from the body. The withdrawal period is the moment an addict begins the detoxification process and continues until the body returns to homeostasis, or normal function.

Detox can also be referred to as "drying out" or going "cold turkey" and can take several days to several weeks, depending on the individual and the substances to which the individual is addicted. In a treatment setting, detox protocols are designed to make the transition to sobriety as smooth as possible for the individual. The main goal of the detox process is the preven-

tion of extreme physical illness, seizures, or any other types of medical compromise.

Treatment centers provide medical screenings and constant supervision of the patients involved in the recovery process. It is important for patients to be completely truthful about all of their addictive substances. As stated earlier, it is impossible to successfully support and advise patients if they are not truthful about their various drug or alcohol interactions. This was a major issue with Darryl's previous interventions, because he was not being truthful about all of his addictions.

The withdrawal process differs from person to person, while the withdrawal symptoms differ from substance to substance. Withdrawal is an excruciatingly painful process! It is the number one reason people should not take a single drug or a single drink or a single puff in the first place. People who drink coffee or smoke cigarettes have an extremely difficult time during their detox process. Can you imagine the suffering involved with those using narcotics, alcohol, and opiates?

People who go "cold turkey" from their nicotine (cigarettes) and caffeine (coffee) addictions will generally feel moody, irritable, fatigued, and will suffer from headaches and insomnia. In addition, they will often suffer from mild cases of depression and dysphoria.

The term "dysphoria" is the complete opposite of euphoria. When individuals suffer from dysphoria, they have an overwhelming distaste for life.

Once the withdrawal process is complete, former smokers will continue battling trigger mechanisms, just like the hard-core addicts. The smell of cigarette smoke can instantly trigger a desire to smoke among nicotine addicts due to the ghost memory of that particular substance.

Addicts have a tremendous amount of anxiety regarding the withdrawal process. They shy away from the idea of detoxification because they do not like the feeling of being uncomfortable. The idea of personal suffering is the reason addicts begin using their illicit drugs in the first place. The idea of internal torment and discomfort paralyzes an addict's thought process. He does not see the big picture; he only lives in the moment. The internal stresses of the detox procedure cause the addict to use more drugs and drink more alcohol, rather than going through the difficult process of getting clean and sober.

If a person sprains his ankle, he knows he needs to rest the ankle so it will heal properly. He will wrap it, ice it, and elevate it. He uses crutches to avoid further damage on his ankle. An addict's thought process is much different. If an addict recognizes that his addiction is becoming harmful to his life, he will abuse his addiction even more to avoid the difficult journey of becoming healthy once again.

Denial plays the biggest role in the addict's ability to address the real issues of his drug or alcohol dependency. In an addict's mind: "If I do something about my addiction, it means I will have to give up something." The addict understands that recovery will take work, and by doing the work, he will be unable to call upon his addictions to help him through the difficult days ahead. He understands that he will be giving up his "old friends" or his addictions.

An addict remains an addict because it is much easier to tip a bottle or snort cocaine to escape the problems of his life. An addict totally understands he is in need of help, but unconsciously abuses his addictions because it keeps him from having to do the difficult work required to make changes. If an addict is convinced he is an addict, then he would instinctively feel as if he needed to make changes. Therefore, addicts deny or rationalize their drug and alcohol use.

Here is an example of an addict's mode of thought based on the aforementioned findings. An opiate addict has surgery on his left foot. He is in severe pain from the surgery, and is given OxyContin to help relieve the discomfort. Three weeks later, the opiate addict is still requesting more OxyContin for his pain. The addict knows he has no more pain, but enjoys the effects of his opiate prescription. He rationalizes the discomfort to receive more OxyContin. The process will continue until the physician calls him out. Reality of the situation convinces the addict to adjust or make the effort to get better. He can no longer hide with the cotton ball inside the prescription bottle.

The symptoms of withdrawal are the reality of an addict's fears to find help and become clean and sober. Withdrawal symptoms vary from substance to substance. An opiate or heroin addict will exhibit anxiety, profuse sweating, diarrhea, and vomiting during the withdrawal process. An alcoholic will exhibit symptoms such as mood swings, fatigue, sweating, shaking, and nausea. Without proper medical treatment, the addict could suffer from delirium and seizures.

The withdrawal symptoms of a hardcore stimulant abuser can be the most intense of all detoxification processes. Crack and meth addicts will suffer from insomnia, emotional irrita-tion and agitation, eating disorders, severe mood swings, depression, and thoughts of suicide.

The withdrawal process is the very reason treatment professionals are required in the addict's journey to sobriety. Although family and friends want to help their loved ones as they battle their addictions, they are often unaware of the true extent of their loved one's disease. Unfortunately, friends and family are also incapable of properly tending to the emotional and physical wreckage of their addicted loved ones during the onset of a recovery process. Family and friends have a genuine desire to help an addicted loved one, but many times, these people's helping hands become enabling hands. Here are a few examples of enabling:

A 25-year-old alcoholic moves into his mother's house. The man is passed out in his bed. His alarm clock incessantly blares like a shrieking siren. His mother enters his room to shut off the alarm clock and finds her son in bed. She attempts to wake him, so he can get to work. Her drunk son finally climbs out of bed, grabs the alarm clock, and fires it through *the window of his bedroom. He yells, "Leave me alone, you bitch!" and climbs back into bed.*

The mother calls his workplace and tells them her son is sick and will be unable to make it to work. She then apologizes to her son and calls a window company to get an estimate on the shattered bedroom window. The next day, she has the window replaced as her newly unemployed son is in the middle of his fifth boilermaker at the bar.

When the mother attempts to pay the window installer, she realizes her credit card is missing from her purse. Meanwhile, her son just finished a pizza at the bar and hands the bartender the credit card. The bartender looks at the credit card, then back to the man at the bar, "You don't look like a Margaret."

The mother broke several cardinal sins of enabling. 1) She should have never let him move back into her house in the first place; 2) She should have never called his place of employment; that is his responsibility; 3) She should have never tolerated his verbal abuse; 4) She should never clean up his messes; 5) She should never be expected to pay for the window; that is his responsibility; and finally 6) She should cancel her credit card and leave his belongings on the front door step.

No mother wants to watch her son or daughter suffer. But by allowing them to run roughshod without consequence, a parent is enabling or allowing the child to continue down the pathway of destruction.

A parent, family member, or friend cannot be held responsible for the onset of recovery process of an addicted loved one.

However, as the recovery process begins under the medical guidance of the treatment center, encouragement, motivation, and love become necessary tools in the recovery process. Parents, family and friends are the centerpieces of this necessity.

Darryl attempted intervention therapy, and although he became drug-free for a short period of time, he was still firmly attached to his addictions. Darryl did not want to be an addict! However, he was also not ready to relinquish his addictions. An addict loves his family and friends. An addict who has never received proper psychiatric treatment through intervention, though, will maintain his one true love—his addiction(s).

Darryl was now facing a new wrinkle in his search for sobriety. Being diagnosed with cancer can seriously jeopardize an addict's path to recovery. When people receive a diagnosis of cancer, they are immediately struck with a sense of impending doom. When addicts are diagnosed with cancer, the news can be detrimental to their recovery, because their immediate thought is, "Why should I go through with this rehab process if I'm going to die anyway?"

Can cancer treatments (chemotherapy and radiation) be affected by illicit drug abuse? There are certain drugs that will not properly co-exist with the cancer treatments. It is vital for an addict to inform his oncologist of any drug use prior to cancer treatments.

Darryl was overcome with emotion when he received the news of his cancer diagnosis. With the support of his family and friends, he understood that his life had meaning and he was important in the eyes of his children, wife, and loved ones. His battle against cancer became the carrot that would motivate him during the healing process.

Darryl's cancer battle was something bigger than his addiction, and he was using the encouragement of his loved ones to own his addictions.

CHAPTER 10

DRASTIC MEASURES

Based on an interview with Rich Capiola, MD

Addicts live with fear on a daily basis. The memories of an addict's past lives have created this fear phenomenon. The fears of being unloved or abandoned, the fears of being neglected, or the fears of being ridiculed and injured, weigh heavily upon the minds of those addicted by drugs and alcohol.

The most common fear of a recovering addict is, "What am I going to do if I relapse?" Addicts have to create the barriers. Addicts have to better manage cuing and trigger mechanisms. Addicts have to recognize with something bigger than their addictions, and they have to fight the urges with every fiber in their being! Sometimes, recovering addicts must become creative in their fight against addictions.

Two female friends were helping one another with their nicotine addictions. One woman was a right-wing Republican, and the other was a devout Democrat. They made a vow that whoever broke down and smoked a cigarette would have to donate her next paycheck to the presidential campaign of the other's political party. These two women were willing to put their addictions on the line by creating a meaningful motivational scenario. The two women were each other's support system, but they also held each other accountable at all times.

Sometimes drastic times call for drastic measures. There once was a man who had a severe gambling addiction. His addiction was so powerful, he lost his family, friends, and all of his money. The man was so addicted to gambling that he sold his company car to have money to gamble. After attending a gambling intervention facility, the man concocted a plan that would ultimately fight off his urges and end his addiction.

The man created a sign with a photograph of himself plastered in the middle. The text on the sign read, "The man pictured here is a gambling addict and is not allowed in this casino. Please escort him out immediately." When the man fell prey to his addictive urges, he would enter the casino with the giant sign. The man then walked around the casino with the sign in his hands, for all to see.

The bouncers of the casino would eventually spot the man with the sign. They would stop him, read the sign, look at the photo, and then look at the man. The man would tell the bouncers, "Please throw me out of here." The bouncers would look at one another and shrug. They would then lead him out of the casino and into the parking lot.

After going through a few of these incidents, the man eventually stopped going to casinos. He had retrained his brain, created a barrier, and in doing so, eventually thwarted the urges of his addiction.

If an addict leaves the door open, he will ultimately walk through it. Recovering addicts must slam the doorway to their addictions SHUT! Drastic times call for drastic measures.

A gambling addiction or any other behavioral addiction will light the brain chemistry in the same, exact manner as a drug or alcohol addiction. Many times, a behavioral addiction will tie in perfectly with other addictions. If a gambler is on a winning streak while he is drinking a Jack and Coke, he may subconsciously believe the alcohol is a part of his winning ways. Therefore, the gambler continues drinking more and more as the evening progresses.

One of the most rewarding aspects of the recovery process is the moment an addict understands he can freely ask for assistance in his fight against the disease. An addict has suffered through many years of guilt and shame. As children, many individuals feel as if they are letting their parents down if they admit guilt or personal problems.

In Darryl's case, he was afraid to show his feelings or thoughts for fear of his father's wrath. But he also did not want to share burdens or guilt with his mother, because he did not want to let her down. Therefore, in this particular situation, no real structure was established, and the personal management of problems and emotions was never truly developed.

Many parents have dealt with the following situation at some point in their childrearing days. A father finds out his college-aged daughter is going to a party. He tells his daughter to call him if she has been drinking so he can pick her up. The daughter agrees to his request.

At 3 a.m., the father's phone rings! He answers and is told his daughter was in a car wreck. The father drives to the hospital to find his daughter in the Emergency Room. She has a small laceration on her chin, but she is fine.

"I told you to call me if you were drinking and I would come get you!" reminds the father.

The daughter drops her head in shame. "I didn't call because I didn't want you to get mad at me for being drunk."

A young person lacks the maturity to comprehend the "domino effect" of a single, bad action.

Such immature thought processes plagued Darryl throughout his baseball career. He did not want to let his team down, so he joined them in their late-night drug fests. He did not want to let his fans down, so he hurried through his intervention therapy to get back to hitting homeruns and driving in runs.

Addicts are notorious for hiding their true emotions. Over time, addicts will realize the importance of sharing their soul with those who genuinely care for them. Caregivers must understand that self-esteem plays a major role in an addict's thought processes and decisions. If an addict was raised in a violent, chaotic household, he or she will continually suffer with self-esteem and self-worth issues.

Fathers play an enormous role in the development of a child's self-esteem and self-worth. Darryl and his brother Ronnie never received any type of positive fulfillment from their father.

Many recovering alcoholics will convey their eagerness to become sober. But unfortunately, these addicts will then follow that statement with a long-term goal or desire such as, "I want to get sober, so one day I can go have one drink at a bar with the fellas and not worry about getting drunk."

Dr. Capiola is adamant that a recovering alcoholic cannot have a drink! He will never be able to pick up a glass of beer without initiating the addiction process all over again. The idea of "I can have just one beer" is the trigger needed to refuel the addiction process once again. One beer may not equal a black-out on the first day, but the machinery is primed for a black-out in very near future. The idea of "normal drinking with the fellas" sends an addict down a slippery slope that leads to alcoholism, especially when the person does not have a recovery plan in place to deal with that initial "one beer" thought or action.

Addicts are constantly dealing with trigger mechanisms. Why do you think beer commercials are so hilarious? Addicts connect humor with fun, which simultaneously connects fun with drinking beer. Why are pizza commercials run so frequently in the evening? The pizza commercial is designed to set off alarms within the brains of those who are addicted to food.

A recovering addict must face the fact that sober means sober. An alcoholic needs to retrain his brain and find something bigger and better than the source of his addictions. Recovering addicts need to become extremely self-observant. They need to build a stronger force-field around the temptations that beckon them on a daily basis in our society.

* * * * *

DARRYL'S STORY

FLY OR DIE

There is no quick cure for addiction. The best way to fight off addiction is to never try an addicting substance in the first place. However, for millions of people, this is not a possibility and in most cases, a foregone conclusion. The negative stresses and emotions of their young lives pull them into such a deep, dark hole. They long for an escape hatch that will free them from their pain. All too often, this escape hatch is drugs, alcohol, or other addictive substances.

Treatment for addiction can help counteract the fixation's powerful hold on the brain's behavior and pleasure systems. The treatment is an ongoing work station that requires unfailing attention. No one battling addiction can fall asleep at the wheel.

People who suffer from addiction needs just one tiny crack in the armor to be exposed to the addictive pleasures of their chosen fix. This statement invites another question: "Does a person's relapse to drug abuse constitute a failure in the addiction treatment?"

Many experts agree that relapsing to drug abuse is not only possible, it is very likely due to the chronic nature of the brain disease of addiction. The treatment of a chronic disease, such as addiction, involves complete changes in a person's past behaviors. The relapse does not indicate treatment failure. The lapses indicate that additional steps were needed in the treatment of the individual.

The best ways to prevent a drug relapse is to continue treatment, no matter how the individual says he or she feels. Lapses can be triggered by stresses brought on by life experiences, people in one's life, work-related issues and depression. However, the main reason for relapse is exposure to the drugs or alcohol the addicted person is attempting to avoid. The exposure to such drugs and/or alcohol are triggers to a recovering addict.

BACK IN THE SADDLE

1999. After several months of chemotherapy, Darryl found himself locked into another spring training in Tampa, Florida. Chemotherapy is a demanding mode of medical treatment for oncology patients. Chemotherapy is composed of chemotherapeutic agents, which are referred to as cytotoxic. The actions of the chemotherapeutic agents are to kill the rapidly dividing cells, which is one of the main properties of cancer cells.

Some of the side effects associated with chemotherapy include anemia, gastrointestinal changes, fatigue, and nausea. Darryl was dealing with all of these side effects as he prepared himself for the following season. He was weak and tired, but continued to push himself toward his goals.

When Darryl began spring training, he was still receiving chemotherapy once a week in Tampa. He would hit, throw, shag fly balls, and work out in the weight room, despite the nagging side effects of the chemotherapeutic agents. He pushed himself, but in doing so, paid a steep price with constant nausea and pounding headaches. There were nights he could not sleep due to the incessant banging in his head.

At the conclusion of spring training, Joe Torre approached Darryl about spending some additional time in Tampa at the training complex. He wanted Darryl to continue recovering from the chemo sessions, and building up his strength levels before returning to New York. Darryl agreed to Joe's wishes, but he was highly disappointed with the team's decision.

Darryl wanted to be with the team in New York, rather than being left behind in Tampa. He promised to continue his chemo-therapy sessions, but he was growing weary of his time spent at the hospital, hooked up to an IV as the toxins coursed through his veins. He was tired of feeling sick and tired, and he was com-pletely over the nausea that had chased him around like an annoying sidekick.

Darryl was miserable. He wanted it to all be finished. Some-times, he would ponder dark, negative thoughts about giving up and letting the cancer take him. He was suffering with depression and slipping into another dark hole. Darryl was beginning to search for the escape hatch. Was it just a matter of time? Would Darryl relapse into the darkness once again?

Despite the constant vigilance of his support network, Darryl was wrapped in a cloak of self-doubt. He doubted his skill sets on the field. He doubted his ability to play the game like he had so many times before. He was hearing the dark, deep grumblings of an old, familiar voice. The Monster was waking, and Darryl could feel the doom approaching like a vicious tornado in the black of night.

His mother called to him from on high. "Stay focused, my child!"

But he could not hear her. He was too far gone.

In April of 1999, Darryl Strawberry fell prey to the demons. Darryl drove to a bar in Tampa and had his first drink in four years.

After four years of sobriety, Darryl stepped onto a path much darker than any he had ever journeyed upon.

It only takes one.

For an addict, one drink can spiral into ten drinks and it can happen within minutes. By taking one sip, the trigger mechanism catapults the brain into an uncontrollable lapse in judgment. One sip is all that is needed to trip the limbic system into a pleasure-craving "seek-and-destroy" mission. One sip is all it took to reconnect Darryl Strawberry with his "old friends." He was hooked!

One drink turned to two, which rapidly became five. In his drunken stupor, Darryl was drawn to the urges for a cocaine fix. Darryl search the streets of Tampa for anything that would take him away. His mind was spinning out of control when he pulled up to a woman on Kennedy Boulevard. He asked her for the "good stuff" and she was more than happy to oblige. That is when Darryl's world began to completely unravel.

The woman was an undercover cop, and Darryl was pulled over for solicitation. Once a search was conducted on his vehicle and person, Darryl was arrested for possession of 0.3 grams of cocaine, which was found in his wallet. His life instantly flashed before his eyes as if he were falling off a cliff.

After spending the night in a Tampa jail, Darryl called his wife, Charisse. It was one of the toughest calls he had ever had to make. The shame that washed over his entire being took his very breath away. How could he be so inconsiderate to his family's feelings? How could he have allowed himself to sink to such depravity once again?

Darryl had officially relapsed. It only takes one sip, one toke, one sniff, one taste. It only takes one trigger.

It only takes one.

THE WOODPECKER

Darryl pleaded "no contest" to the drug charges, and received eighteen months of probation. He was also suspended by Baseball Commissioner Bud Selig for 120 days for his destructive actions. No penalty was stiffer than his own self-induced sentence.

Darryl was walking down the darkest of paths and with each plodding step, he sank deeper into the quagmires before him. He found no joy in his heart. He was not living with purpose, like he had when he was battling for his life. He was not living for his family. He lived selfishly, thinking only of his next fix, his next drink, or his next sexual conquest. His words and actions mirrored his thoughts.

"The heck with it! Being good didn't work. I'll go back to being bad."

These words would be referred to as Darryl Strawberry's official surrender. His addictions were victorious, and his "old friends" cheered his defeat. What kind of friend would cheer for your defeat? What kind of friend would want to find you lying face down in your own vomit? What kind of friend would want to see you wallowing in pain while trembling in fear? What kind of friend would want to watch you die?

Darryl's addictions had slowly, but surely, chipped away at his mind like a woodpecker on a tree.

RAT-A-TAT-TAT! RAT-A-TAT-TAT! RAT-A-TAT-TAT!

The rapping sound inside his head was incessant! It pounded his brain like a sledge hammer!

RAT-A-TAT-TAT! RAT-A-TAT-TAT! RAT-A-TAT-TAT!

The addictions chased him. They were relentless in their pursuit.

In time, Darryl would break and give in to the addictions' constant bombardment. He would frantically reach for his crack pipe, and within minutes of its use, the woodpecker would fly away. The woodpecker was free to spread its wings and swoop across the pitch-black skies.

Silence then drifted through Darryl's head and he would find momentary solace. He knew, though, that the silence would be a fleeting reward compared to the addictions' powerful pull. He understood that the rewarding stimuli would be short-lived, and he also well aware that the ugly consequences would be overwhelming.

Darryl also knew the punishment for his actions would be brutally painful. He did not know what was worse—the aftermath of his deeds or the incessant pounding of the woodpecker and growling voice of the Monster. He could taste the venom spewing from the devilish ghoul's intoxicated breath.

"WHAT DID I TELL YOU, BOY?
YOU'RE WORTHLESS!
YOU'RE NOTHING!"

Darryl could not escape the barrage of its insults and hateful images bombarding his mind!

THWACK! THWACK! THWACK!

The hatred he felt for his father was buried deep inside his soul as he imagined the leather belt ripping through his skin. Why would you injure your own child, Father? Why would you cause me such pain? Why would you treat me with such contempt?

Darryl was also ravaged by the media. Their vicious ink lashed out at him as if he were a murderer, their words crucifying him for his shortcomings. People booed him and called him names. He was persecuted by individuals who never understood his heart or had walked in his shoes.

"HEY STRAWBERRY, YOU SUCK! YOU PIECE OF SHIT!"

Darryl's life was in total disarray. Nevertheless, he refused to abandon his "old friends." They were kind to him. They brought him solace. They gave him peace. They rewarded him with pleasurable escapes.

"Where's the escape hatch?! WHERE IS IT!?"

Darryl felt hopeless. He knew he would never find his way off the spinning carousel. It was going way too fast. He could not see the ground, for it was just a blur. He was scared to hold on, but even more frightened to jump off the whirligig that was his life. His addictions owned his every thought, and he had no more strength to fend them off. He could not look into the mirror, for he had shattered it into a million pieces.

RAT-A-TAT-TAT! RAT-A-TAT-TAT! RAT-A-TAT-TAT!

As the addictions progressed, Darryl became more careless with his actions. The consequences of his acts were not a concern to him any longer. The drugs and alcohol had whittled his brain into a self-loathing coward, unable to provide love to anyone, most notably himself.

Darryl wanted to fly away like the woodpecker. He just wanted to be set free.

"LEAVE ME ALONE!"

ASK AND IT WILL BE GIVEN TO YOU

Within eighteen months after that fateful first drink, Darryl was no longer a professional baseball player. He was offered several independent league contracts, but he had no interest in playing the game any longer. He was offered business investment opportunities, but he was not in the right state of mind to be involved in such capital ventures.

He attempted rehabilitation for a third time at the Hazelden Addiction Treatment Center in West Palm Beach, Florida. He lasted there three and a half months, before asking for his release from the Center. He had no intention of ending his drug and alcohol abuse. He would rather spend his money on his addictions than getting well.

Darryl Strawberry had a death wish.

In July 2001, Darryl went to the hospital for a routine, post-surgery checkup. He received a CAT scan as part of the procedure, and the findings of the test revealed that his cancer was not only back, it was spreading.

This was Darryl's chance to truly end his life. He could honor his death wish, and let the cancer devour him once and for all. Darryl would finally be able to end his pain and struggles. He could finally hush the woodpecker and silence the Monster. He could slip away from his "old friends" and finally relinquish their holds on his life. This was his chance to escape for good! He could finally die.

His loving wife, Charisse, however, would not let him go. She encouraged him to look inside his heart for the strength. She asked him to look into the eyes of his beautiful children and think about their shattered hearts and dreams. When Darryl looked at his babies, he knew he had no choice in the situation. He had to fight for them. He wanted to be there for them.

"Was there a bigger purpose for Darryl Strawberry in this world?" Was God sending him another message? Was he being given another chance to become victorious?

Within a month of his diagnosis, Darryl reported to Columbia Presbyterian Hospital, where he underwent his second cancer surgery. The procedure was successful. The doctors removed all the affected tissue, but Darryl lost his left kidney in the process. He would have to complete another rigorous six-month bout of chemotherapy, which did not sit well with him.

Darryl was extremely sore for weeks after the surgical procedure, and was prescribed Vicodin and Percodan for the pain. He could not sleep, so he was prescribed Ambien. Within time, Darryl was hooked again. But this time it wasn't cocaine or crack or amphetamines or alcohol. He was now addicted to his prescribed pain medication.

Charisse confronted Darryl about his pain medication abuse, but he was defiant! He said he was in pain and needed the medication. Charisse blew up and threatened to report him to his probation officer if he didn't stop using the drugs!

Darryl was also in denial. He honestly thought he was not doing anything wrong. He argued that he was not a criminal! He had no idea that pain medication could also trigger a dopamine response in the brain's pleasure circuit.

After their argument, the next morning, Darryl drove his Ford Expedition into a telephone pole before being stopped by police officers. He was totally spaced out with Percodan, Vicodin, and Ambien floating through his system. He had no illegal substances in his body, but did receive an additional eighteen months on his probation status for his dangerous actions.

Because of the traffic incident, Darryl was court ordered to an intervention center for serious addiction abuse treatment. He was placed under house arrest at the recovery center. He wore an ankle bracelet to restrict him from fleeing the facility, and was required to finish a five-month treatment course. He would also receive his chemotherapy treatments while under house arrest at the center.

At the conclusion of his 5-month stint, Darryl asked to be discharged from facility. He was not allowed to leave the premises. Darryl argued with the office staff and asked Charisse to come pick him up. But, Charisse would not agree to such an arrangement. She was no longer going to be a part of Darryl's life.

Darryl was furious. He exploded with anger! He told her to come get him! But, she refused. She was taking the kids and leaving him. She needed stability for herself and for her children. Charisse had been pushed to the brink, and now that she was out the door, there was no looking back.

Darryl was told he would be held in the facility for an additional seven months, but Darryl was not having any part of it. Darryl lost his mind! He needed the escape hatch more than ever now! He was tired of being cooped up like a bird in a cage. He was tired of the chemo chemicals being pumped into his veins and he was tired of shunning his "old friends."

From the center, he called a former drug-using acquaintance and asked her to pick him up at the facility. He did not care if he lived or died that night—he just knew he had to escape! The woodpecker was at it again with its incessant banging!

RAT-A-TAT-TAT! RAT-A-TAT-TAT! RAT-A-TAT-TAT!

Darryl grabbed the phone again. This time, he would call his counselor and friend, Ron Dock. When Ron answered the phone, Darryl's deep voice muttered his thoughts into the phone, "I'm done, Ron."

Darryl could hear Ron's excited voice shouting in his ear, "What are you talking about, Darryl?"

Darryl's voice cracked as he battled for his next words, "If I escape this place, I'm going to kill myself."

"What are you talking about?! Darryl, don't be stupid!" yelled Ron. "DARRYL!"

Darryl's voice stalled into silence. His heavy breathing was all that could be heard over the phone line. He whispered to his friend, "I'm ready to die, Ron," then hung up the phone.

Darryl looked at the four walls of his tiny room. He could feel the walls shrinking around him. The pain was brewing inside him as his hands shook with fear. He shouted to the heavens!

"JUST GIVE ME PEACE!"

His words echoed off the walls of the room, but were quickly silenced beneath the overpowering hammering of the woodpecker!

RAT-A-TAT-TAT! RAT-A-TAT-TAT! RAT-A-TAT-TAT!

Darryl banged his fists into the concrete wall to drown out the ceaseless banging of the woodpecker!

RAT-A-TAT-TAT! RAT-A-TAT-TAT! RAT-A-TAT-TAT!

That night, Darryl Strawberry escaped HealthCare Connection.

RAT-A-TAT-TAT! RAT-A-TAT-TAT! RAT-A-TAT-TAT!

That night, Darryl Strawberry would either fly or die.

COMMENTS TO CHAPTER 10

with John Picciano, LCSW, MSW

Darryl was spiraling out of control. The weight of the world was crushing him, and he was running out of places to hide. Why couldn't he just do the work? Why couldn't he just quit the addictions? What speaks to an addict? What controls his mindset? For Darryl, it was the Monster, the "old friends," and the woodpecker.

The Monster of Darryl's life was the source of his addiction. His father's abuse and neglect altered the young boy's self-esteem and self-worth. Whenever Darryl lacked self-confidence or doubted his abilities, he became more vulnerable to his subconscious. When he closed his eyes, he was being chased by the visions of his father and his abusive hands. When he shut his eyes at night, Darryl felt he was being pursued by a brutal defiler. Every addict has a similar monster in his dreams.

The "old friends" of Darryl's life were his addictions. The drugs, alcohol, and bad behaviors were directly responsible for his happiness and emotional relief. He learned to rely on his "old friends" when his life began unraveling. Unfortunately, the "old friends" created a narcissistic self-love within Darryl. When he was in a dark, emotional state, he became selfish. The only thing that mattered to him was getting high, drunk, or both. He thought of no one but himself.

In time, Darryl mistook the powers of his addiction for the caring touch of a loved one. Drugs and alcohol did not judge him or ridicule him. Drugs and alcohol were his source of freedom. In Darryl's mind, drugs and alcohol were his only true friends. Every addict has a group of similar friends. Drugs and alcohol are a curse and the scourge of a person's mind.

The woodpecker of Darryl's life was his incessant need to satisfy his addictions. When he heard the pecking in his head, he started "Jonesing" for his fix. The woodpecker was loud! It was relentless and it was not going to stop until Darryl satisfied its beckoning. The woodpecker caused endless headaches that could only be relieved by the substances that controlled Darryl. Every addict has a woodpecker!

Addicts avoid many emotional obstacles. Addicts do not want to deal with the underlying issues caused by their own individual monsters; they just want to hide or avoid the images altogether. Addicts dread the concept of recovery, because it is so much easier to call on their "old friends." Recovery is long and difficult, whereas the "old friends" provide instantaneous relief. Addicts are tortured by the incessant pecking of the woodpecker, but understand the necessity of its ceaseless rapping. Addicts avoid everything but their addictions. Some addicts would rather perish than ask for help.

Darryl could have easily given in to his second bout of cancer. He could have let the disease run its course and eventually end his suffering for good. He could have given up and let the sickness consume him. However, Darryl had something many addicts do not have in their broken lives. He had family, friends, teammates, and sponsors who would never let him give up the fight. These people pushed and prodded the Mighty Thor.

Many addicts fail to realize the full-scale power of their substance abuse. Alcoholism and drug dependency are beyond most sober people's comprehension. If an addict is a pawn in a chess game, then the addiction is the box in which the game is stored. It may have only taken one individual to initiate the onset of drug or alcohol abuse, but it takes a team to eliminate the addiction's stronghold on that individual. Darryl was staring into the eyes of death, but was still unable to break free from the substances that continually ruled his life.

An addiction buries its fangs in the body of an addict and will not release its hold until an individual is either incarcerated or dead. Darryl had lost two wives to failed marriages. His children were taken from him. He lost his career, his livelihood, and would eventually become penniless.

Do you think Darryl Strawberry wanted to lose everything? No! He did not.

Do you think he wanted to stop using drugs and alcohol? The answer is once again, "No! He did not."

The fact that Darryl lost everything in his life, and was still unable to walk away from his addictive substances illustrates the power of his addictions. Darryl needed professional intervention to wage battle against his old friends. He needed additional firepower to silence the woodpecker. He needed a team of doctors, nurses, psychiatrists, counselors, and sponsors to help chase away the Monster.

Darryl needed structure. He need a plan of attack during his intervention, but most importantly, he needed a more successful scheme against the trigger mechanisms upon his release from the recovery center. He needed to construct better barriers and find something bigger than his addictions! Darryl had to retrain his brain while convincing himself that sobriety was much more important than his addictions. He had to believe that being clean was a more powerful and meaningful state of mind. He could not let the disease win!

There are numerous addicts in our great nation who live in cardboard boxes beneath train tracks. Many addicts live inside dilapidated crack houses that are not even fit for vermin or cockroaches. These people are like the lab rats choosing the crack pellets over food and water. They live like zombies, shuffling about in their filthy clothes, caked with urine and feces. These people have given into the disease and are just one hit away from an early grave.

There are no news reports of the hundreds of people who die every day from substance abuse. These people have been sadly forgotten and discarded by our world. The bodies of these addicts are quietly reclaimed by the parents and caretakers who were simply overmatched and ill equipped to battle the ghoulish grips of substance abuse.

All addicts begin their lives as innocent children. However, when young boys or girls are beaten, abused, or abandoned, the lives of those innocents are forever altered. If young children are bombarded with dysfunction, chaos, and violence at an early age, they must receive psychological treatment to aid in the minimization of their trauma. If they have not received emotional stabilization by their teenage years, they will most likely seek out alcohol and drugs as a means of escape and pleasure.

If addicts fail to receive proper intervention from their substance abuse, their lives will continue to spiral out of control. When a person (addict or caregiver) gives up on the recovery process, the addict will ultimately give up on his or her life. Addicts who give up on their lives often disappear into a dark realm.

When addicts accept defeat in their battles against substance abuse, they will turn to prostitution and crime to fund their addictions. Addicts are willing to live amongst sewer rats and garbage as long as they can secure their much-needed fixes. Street people ultimately die from their addictions. Often, they are found to have substandard mental and physical health, penniless and alone. They are discarded like bundles of garbage.

There should be a ticker-tape parade in New York City honoring the many victories of crack, cocaine, meth, alcohol, and amphetamines! These addictive substances have dominated the competition for years! Over ten percent of our nation is suffering from some form of drug or alcohol addiction and the numbers are rising! That is why it is imperative that our *families and friends begin rising up to the aid of those who are suffering in our schools, neighborhoods, and homes.*

"Rising up" means becoming pro-active in our children's lives. When children have been abused, find help for them right away! Do not let them suffer throughout their lives, searching for ways to find happiness! Abused, bullied, and neglected children will constantly search the world for a glimmer of self-worth and self-value. Parents and caregivers need to become more aware of the damages being caused to the innocent.

If children have been victims of abuse, they need psychological and psychiatric assistance immediately! Our children need to understand they are important and loved! When they are abused, they can feel overwhelming guilt for possibly provoking the violent act in some way. They feel shame for causing such hatred in the caregiver's life. Over time, abused children believe they are terrible people who deserve such deplorable treatment. These children begin losing self-esteem and self-worth due to the abuse.

Often in cases of domestic abuse, the mother will be the victim of physical maltreatment by the husband. The woman will not react to the husband's abuse until her children begin to be physically harmed. Sometimes, the mother will rise up against the husband, resulting in further abuse by the father. Sometimes, the mother will not do anything at all. This is her way of protecting her young, as if she were matched up against a bear. This was Ruby Strawberry's mode of protection for her children. She knew if she antagonized the bear by fighting back, the bear could have become more violent and possibly injured or even killed one of her children.

Many abused family members suffer from Post-Traumatic Stress Disorder, or PTSD. PTSD develops in people who are exposed to recurring trauma. This disorder is typically found in people who have be engaged in warfare, horrific traffic collisions, or terrorist attacks. PTSD can also be found in spouses and children who have been physical beaten or sexually abused.

When people suffer from PTSD, they will have recurring flashbacks, deleted memories, or hyperarousal to events similar to their own life experiences. A child can also suffer from PTSD because of constant bullying at school. Many children who suffer from PTSD may develop some type of addiction later in life in order to ease their pain, according to John Picciano.

If youngsters are not given proper psychological treatment at a young age, they will carry the effects of PTSD throughout their lives. Many children who do not receive proper treatment at a young age will begin using drug and alcohol use by the time they are in fifth grade. This age is a critical psychological juncture for children!

If children do not receive the psychological treatment required, they have a greater likelihood of becoming addicts in their later lives. If a parent, caregiver, or family member recognizes the possibility of addiction, they must become proactive in that person's intervention and recovery process.

The first step in preventing addiction is getting your loved one psychological help, whether it is in a clinical setting or in a treatment center.

Once an addiction is cemented in a person's life, the addict will be unable to properly treat his own addictive behaviors. A caregiver needs to be loving, understanding, and cognizant of the pain the loved one is experiencing. However, a caregiver must not become an enabler.

In many addiction cases, addicts must be allowed to hit rock bottom, before they are able to properly rebound from their substance abuse. Addicts will become defiant and demanding, but parents or caregivers must stand strong, create boundaries, and refuse to give in to their loved one's demands. A line in the sand must be established in the home, and if the young person crosses that line, he or she must be dealt with in the appropriate manner.

Here is an example of how to deal with an addict who is overstepping his bounds in a household. An 18-year-old son comes home after a summer party. He is drunk and obnoxious as he roots through the refrigerator for sandwich ingredients. In his haste, he drops a mayonnaise jar on the kitchen floor. The jar explodes into a million pieces of creamy white glass fragments.

The boy's father walks into the kitchen and asks his son to clean it up the mess. The son refutes his request, and yells at *his father, "Screw you! I'm outta this prison!" The son storms through the house, opens the front door, and runs outside. The father watches his son sit under a tree. Within seconds, the son passes out in the front yard.*

Should the father go wake his son and bring him inside? No chance—let him sleep it off with the squirrels and the fire ants. If the father had tried to bring his son inside, he would be sending the wrong message. The father would have been conveying that his son can do anything he wants, and no matter what type of mess the son gets himself into, the father or mother will be always be there to clean it up for him.

The action of the father is referred to as "tough love." When the son wakes up from his drunken stupor, he feels awful. He wonders how he got outside and why he used a branch as a pillow. The son crossed the line in the sand, and he paid the consequences for his actions.

The father's message was clear—"Your addiction will not rule both of our lives." The father was there for his son, but he was not going to allow his son's blatant disregard for authority become a habit in his household. The father held firm to his commitment, and the son held firm to the whiskbroom, mop, and bucket of Mr. Clean.

Another tough-love example. A mother was dealing with her addicted 19-year-old daughter who refused to obey the rules of the house. The mother constantly warned her daughter to stop bringing men and drugs into her house. The daughter ignored her mother's wishes, so the mother changed the locks on the front door.

The daughter banged on the front door and cursed her mother. The mother told her daughter, "If you live in my house, you live by my rules. I love you, and you can stay here, but if you can't abide by the rules of the house, then you need to go find your own place." The angry girl turned and walked away.

Two weeks later, the mother was walking through the downtown area of her city. She came upon her daughter panhandling on the street corner. The daughter looked at her mother with anger. The mother said, "I love you, and you can always come home. But first you need to get your life straight. You can either go to a recovery center, or sleep on this side-walk. It's up to you" The mother then turned and walked away.

This action affected the mother greatly. She was very sad, but she had to draw a line in the sand. The girl had to make a choice. She could get help and return to the comforts of her home or continue sleeping in the streets. The daughter had to make sobriety a more meaningful and powerful part of her life.

Sometimes, hitting rock bottom is the only way to reach those who are fully vested in addiction. Darryl had lost his wives, children, money, and career, but he was still not ready to come in from the cold. Denial ruled his thought process and the projection of blame was still firmly rooted in the memories of his past life.

A parent or caregiver should not allow an addicted son or daughter the ability to rule the roost with defiant acts and substance-fueled disobedience. Caregivers must demonstrate tough love to their child, as long as they maintain a "prodigal son" mentality that allows the child to return safely and without judgment.

We must never give up on those we love, no matter how hopeless the situation appears.

CHAPTER 11

TREATMENT

Based on an interview with David Blair Miller, PsyD

Early detection of an addiction is a key step in the prevention and/or the recovery process of a loved one who has fallen prey to addiction or addictions. It is vitally important for parents and caregivers to first understand and identify the warning signs involved with those suffering from addiction. Prevention is integral for managing situations before they become unmanageable.

As stated earlier, a parent or caregiver must pay close attention to those who possess low self-esteem or have overwhelming feelings of hopelessness. Addicts will have a strong sense of helplessness, and may feel trapped in their lives. Addicts will express these various symptoms in every aspect of their lives.

Addicts will struggle in relationships and marriages. They will have difficulty raising their children and succeeding in their workplace. They will begin to lose interest in self-care and cleanliness around their homes. Addicts will have financial woes and become ill more often. They will become irritable, volatile, melancholic, anxious, and highly emotional. They will have enormous mood swings with intense outbursts of anger. They will begin to lie and deceive others to cover their tracks, and their life decisions will become confusing and inconsistent.

However, the most glaring symptom of addiction is the addicts' inability to properly care for themselves. This lack of self-care is brought about by the deep wounds and trauma that continually haunt them. Addicts turn to self-medication through drugs and alcohol to hide the pain, instead of properly dealing with the issues causing the emotional suffering. These deep, furrowed emotional scars must be treated by highly skilled professionals through psychoanalytic therapy if an addict is ever going to find internal freedom.

"Psychoanalytic Therapy" is both a treatment and a process of better understanding and regaining control of unconscious thinking. This type of treatment concentrates on a patient's conscious feelings and behaviors, as well as the repressed unconscious motives and desires of the individual. Psychoanalysis is traditionally conceived as an opportunity for a motivated individual to reflect deeply about everything he or she is thinking and feeling without censorship.

The goal of the psychoanalytic treatment is to strengthen the Ego, which is the most important unconscious mental aspect of our brains. As stated earlier, the Ego is our sense of self. The Superego is our conscience. It is our rigid commitment to morality and the rules and regulations of society. The

Id is our desire for pleasure and immediate gratification. These three unconscious mental expressions of our brains make up our individual views about our own character, as well as our personal outlooks on the world.

The Ego responds to our Id (desires) and Superego (staying within boundaries) impulses by modifying them to manage possible conflict and danger. If the Ego is not functioning properly, the Id will run wild and addictions will become a source of escape and fulfillment. If the Ego is not functioning properly, the Superego will be unable to fight off the Id's uncontrollable desires, resulting in broken rules and immoral acts of gratification.

The goal of psychoanalytic treatment is not only to strengthen a person's Ego, which is vital in the recovery process of those suffering from addictions, but also improve relationships. By strengthening the Ego, addicts have greater self-control over the Id and more independence from the Superego.

Most mental disorders (anxiety and depression) are due to feelings associated with a loss of control, helplessness, hopelessness, and low self-esteem. By increasing mental awareness through psychoanalytic treatment, people become more tolerant to emotional struggles and ultimately become less self-destructive.

A second goal of psychoanalytic treatment is to augment emotional growth by improving one's understanding and acceptance of oneself. Emotional growth requires self-acceptance and self-understanding. By becoming more in tune with his or her emotional state, an addict becomes better equipped to avoid triggers and unconscious desires. Addicts must learn to properly deal with the external traumas of their lives (both past and present) to avoid feelings of helplessness and hopelessness.

Addiction is described as a defensive process for addicts. Drug users and alcoholics avoid painful thoughts and memories by drowning themselves in the temporary numbness provided by their particular substance choices. Substance abuse is a futile attempt to compensate for inner feelings of shame and emptiness. The release is temporary and causes a false sense of relief or escape. These actions ultimately create a "false self." The price for this type of self-preservation is an over-developed resilience regarding the desired substances.

A third goal of psychoanalytic treatment is to lessen the internal fears of a person suffering from addiction. The feelings of fear intensify when a person is unable to cope with challenging life events, painful moments, or personal criticism. The inability to cope with external traumas causes devastating feelings of inadequacy and powerlessness. If a person lacks the ability to cope with such negative situations, fear is created and desperate actions are taken to avoid the despair.

Another important goal of treatment is providing insight into the need to change one's environment. By changing the environment, the addict is practicing abstinence from his addiction, as well as all people associated with his substance abuse. An addict cannot become successful in the fight against addiction without these vital changes. The addict will require a strong support system from family and friends during this important time of abstinence.

Addicts often perpetuate justified reasoning for their substance abuse. If an addict insists he is not an alcoholic, he is creating fantasy as a survival skill and resistance to the reality of his addiction. The addict lives in a world of denial, resulting in a temporary decrease in fear and anxiety, from underlying feelings of emotional deprivation.

The relationship between the therapist and the person suffering from addiction must be built upon trust, before genuine vulnerability can be shared. It is extremely important that family, friends, and caregivers are supportive of the treatment process. No change can occur within an addict without total teamwork, patience, and deep commitment.

The work of recovery includes a complete assessment of the patient's emotional history. Patients must be able to expand their emotional vocabulary, as well as insight, by releasing names, places, and feelings that have controlled their minds, hearts, and spirits. People who feel deeply wounded need a safe emotional space and a good listener.

In addition, patients must be allowed to vent frustrations, sadness, and anger to properly kick-start the healing process. It is important to understand the healing process will have its share of bumps in the road. It may even have road blocks, but well-intentioned commitment and support by loved ones will allow addicts the opportunity to overcome deep-rooted life adversities.

The process of working through the emotional status of a patient requires deep mental exploration. Deep-seated pain must be released to the surface. This type of work demands patience, endurance, and tenacity. The ultimate goal of such emotional exploration is to change passive thinking and past suffering into greater insight, improve problem-solving, and discover better modes of self-soothing and self-care. By creating these changes, a recovering addict has a better chance of defying fears and living with an improved sense of self-worth.

* * * * *

DARRYL'S STORY

LOCKED AWAY

Ask, and it will be given to you.
Knock and the door will be opened to you.
—Matthew 7:7

FOUR DAYS LATER

Ron Dock drove from Tampa to Daytona Beach in the dead of night. Ron's car could not go fast enough as he sped across the state at 95 miles per hour. Ron had received word from Darryl and learned his whereabouts, and Ron needed to get to him before he was found and taken into custody by law enforcement officers.

When Ron arrived in Daytona Beach, he found Darryl slumped over behind a garbage dumpster. Darryl was covered in filth. His watch and rings had been ripped from his person. His face was gaunt, his body starved. He was weak, exhausted, and empty. Darryl was not dead, but he was definitely knocking on the Reaper's door.

Tears streaked Darryl's dirty face as he rode in the passenger seat of Ron's car. Ron was relieved he had found his friend alive, but was concerned with his friend's life expectancy. How many more close calls would there be before it was finished? Darryl stared out the window of the car, then turned to Ron, "Why do you care for me so much? I am nothing."

Ron looked at Darryl, tears welling in own his eyes, "Because we've been in the trenches together for a long time now, and you are my brother. And I will not give up on you!" His eyes were intense and a single tear rolled down his cheek. Ron reached out to Darryl and squeezed his arm. Ron would not let him go.

Four days after escaping the treatment center, Darryl quietly surrendered to the authorities. As Darryl was being led away, he looked at Ron, "I want to be free of this. I want to surrender."

Ron hugged his friend one last time. "When the pupil is ready, the teacher will appear. I love you, brother," and Ron let him go.

Was Darryl Strawberry a danger to society? Were his actions worthy of a prison sentence? Was he a threat to his family? Or was he just a threat to himself?

When he was a middle-school student, Darryl shook down other kids for their lunch money. He set fires in the bathroom of his school to get out of his first-period class. He drank and smoked weed as a young teenager to escape the horrors of his home. Through it all, he swore he would never be anything like the Monster. Was it too late? Had Darryl truly become his own monster?

Darryl was running on fumes. He was tired of living, but too tired to die. The loss of his family crushed his spirit. The end of his illustrious career caused him great concern because it had always been his refuge. Where did he belong? There was just one certainty for Darryl—the disease had officially locked him up and the key had been thrown deep into the ocean.

Darryl had been detained for several months at various rehabilitation centers, but his time spent in the facilities always ended in a relapse. One of the reasons for his treatment failures could be blamed on the fact that he was a celebrity. In society, celebrities live their lives with a sense of *"carte blanche,"* anything goes.

Celebrities are commonly known for their riches, yet oddly enough, they are the ones who receive the most compensation. In other words, if a celebrity goes to a restaurant, the owner or manager of the restaurant will nearly always comp a celebrity's meal. Why would a restauranteur do this? Celebrities make more money than anyone in the joint!

The status of a celebrity mysteriously captivates common folk. Autographs, photographs, and status selfies are all the rage, and have been for years. Thus, when a celebrity enters an addiction/rehab center, there is a good chance he or she will be treated differently than the other patients. He or she will be secretly compensated in exchange for autographs or photographs. Such actions send mixed messages to the person requiring serious treatment. It is difficult for celebrities to stay focused when they are treated better than the other patients.

However, Darryl's relapses cannot be solely blamed on the treatment centers he attended. His addictions were affixed to his very core, and his self-loathing and lack of self-esteem were still the major culprits in his treatment failures. Darryl's addictions appeared to be unstoppable, but the last thing he wanted was to be sentenced to another treatment center. He would rather be locked away in prison than waste his time at a facility from which he could easily escape. He needed hardcore treatment! He needed to be put away.

When Darryl was asked which sentence he would prefer, his comments were harsh "Send me to prison! I would rather be locked away." The judge did not think Darryl was a criminal. She knew he was sick and needed treatment, but she didn't believe he deserved a prison sentence. So, she ordered Darryl to serve eighteen months at a hard-core addiction center in Ocala, Florida.

Darryl struggled mightily in the facility. He became defiant and broke several house rules. He was fed up with the strict regulations, and was eventually dismissed from the property for improper sexual relations with a young woman resident. He had violated his treatment once again.

After failing to comply to the rules set by the Ocala treatment center, Darryl got his initial wish. However, it wasn't a "blow-out-your-candles" birthday wish by any stretch of the imagination. Darryl was given the choice of spending a year in another rehabilitation facility, with an additional five years of probation, or he could serve eighteen months in the Florida State correction system.

Darryl responded, "To be honest with you, Your Honor, I would rather be dead." The judge sentenced Darryl to 30 days in jail to think about that choice.

Within a month, Darryl was sentenced to 18 months in prison and eventually assigned to the Gainesville Correction Institute in north-central Florida. The prison was a minimum- and medium-security campus that housed inmates involved with theft, drug dealing, and various other non-violent crimes. Darryl was assigned to the drug treatment center of the prison.

WHY AM I STILL HERE?

As Darryl Strawberry sat inside his dank cell, his mind wandered.

"Here I sit, an eight-time All-Star, a four-time World Champion, a man who has made millions of dollars. I was a husband, a father, and a teammate, but look at me now. I have nothing but these four walls and a bed too small for my body. I don't even have my freedom anymore. Or did I ever truly have freedom in the first place? I swore I would never be like him, but here I am, no better than he was. I swore no person would ever control me like my father did. I have lost two marriages because of that thought process. Drugs have robbed my six kids of their father. I craved my addictions more than I craved being with my family and here I am, sitting all alone. Why did I let this happen?"

By being locked away, Darryl was forced to learn acceptance of himself. He had never believed in himself because of the brutal verbal attacks he had received from the Monster, growing up. He had deep-rooted self-esteem issues that helped push him into the drug scene. When individuals feel they are unworthy of love, they will try anything to feel good about themselves.

Darryl had to find love for himself. He had to forgive himself for all his transgressions and wipe the slate clean if he was ever going to fend off the addictive shackles of his life. He had to believe in himself, and fully understand his worthiness on this planet. He had to believe that God had a plan for him. Darryl had a lot of work ahead of him.

As the days moved forward, Darryl found an eerie peace behind bars. He was clean and sober throughout his imprisonment, and his mind was free to think clearly once again. Ron Dock visited Darryl every Sunday throughout his sentence.

Ron's visits lifted Darryl's spirits. Darryl thanked his friend for his vigilance, and asked him one simple request. "Don't give up on me."

Ron always replied, "Never, my brother."

Ron was also a recovering addict, so he knew the pain Darryl constantly lived and breathed. "Addiction will make you do things you would never imagine. It will make you sell your own family," said Ron.

Darryl could feel Ron's compassion, and he fed off the strength Ron supplied. Ron was one of the few people who never wanted anything from the New York sports star. He just wanted Darryl to be free of the pain and get well.

Darryl missed his wife and his children terribly. Their beautiful faces were the constant focus of his dreams. When he closed his eyes, he could see them smiling and laughing. He could see them dancing and twirling.

He focused on the beauty of his world. He thought of his mother and his siblings. He thought about his high school baseball days, when he helped lead his Crenshaw Cougars to the state finals. He thought about the day he quit the team, and how terrible it felt to be without his teammates. He was grateful he had been allowed to re-join the team, and he swore he would never quit anything again.

His "old friends" and the Monster were on sabbatical. The Woodpecker had no more wood to peck, and Darryl was slowly finding peace within himself. He had no time to think about the negative aspects of his life, and knew he had to concentrate on his treatment if he was ever going to get mentally healthy.

Was Darryl Strawberry a danger to society? Was he a danger to his family? Or was he just a danger to himself? Darryl prayed that he would never be a danger to anyone, especially himself. To say he was out of the woods with his addictions would be wishful thinking. His addictions were like terrorists, and he never knew when they were going to attack.

After serving eleven months in prison, Darryl Strawberry was released from his state-ordered confinement. As Darryl exited the facility, he noticed the media stalking him once again from beyond the front gate of the facility. He could only imagine what they would write about him now. For the first time in his life, he didn't care what they would print, their ink pens and pencils had cut him bloody for far too long.

He just wanted to see his children.

WHERE NOW?

After Darryl was released from Gainesville, he made his way down Highway I-75 to be reunited with his children. When he arrived in Tampa, his main goals were to reconnect with his kids and find a way to earn Charisse's respect and love once again. He wanted to be a better husband, a better father, and a better person. He had tried this route so many times before. Could he actually pull it off this time?

The emotional work he completed in prison was continued in his home. He worked hard at being more involved with his family life and with his spirituality. He attended church and worked hard at being more of a positive factor in his children's lives.

Sadly, the damage was far too great for reconciliation. Darryl and Charisse eventually separated and a divorce was not too far behind. His mind was swirling. He could feel himself sliding, his mind drifting. He needed to take immediate action to chase away the villains of his life. If he could ask God for one thing, he would ask for the "peace that passeth all understanding."

Darryl moved from his Tampa home to West Palm Beach. There, he surrounded himself with a group of recovering addicts whom he had befriended along his journey. He needed to be enveloped by people who would watch over him and protect him from backsliding into a relapse. A support group can offer enormous assistance to a single person fighting off the demons. There is definite strength in numbers.

Darryl faced several demons during his divorce proceedings, and he was thankful for the stability provided by his sponsor Will G and the others from his support group. However, during an extremely difficult week, Darryl fell. He went on a four-day crack binge before being found and saved by Will G.

Cocaine and crack are short-acting stimulants. The highs are intense, but they don't last as long as highs from other drugs. Therefore, crack addicts will binge on the drug, taking it as many times as possible in a single session.

Will G took Darryl to a Narcotics Anonymous meeting with the hopes he could nip the situation in the bud. As Darryl mingled with folks at the gathering, they were more enamored by his celebrity status than the fact he was a drug addict. They could not believe they were talking to All-Star Darryl Strawberry! They could have cared less about the fact that he just got off a four-day crack-fest in a sleazy, flea-bitten hotel.

Darryl quickly got bored with the group and his mind began to wander. His cravings were starting to kick in, and he was beginning to shake with the idea of getting high. Darryl searched for the exit sign. As he looked around, he spotted a blonde woman walking toward him with another woman in tow. The blonde's name was Tracy Boulware.

Tracy was a recovering addict who had been clean and sober for one year. She was very pretty, but all business as she made her way toward Darryl and Will G. She stopped near the men, and told her friend that she was ready to leave. Darryl studied Tracy as she was politely introduced to him by Will G.

"Tracy, this is Darryl Strawberry. He's a famous baseball player."

Tracy was not impressed. She shook Darryl's hand and turned to her friend, "Do you have my keys?" Darryl did not want her to leave. After a few minutes of pleading and coaxing, Darryl finally convinced Tracy to stay for a little bit longer. The two exchanged their stories of addiction. He then asked her for her phone number. She was reluctant to give it to him, but ultimately did.

Darryl and Tracy began a friendship. They talked on the phone and shared thoughts and concerns. He warned her of his past, and she did the same to him. Their relationship was not based on romance and sex, but rather was founded on a common thread—nonjudgmental friendship. Within months, the two fell in love with one another.

Darryl could not help but wonder, "Is God putting this woman in my life for a reason?"

He had been an eight-time All-star, a four-time World champion, he had been a millionaire, but he had nothing inside his heart. He was devoid of the feelings that make a person feel alive. He had always been empty in that regard.

Tracy was different. He looked at her in a completely new manner. Her strength was a powerful aphrodisiac. Her loving heart spoke to him. She was not enamored with his celebrity status. She only cared about Darryl Strawberry the person, not the former super-star outfielder.

Darryl was broke. Not only was he broke, he was going through another divorce and was $3 million in debt. The only thing he had to offer Tracy was a broken-down drug addict. However, Tracy saw something far greater than worldly possessions, fame, and fortune. Tracy saw a loving man who had been spared by God. Darryl was a lost soul, and she was his shepherd. God was indeed providing the peace that "passeth all understanding."

Darryl was locked away once again- but this time, it was inside the heart of his new best friend, Tracy Boulware.

COMMENTS TO CHAPTER 11

with John Picciano and Ron Dock

Darryl was found behind a Dumpster in a filthy alley. He had been robbed of his personal effects, as well as his dignity. When Ron Dock cautiously approached his friend, he came face to face with a sick, feeble, gaunt, gray man. Darryl had finally hit rock bottom. He had two choices: 1) end his life or 2) call for help. He called for help.

Ron had been Darryl's sponsor for many years. He had seen Darryl broken and bruised many times before, but even Ron was not prepared for what he was witnessing. Ron's heart was broken. Ron was no different than the saddened mother who watched her drug-addicted daughter sleep on the cold streets of the city. Ron was no different than the father who allowed his inebriated son to spend the night in the front yard. There comes a time when the caregiver must provide "tough love" to those who are defiant and lost.

The fact that Darryl was ready to die rather than taking another drink or hit was actually a positive stride toward a possible recovery. This mindset meant he was tired of losing the fight against his addictions. Darryl's call to Ron Dock instead of ending his life was a monumental step toward conquering his addictions, for it meant he was now ready to receive help from others. Would these two important steps finally lead to the end of Darryl's drug and alcohol use?

Although Darryl's steps were pointed in the right direction, there was a strong possibility he would require multiple rehabilitation stints before his disease was properly contained. In fact, an addict may fail numerous times before he ultimately discovers the correct formula for his particular substance cessation.

Caregivers, family members, and friends of the addicted must understand the aforementioned information. The recovery process is unique to every individual. Each person's treatment takes time and what works for some will not work for others. The words, "Don't give up on me," apply to anyone suffering from addiction! It is an addict's secret plea to all.

Denial and blame plagued Darryl's heart. If he was ever going to find sobriety and truly defeat the powerful hold of addiction, he would have to eliminate or minimize these two extremely active defense mechanisms.

Denial weighs heavily upon an addict's illogical mindset. Why does a drunk driver feel he is perfectly capable of driving while under the influence of alcohol? The answer is denial and rationalization.

A drunk driver rationalizes his decision to drink and drive because of the depressing effects caused in the central nervous system of the individual. A drunk driver feels relaxed when he gets behind the wheel, which gives him a false sense of awareness and judgment. In truth, the drunk driver has decreased coordination, slower reflexes, and blurred vision. However, the worst side effects of driving drunk are the driver's erratic memory lapses and the possibility of passing out behind the wheel at any time.

During the recovery process, the treatment team works diligently to subtly eliminate an addict's defense mechanisms. The treatment team has three major barriers to overcome in the recovery operation:

1. *Break the chain of denial,*

2. *Eliminate defense mechanisms, and*

3. *Begin restoring or building an improved sense of self-esteem and self-worth for the patient.*

These three crucial steps will not create individual change in an addict's mindset without diligence and truth in the intervention process. An addict must be committed to the treatment process.

Therapists cannot want sobriety for an addict more than the addict wants it. The treatment team works toward a common goal in each addicted individual. Therefore, patients must exercise the same intensity and efforts toward the shared goal of finding sobriety.

What type of therapy can an addict and his caregiver expect from a recovery/intervention center? There are many types of therapy and programs for both addicts and their caregivers.

Medical, psychological, and psychoanalytical examinations are required upon an addict's arrival to the facility. Patients will be designed medicinal or psychological therapy based on the each of the physicians' findings. All therapy sessions are individually designed for each patient and the person's individual substance abuses.

"Cognitive therapy" is an important process in an individual's recovery. It allows addicts to make positive changes in their lives by overcoming pre-existing attitudes and speculations. Cognitive therapy allows addicts to become pro-active in their own personal thought processes. By altering their previously distorted mindsets, addicts are able to work through their negative self-imagery, bad behaviors, and gnarled emotional viewpoints.

Cognitive therapy implies that thoughts, feelings, actions, and behaviors are linked. By changing the initial impressions of an addict, a therapist can alter any preconceived notions or perceptions made by that individual. The following is an example of cognitive therapy and its impact on a recovering patient:

Abused children will feel shame for the acts of violence perpetrated upon them. They actually believe they are responsible for their own abuse. In their minds, they have provoked the assailant and deserve the beatings, because they are bad, horrible children.

Through cognitive therapy, the addicts' previously conceived thoughts are redirected. The addicts look at the abuse through their adult eyes and not their childhood eyes. The addicts realize they were not responsible for the violent abuse *they endured and are able to finally absolve themselves of the guilt that forever imprisoned them.*

By eliminating the fear involved with such horrid images, addicts are finally capable of ridding themselves of the monsters that reside in their thoughts and dreams.

"Group Therapy" is another important stepping stone in the recovery process. "Hi, I'm John and I'm an alcoholic" is the commonly used opening in every Alcoholics Anonymous (AA) meeting. This welcoming phrase lets a person know he or she is not alone. Group therapy allows people to speak freely about the trauma or abuse they have endured. When addicts hear the heart-rending story of another person's torturous upbringing, they find a certain peace within their own hearts and minds.

By sharing their life stories in a group setting, addicts come to realize they are not alone in this world. They come to realize and understand that every person in the group is a victim searching for peace, love, and understanding. The group setting allows individuals to share their feelings without fear of embarrassment, shame, or guilt.

In time, the therapy group becomes a family. For some addicts, it is the only family they have ever known. This family works towards the same goal and will valiantly protect one another from the temptations and triggers constantly pursuing them.

As the recovery process continues, an addict is eventually assigned a sponsor or an interventionist. The sponsor is a mentor or a "recovery coach" to the patient. A sponsor has years of experience in drug abuse and recovery because most sponsors have already lived with addiction themselves.

A sponsor is a sounding board to a recovering addict. The sponsor is extremely familiar with the trigger mechanisms that summon the addict. The sponsor has maintained his sobriety through hard work and determination and is a working example to the recovering addict. Sponsors provide inspiration through words of encouragement, and positive expressions such as "You are an important person!" and "I am not going to give up on you!"

Ron Dock was assigned to Darryl Strawberry as a member of the New York Yankees. It was during that time Ron made a vow to Darryl. "I am not here for me and I'm not here for the Yankees. I am here for you! And as long as you are under my care, I will never give up on you. And you're not going to give up on yourself either!"

That vow meant something to Ron Dock, which is why Darryl called for him the day he woke up behind the Dumpster. Ron was Darryl's sponsor, but more importantly, Ron was Darryl's brother. "Tough love" is often a vital strategy in the war against addiction.

Please remember, there is no such thing as "tough love" without exhibiting true love when it is needed most.

CHAPTER 12

WHO AM I?

DARRYL'S STORY

Over time, Darryl and Tracy started dating. Early on, Tracy made it crystal clear to Darryl that they were equals in their relationship. She was not looking to be wined and dined, she just wanted to stay clean, and she wanted Darryl to do the same. She was strong and loyal to her cause, and she could not accept anything less from the man in her life.

Darryl was not in the same place as Tracy. She had been clean and sober for over a year, while Darryl was still fighting the urges on a daily basis. He had been clean and sober for over a year in previous years, but it was exceptionally difficult for him to maintain his sobriety. When it came to Darryl's addictions, he had a hair trigger. His addictions were bold, and his ability to restrain himself from his "old friends" was shaky at best.

Darryl later stated, "Drugs will take you farther than you want to go, and it will keep you longer than you want to stay." Tracy needed to keep Darryl from taking any more trips. Darryl needed to forego the dark paths that called to him, and follow Tracy's lead. He could not venture down any more shadowy trails. His very life depended on it.

Tracy was pursuing a real estate license. She was attending seminars, taking classes, and studying for her examinations. She wanted a better life for herself. Meanwhile, Darryl was getting high. He had too much idle time on his hands, and the temptations were too abundant.

Tracy was infuriated by his actions. She stormed through crack houses in South Florida until she found him. She would find him passed out in a disgusting bathroom, his face pinned to the urine-stained linoleum as drool seeped from his mouth. She would find him slumped against a graffiti-covered wall, his incoherent eyes rolling back in his head.

Tracy rescued this 6-foot-6, 220-pound man from rat-infested hovels. She was tough and determined, like a Navy SEAL on a mission! However, she was quickly reaching her search-and-rescue limitations. Darryl had to stand on his own two feet; she could not be his crutch any longer.

"If I can get clean, so can you!" she yelled.

Darryl studied her ardent words. He reflected about his brother Ronnie, and how he and Mike would pull him from similar crack houses in Southern California. How could he do the exact, same thing to Tracy? She is the only person who had ever cared for him enough to kick in a crack house door and pull him out by his ear. How could he do this to her?

Darryl stumbled one last time. It would be the last time he would be rescued by Tracy. Her limit had been reached. She told Darryl she was getting out of Florida and moving to Missouri, and he was not allowed to follow her. Darryl was heartbroken. He moved in with his godparents while Tracy finished packing her things for the move. Darryl did not want her to leave him.

Once again, an overwhelming sense of remorse swept over him, but this time it was different. He was repentant. Never had his mind allowed such sadness. He could not let her go without him. He needed her, he loved her, and he could not live without her. His regretful tone spoke to Tracy's heart.

On the day Tracy was leaving, Darryl asked one last time if he could go with her. She tried to deny his request, but as she looked upon his face, she could feel the genuine pulse of his conscious-stricken heart. The two embraced and within moments, Darryl and Tracy were on their way to Missouri.

Darryl had no money, no job perspectives, and he didn't even have a driver's license. The two loaded a U-Haul trailer on the back hitch of Tracy's Toyota Camry and made their way across five states to their ultimate destination.

St. Louis, Missouri, was one of those National League cities that had heckled Darryl during his playing days. In fact, St. Louis probably taunted him more than all the other cities combined. Darryl was "pond scum" to "Cardinal's Nation," and now he was driving right into the inner sanctum of the city that once despised him.

Darryl and Tracy arrived at her parents' home in St. Charles and moved into the basement. The basement bedroom was cramped and dark. Darryl peered at the worn carpet and peeling paint chips on the walls. This was to be his new home, and the tiny room was as damaged and threadbare as he was.

Darryl stared off into space as he attempted to make sense of the reality of it all. Tears soaked his face as he silently begged for guidance. He was a 40-year-old man who had nothing. He once had enjoyed a storybook life filled with fame and riches. At one time in his life, he could have bought anything he desired, he could have had anything or anyone he fancied.

Now he had nothing. He had no money for an apartment. He had no money for taxi fare, let alone a car. He had no ability to take care of the woman he loved, and to top it all off, he was a drug addict and alcoholic.

"How did this happen?" Darryl asked himself. "Who am I?"

It was up to him to find God's message within this room. He had to understand that he was getting a second chance, a "do-over," if you will. And this time, it was up to Darryl to apply the knowledge he gained through the pitfalls he had endured. It was time to change his thought process and embrace his shortcomings, if he was ever going to rise above his circumstances.

Darryl had to use the victories of his life as guideposts toward making sound life choices. It was up to Darryl to create his own peace. It was up to Darryl to discover once and for all who he really was as a person. Darryl needed to conquer his fears and deny all temptations, so he could bring genuine glory to his name.

But more than anything, Darryl needed to find his purpose in life.

A TRUE BLESSING

Darryl and Tracy co-existed as boyfriend and girlfriend for some time in the basement bedroom. Inevitably, there came a day when the two would have to finally discuss the sanctity of their relationship. Tracy had been deeply planted in the word of God. The thought of the two of them living together without being married brought major concerns to the spiritual aspect of her Christian beliefs.

Darryl relied on Tracy for his strength, whereas Tracy relied on God's word for her strength. She felt torn with the idea of living with Darryl unwed. One other thing still weighed heavily on Tracy's heart. Darryl was still not clean and sober. Despite the fact that he was trying hard to stay clean, he still had his tiny relapses.

After a difficult heart-to-heart discussion, Darryl and Tracy decided to separate. They truly loved one another, but both were well aware of Tracy's devout concerns. Darryl loved Tracy with all his heart, but understood the conviction in which she spoke. Within days, Darryl was on a plane to California. The two were now entering the "faith game" and only time could reveal the couple's fate.

Darryl moved from the basement bedroom to his sister Regina's home in San Dimas, where he lived with Regina and her kids. He lived with his sister for six months, and stayed clean and sober throughout his time in San Dimas.

Tracy was always the centerpiece of Darryl's thoughts. He was so grateful for her presence in his life. Tracy taught Darryl the true meaning of being a father. She taught him how to live, and what was truly important in life. She gave him hope. She showed him the importance of the little things in life. "The little things create the grandest memories; they are the reasons for our smiles."

She reminded him of his younger days and the powerful choices that once confronted him. "Lay down and the world will trample over or you. Or find your courage and chase fear out the door, even if it means grabbing a skillet, a butcher knife, and frying pan to do it."

More than anything else, Tracy taught Darryl how to be a man.

As an adult, Darryl had lived on a grand scale. He had it all! He had trophies, the newspaper clippings, and signed auto-graphs for star-struck fans as if he were a king. He had cars, and money, and elegant homes, but he failed to find peace in these worldly treasures.

The reason for his unhappiness was simple. Darryl was always empty inside. He needed to make a vow to himself, and carry it out to the end of time. He needed to create the challenge and see it through.

He needed to look in the mirror and watch as the shadows of his former self lifted from his reflection. He needed to love the person staring back at him.

When a child is constantly beaten and verbally abused by a parent or a person of authority, the heart and mind of that little boy or girl is destroyed. Every type of physical and emotional abuse causes individuals to feel as if they are on deserted island. They have so much to say, but no one to tell it to. They are fearful and become distant because of the shame that has been wrongfully placed upon them.

THWACK! THWACK!

Abused people cannot escape the terrors that dwell within. They are forced to mask their pain by reaching out to drugs, alcohol, or other mind-numbing fixes. These abused souls lose trust in others, and find it hard to release the poison they have endured.

"YOU ARE NOTHING! AND YOU WILL NEVER AMOUNT TO ANYTHING!"

But there comes a time when a person must summon the strength from deep within to help combat the "old friends" and the "Monsters." A person must dig deep to find the tenacity required to silence the woodpecker's incessant pecking!

RAT-A-TAT-TAT! RAT-A-TAT-TAT! RAT-A-TAT-TAT!

Darryl was introduced to a person who knew his pain. She was a person who was willing to risk her life to save his. She kicked in crack house doors and physically removed him from the drug dungeons that had shackled him to the wall. And as his eyes rolled back into his head, and drool oozed from the corners of his mouth, he begged for his life. He begged for her love.

"DON'T GIVE UP ON ME!"

Tracy Boulware was a *bona fide* blessing from God. She gave Darryl the strength needed to design his battle plans for his own personal war on the disease that had consistently attacked him for over twenty years. She gave him the backbone to find an inner power that was durable enough to squash his addictions once and for all.

When Darryl finally surrendered his life to God, he found his inner power. From this inner power, he derived the tenacity required to finally say "NO!"

- ◆ NO to amphetamines!
- ◆ NO to marijuana!
- ◆ NO to alcohol!
- ◆ NO to cocaine!
- ◆ NO to crack!
- ◆ NO to sexual conquests!
- ◆ NO to all temptations!

Darryl also had to change his mindset regarding the "blame game" of his life. He could not make excuses for his downfalls any longer. He could not pin blame on those in his past. His life was in a different realm, and he had to forgive those who had trespassed against him.

He could no longer blame his father. The Monster has been defeated.

He could no longer blame his wives. They were the mothers of his beautiful children.

He could no longer blame the IRS. He was responsible for his own lack of judgment.

He could no longer blame the media. They were only doing their jobs.

The only way he could find true peace was to surrender it all, and Darryl did just that.

FINDING PURPOSE

Ron Dock had told Darryl long ago, "When the pupil is ready, the teacher will appear." A statement has never retained more truth. Darryl was certainly ready, and when he made the important choice to end the suffering, he was met by others with open arms. Darryl is an inspiring reminder that it doesn't matter how far a person travels in the wrong direction, he can always turn around.

Darryl Strawberry hit hundreds of home runs in his career. He drove in hundreds of runs. He hoisted World Series trophies and rode in ticker-tape parades as fans chanted his name. He was adored by the fans of his hometown teams, and created unforgettable memories with his towering blasts.

But Darryl was never impressed with these things. He played baseball because he was a natural. He had the size, athleticism, and God-given instincts to play the game and he played it very well. It was difficult for Darryl to admit his dominance in the game, because he despised himself. He had everything a king could desire, yet he felt a void deep in his soul.

Darryl has been clean and sober for many years now. He is no longer a superstar athlete, being chased by groupies and autograph hounds. No, he is something much more accomplished than that. Darryl Strawberry is a survivor.

Darryl Strawberry has miraculously survived two bouts of cancer. He has survived severe drug and alcohol addictions that should have killed him. He was locked away in a cell with iron bars, and was mentally imprisoned by a Monster who brutally attacked him. He has battled through several torturous rounds of depression and has been consumed by self-hatred.

"I don't know why God kept me here, but I'm here." Darryl stated. "God has always had something more important for my life, and now it is here." Darryl has found his purpose in life, and his words are giving faith to those who are in need.

As a baseball player, Darryl Strawberry could strike out 9 times in a row, but hit a game-winning homer his 10th time at bat. Nowadays, when Darryl strides into a room with his stoic face and long body, people know they have a fighting chance.

Darryl preaches the importance of people owning up to their addictions. He speaks of forgiveness and love that must be shown to others, as well as themselves. Darryl will not let them quit! He will not let them go. He will not give up on them.

Darryl helps patients look inside their hearts for strength and courage. He shows them compassion as he guides them to a lighted path, far from their "old friends" and the dreadful pitfalls hidden inside the darkness. Darryl helps young people find a way to end the self-destructive behaviors that commonly parallel the use of drugs and alcohol.

Tracy and Darryl Strawberry's messages to our youth about drug and alcohol abuse are very clear and succinct.

- The best way to deal with drug abuse is to not begin drug and alcohol use in the first place.

- Don't lose yourself. Always be in control of who you are and what you stand for. Your life is important, take it seriously.

- Genetics play a major role in drug and alcohol abuse. Be aware of that fact, and find alternate ways to deal with painful thoughts and negative feelings of self-worth and self-esteem.

- Think about what you are doing at all times, and understand the consequences that will follow every bad decision you make.

- The damage and pain you cause others, can never be taken back.

- ◆ Find support immediately, when abuse is taking place in your life.

- ◆ Find your purpose in life. Embrace it, and share it with the world.

- ◆ Stay alert and avoid external distractions.

- ◆ But most importantly, **Stay Focused!**

Darryl also shares the heart-rending stories about him and his brother Ronnie. He talks about the selfless love given to him by his mother Ruby, his brother Mike, and his two sisters. He talks about positive images and the inspirational influences of his life. He reminisces about the many earthly angels who guided him during his darkest days: Will G, Bill Goodstein, George Steinbrenner, and Lloyd McClendon. It was their footprints he saw upon the sand, and knew he was not alone.

Darryl talks of Tracy's undying love and her grand inner strength. He reminds audiences of the poignant words she lovingly yelled at him, "If I can stay clean, so can you!"

Darryl also speaks of the overwhelming grace bestowed upon him by the cancer-ward children at Columbia Presbyterian. Their beautiful well-wishes proved that the world was not devoid of goodness.

He reminds people of the day he was found behind the Dumpster in Daytona Beach. He was a filthy, broken mess. He was garbage! But, in his damaged mind, he had always been garbage.

Darryl was ready to die. He was sick of being tired, and tired of being sick. In his mind, he had nothing more to give this world. But unbeknownst to Darryl, the purpose of his life was just starting to unfold. His life was not even close to being finished, and the gifts he would one day share with the world, would dwarf any of the thrills he ever created on the ballfields of America.

As the sun's bright blaze warmed the alley way, a beam of morning light bounced off his face behind the Dumpster. Darryl thought about the homeless people he helped feed when he attended the Church of St. Stephen. He wondered how tough their lives must have been to have searched for nourishment inside trash cans.

Darryl was now connecting with their hopelessness, but did not want to be piece of garbage waiting to be swept away and buried in the cold, dark earth. He wanted to live! He wanted to be a beacon for others. He wanted his story to be told, so his words could touch those who silently suffer from addictions.

Darryl Strawberry wanted the world to know: there is hope and love and forgiveness for all.

As Darryl stared into the blinding sun, he could see an angelic silhouette before him. With a slow and trembling hand, Darryl reached towards the shadowy man, who grabbed his hand and pulled him to his feet. The two men embraced, as tears streamed from their eyes.

With a gaunt face and a tear-stained face, Darryl made a sincere request of his friend. "Don't give up on me."

Ron Dock replied, "Never, my brother."

Comments to Chapter 12

with John Picciano, Rich Capiola, & Ron Dock

Is Darryl Strawberry forever free of his addictions?

"No addict is ever free from the disease of addiction," states Dr. Rich Capiola. *"The disease will live in the shadows of every addict's mind, patiently waiting for a chance to strike again. The brain may not light up to every trigger it comes across, but it is constantly flickering. An addict will never be able to drop his guard, for he must remain vigilant in his battle."*

In the 1800s, a young boy came across a soldier in the look-out tower of a small Army fort. The young boy studied the soldier from the ground below. He watched as the soldier held his rifle in one hand and his binoculars in the other. The boy shouted up to the soldier, "Hey, Mister! Why are you holding your gun like that? Don't you know the war is over?"

The soldier looked down at the boy, and shouted, "You must always stand guard, son. They may be gone now, but you never know when they'll attack again."

Ron Dock is very familiar with this truth, because he is a recovering addict as well. In fact, Ron has lost three brothers to addiction. Ron's mother gave birth to triplets, and Ron was one of the three baby boys. One triplet brother died of a drug overdose, and the other deceased triplet brother succumbed to kidney failure due to his drug and alcohol use. Ron's older brother hung himself due to the maddening disease.

Ron was the only male child who would rise up against the disease and survive. What drove Ron to become sober and clean? Was it the deaths of his three brothers? Or did he have a greater purpose for survival? Ron looked at his grieving mother and knew that he could not put her through another tragedy. He made her happiness bigger than his addiction.

Ron pushed himself to stay clean. It was not an easy process. But, in time, Ron was able to conquer his triggers, temptations, and needs for the same substances that had claimed his brothers' lives. He made a solemn oath to his mother and to himself to stay clean. "If I don't pick up the beer, I can't get drunk. If I don't pick up the joint, I will not get high," states Ron.

Ron has been a sponsor for many years now, and he has remained sober and clean throughout it all. Ron reminds us, "A drug addict can become dry or sober, but he is never free from the strongholds of his addiction. Remaining drug-free requires hard work and dedication." Ron Dock is living proof of the power of intervention, recovery and treatment. He has been a devout follower of the 12-step program, and lives his life free of addiction.

Ron wants the same for Darryl. It is the reason he pushed Darryl when he needed to be pushed and stepped away when he needed to step away. Addicts must relent or they will never be able to control their actions. Sometimes addicts need to crash to see the big picture of their issues.

"As a sponsor, I have to be there for those who are calling out. Addicts can never conquer the disease without knowing they are truly loved and important in this world," states Ron. "I learned that from my sponsor, many years ago."

Darryl is now a key figure of the Darryl Strawberry Recovery Centers, managed by the Oglethorpe Corporation. The company's CEO, John Picciano, was asked why he would give Darryl Strawberry a managerial position in his company.

John's answer: "Darryl's story helps people understand that addiction can happen to anyone. He has learned from his mistakes, and has become a national mouthpiece for the disease. Darryl is helping people understand the power of addiction and how to fight for your life, even when the world looks bleak. Darryl is taking his story and using it to help others. He is doing the work, so why shouldn't we give him a second chance in life? We are all humans and we make errors, but who are we to judge those who have suffered so greatly?"

"I hope people come to understand the truth about addiction. I hope they understand that no one wakes up one morning and says, "I want to be a drug addict today!" But more importantly, I hope people understand the importance of these five words: "DON"T GIVE UP ON ME!"

Love your children. Give them hope. Quell their fears and never let go of their hand.

ACKNOWLEDGMENTS

Thank you to all who have helped and supported this valuable project: John Picciano, Bob Cohen, Lou Maggio, Dr. David Blair Miller, Dr. Rich Capiola, Darryl and Tracy Strawberry, Ron Dock, Denise Amos, Warren Knight.

In addition, I would like to thank the Kahwa Coffee Shop and the Charles J. Fendig Public library in Tampa.

ABOUT THE AUTHOR

Shawn Powell has worked in professional sports since 1989 with three different sports franchises: New York Yankees, Chicago White Sox, and New Jersey Nets. His storied resume contains lead roles in Strength & Conditioning, Scouting, and the Front Office.

Powell's vast experience in professional sports has enhanced his passion for writing. His first two published books, *Classical Madness* and *August Moon,* were instrumental in jump-starting his writing career. Since 2006, Powell has become a screenwriter and ghostwriter. Powell's first two ghostwriting assignments gained critical acclaim in the Children's Literature genre.

In screenwriting, Powell has had numerous movie scripts optioned in the past eight years, and has been hired to write several sports-related screenplays.

ABOUT THE CONSULTANTS

DAVID BLAIR MILLER, PSYD

Dr. David Blair Miller is a licensed psychologist and psychoanalyst practicing in Boca Raton, Florida. He is a Fellow and Diplomate of the American Board of Professional Psychology and Board Certified in Psychoanalysis by the American Board and Academy of Psychoanalysis. Dr. Miller earned his Clinical Psychology Doctorate Degree from the California School of Professional Psychology. He trained at the University of Miami, School of Medicine for his Internship training in Adult Clinical Psychology, Neuropsychology and Behavioral Medicine. He completed Residency and Fellowship training in Pediatric Clinical Psychology, Psychoanalytic Psychotherapy and Contemporary Psychoanalysis. Dr. Miller's Medical Staff privileges are at Boca Raton Regional Hospital. He is formerly an Affiliate Assistant Professor at Florida Atlantic University, College of Medicine, Division of Psychiatry and Neurology.

RICHARD CAPIOLA, MD

Having triple board certification in General Psychiatry, Addiction Psychiatry, and Forensic Psychiatry, Dr. Capiola has been in practice for over 20 years. In his years of training at Tulane Medical School and UCLA, Dr. Capiola developed a keen interest in the treatment of Depression and Anxiety overlapping with Drug and Alcohol Abuse. His focus on how addictive substances impact brain chemistry, structure, and function led to his present role as Chief Medical Officer for Oglethorpe, Inc., a healthcare company specializing in the treatment of mental health and addiction. He has been instrumental in the clinical development of 10 specialty treatment centers in four states.

Dr. Capiola is the Chief of Psychiatry for Physicians Regional Medical Center and the Medical Director of The Willough at Naples. He also has a 10-year history of service with the Joint Commission, which evaluates hospitals around the country for quality of care and patient safety. In addition, Dr. Capiola consistently receives high praise for his confidential private practice, which focuses on using each person's unique strengths to achieve happiness and a well-balanced life.

JOHN PICCIANO, LCSW, MSW

John Picciano currently serves as chief executive officer of Oglethorpe, Inc. In 1969, John graduated from Saint Leo College. While at St. Leo, he achieved recognition from the Student Government for being the Outstanding Sophomore and Outstanding Junior. He also served as president of Phi Theta Chi, and was honored to be the president of the Inter Fraternal Society Council. In his senior year, John was presented with the Frank Slane Memorial Award for Outstanding Executive.

Upon graduating from Saint Leo College, John attended St. Vincent de Paul Major Seminary in Boynton Beach, Florida. In 1973, he was ordained a Catholic priest for the Diocese of Orlando; where he served for over 14 years.

By 1978, John was appointed director of Ministry for Disabled Persons in the Diocese of Orlando. He was also responsible for drug and alcohol counseling and performing interventions while working for the church. During this time, John earned a master's degree in Social Work from Barry College.

Since leaving the priesthood, John has served as the chief executive officer of many psychiatric hospitals and recovery centers. In 1989, he opened the first in-patient treatment center in Clearwater, Florida. for hearing-impaired patients. It was one of the most successful in-patient substance abuse programs for hearing-impaired individuals in the country.

John's inspiration for conceiving this book was Dr. Stanley Conrad, MD, International Psychoanalyst, both a friend and mentor to John.

RON DOCK, CAC/CIP/CRC

As the owner of Sober Coach and Stars R Sober, Ron Dock prides himself in being an expert in the field of sobriety. He has walked miles in similar shoes of current and potential clients. Ron aims to help clients overcome and navigate the obstacles of addiction and recovery. He also helps those in recovery to effectively meet their emotional, physical, and spiritual needs while taking full responsibility for their choices in life.

Ron often utilizes a blend of learned therapies to meet the needs of clientele. This includes the use of Confrontational Therapy/Counseling, which confronts behaviors, attitudes, and belief requiring clients to take ownership for their behavior; and Reality Therapy, which helps clients work on things that they are in control of here and now.

He is also an interventionist at the Darryl Strawberry Recovery Center in St. Cloud, FL, where he utilizes his extensive experience with and knowledge of the 12-step program to aid clients in their recovery process. Ron offers personalized treatment to ensure clients and their families, when appropriate, are engaged in the recovery process.

About Oglethorpe and the Darryl Strawberry Recovery Centers

Oglethorpe is a corporation that currently owns and manages ten psychiatric hospitals throughout the United States, including two Darryl Strawberry Recovery Centers. Oglethorpe is about helping patients who are struggling with mental illness and addiction to improve their quality of life.

Oglethorpe recognizes that each person is unique, and through a multidisciplinary team of healthcare professionals, embraces an individualized approach for greater long-term success.

Darryl Strawberry is an inspiration and role model for people struggling with addiction. Oglethorpe has partnered with Darryl to work together to shed light on addiction and help alleviate the hold that it has over so many lives.

For more information, please call 866-655-2670 or visit the Strawberry Center website at https://strawberrycenter.com

CPSIA information can be obtained
at www.ICGtesting.com
Printed in the USA
BVOW09s1539051017
496816BV00003B/3/P